"This book tackles an issue that does not get the deserved attention. While many books study the benefits of economic freedom, this project studies the origins and persistence of economic freedom. Any attempt to increase our economic freedom needs to understand the roots and necessary condition for economic freedom to flourish and persist in time. This book offers a timely endeavour carried out by one of the most reputable authors in the field."

— Nicolás Cachanosky, Metropolitan State
University of Denver, USA

Economic Freedom and Prosperity

Economic theory and a growing body of empirical research support the idea that economic freedom is an important ingredient to long-run economic prosperity. However, the determinants of economic freedom are much less understood than the benefits that freedom provides. *Economic Freedom and Prosperity* addresses this major gap in our knowledge. If private property and economic freedom are essential for achieving and maintaining a high standard of living, it is crucial to understand how improvements in these areas have been achieved and whether there are lessons that can be replicated in less free areas of the world today.

In this edited collection, contributors investigate this research question through multiple methodologies. Beginning with three chapters that theoretically explore ways in which economic freedom might be better achieved, it then moves on to a series of empirical chapters that examine questions including the speed and permanence of reform, the deep long-run determinants of economic freedom, the relationship between voice and exit in impacting freedom, the role of crises in generating change, and immigration. Finally, the book considers the evolution of freedom in China, development economics, and international trade, and it concludes with a consideration of what is necessary to promote a humane liberalism consistent with economic freedom.

Economic Freedom and Prosperity will be of great interest to all social scientists concerned with issues of institutional change. It will particularly appeal to those concerned with economic development and the determinants of an environment of economic freedom.

Benjamin Powell is director of the Free Market Institute and Professor of Economics at the Rawls College of Business Administration at Texas Tech University, USA. He has authored or edited five other books and more than 50 scholarly journal articles, his research findings have been reported widely in the popular press and he has been a regular commentator on national television.

Routledge Foundations of the Market Economy

Edited by Mario J. Rizzo, New York University, and Lawrence H. White, George Mason University

A central theme in this series is the importance of understanding and assessing the market economy from a perspective broader than the static economics of perfect competition and Pareto optimality. Such a perspective sees markets as causal processes generated by the preferences, expectations and beliefs of Economic agents. The creative acts of entrepreneurship that uncover new information about preferences, prices and technology are central to these processes with respect to their ability to promote the discovery and use of knowledge in society.

The market economy consists of a set of institutions that facilitate voluntary cooperation and exchange among individuals. These institutions include the legal and ethical framework as well as more narrowly "economic" patterns of social interaction. Thus the law, legal institutions and cultural and ethical norms, as well as ordinary business practices and monetary phenomena, fall within the analytical domain of the economist.

For more information about this series, please visit www.routledge.com/series/SE0104

Economic Freedom and Prosperity

The Origins and Maintenance of Liberalization

Edited by Benjamin Powell

Routledge
Taylor & Francis Group

LONDON AND NEW YORK

First published 2019
by Routledge
2 Park Square, Milton Park, Abingdon, Oxon OX14 4RN

and by Routledge
711 Third Avenue, New York, NY 10017

Routledge is an imprint of the Taylor & Francis Group, an informa business

British Library Cataloguing-in-Publication Data
A catalogue record for this book is available from the British Library

Library of Congress Cataloging-in-Publication Data
Names: Powell, Benjamin, 1978- editor.
Title: Economic freedom and prosperity : the origins and maintenance
    of liberalization / edited by Benjamin Powell.
Description: Abingdon, Oxon ; New York, NY : Routledge, 2019. |
    Series: Routledge foundations of the market economy ; 36 |
    Includes bibliographical references and index.
Identifiers: LCCN 2018029514 (print) | LCCN 2018030620 (ebook)
    | ISBN 9780429443817 (Ebook) | ISBN 9781138335394
    (hardback : alk. paper)
Subjects: LCSH: Free enterprise. | Liberalism—Economic aspects. |
    Free trade. | Economic development. | Economic policy.
Classification: LCC HB95 (ebook) | LCC HB95 .E256 2019 (print) |
    DDC 330.12/2—dc23
LC record available at https://lccn.loc.gov/2018029514

ISBN: 978-1-138-33539-4 (hbk)
ISBN: 978-0-429-44381-7 (ebk)

Typeset in Bembo
by Swales & Willis Ltd, Exeter, Devon, UK

Contents

Figures

Tables

Contributors

Peter J. Boettke is Professor of Economics and Philosophy at George Mason University (GMU), as well as BB&T Professor for the Study of Capitalism, Vice President for Research, and director of the F.A. Hayek Program for Advanced Study in Philosophy, Politics, and Economics at the Mercatus Center at GMU. He is the author of 11 books and more than 200 scholarly studies. He earned his Ph.D. from GMU.

Jamie Bologna Pavlik is Assistant Professor of Agricultural and Applied Economics in the College of Agricultural Sciences and Natural Resources, and a research fellow at the Free Market Institute at Texas Tech University. She earned her Ph.D. from West Virginia University.

J.R. Clark is Probasco Distinguished Chair of Free Enterprise at University of Tennessee Chattanooga. He is author of six books and scores of scholarly studies. He earned his Ph.D. under the direction of Nobel Laureate James Buchanan at Virginia Polytechnic Institute.

James A. Dorn is a senior fellow and China specialist at the Cato Institute. He is the author or editor of more than ten books. He earned his Ph.D. at University of Virginia.

William Easterly is Professor of Economics at New York University (NYU) and a co-director of the NYU Development Research Institute. He is the author of three books and has published more than 60 peer-reviewed academic articles. He earned his Ph.D. at Massachusetts Institute of Technology (MIT).

Stephan F. Gohmann is Director of the Center for Free Enterprise and BB&T Professor of Free Enterprise in the Department of Economics at University of Louisville. He earned his Ph.D. at North Carolina State University.

Joshua C. Hall is Associate Professor of Economics at West Virginia University and director of the Center for Free Enterprise. He is co-author of the *Economic Freedom of the World* annual reports and the author of scores of scholarly studies. He earned his Ph.D. at West Virginia University.

Douglas A. Irwin is John French Professor of Economics at Dartmouth College and a Research Associate of the National Bureau of Economic Research. He is author of six books and many articles on trade policy in books and professional journals. He earned his Ph.D. at Columbia University.

Robert Lawson is Jerome M. Fullinwider Endowed Centennial Chair in Economic Freedom and is director of the O'Neil Center for Global Markets and Freedom at Southern Methodist University Cox School of Business. He is co-author of the *Economic Freedom of the World* annual reports and author of scores of scholarly studies. He earned his Ph.D. at Florida State University.

Adam Martin is Assistant Professor of Agricultural and Applied Economics in College of Agricultural Sciences and Natural Resources and a political economy research fellow at the Free Market Institute at Texas Tech University. He earned his Ph.D. at George Mason University.

Ryan Murphy is Research Assistant Professor at the O'Neil Center for Global Markets and Freedom at Southern Methodist University. He earned his Ph.D. from Suffolk University.

Deirdre Nansen McCloskey is Distinguished Professor of Economics, History, English, and Communication Emeritus at University of Illinois at Chicago. She is the author of 16 books and more than 300 scholarly studies. She earned her Ph.D. at Harvard University.

Alex Nowrasteh is an immigration policy analyst at Cato Institute's Center for Global Liberty and Prosperity. He earned his M.A. in economics at George Mason University.

Liya Palagashvili is Assistant Professor of Economics at State University of New York Purchase, and a law and economics fellow with the Classical Liberal Institute at New York University School of Law. In 2016, she was named one of Forbes' "30 under 30" in law and policy. She earned her Ph.D. at George Mason University.

Benjamin Powell is Director of the Free Market Institute and Professor of Economics in the Jerry S. Rawls College of Business Administration at Texas Tech University. He is the author or editor of five other books and more than 50 scholarly studies. He was the principle investigator in charge of the grant investigating the origins of economic freedom and prosperity. He earned his Ph.D. from George Mason University.

Alexander William Salter is Assistant Professor of Economics in the Jerry S. Rawls College of Business Administration, and a comparative economics research fellow at the Free Market Institute at Texas Tech University. He is the author of more than 30 scholarly studies. He earned his Ph.D. at George Mason University.

Russell S. Sobel is Professor of Economics and Entrepreneurship at the Baker School of Business in the Citadel. He is the author of more than 200 scholarly studies and a best-selling textbook on the principles of economics. He earned his Ph.D. at Florida State University.

Andrew T. Young is Professor of Economics in the Jerry S. Rawls College of Business Administration, as well as director of Graduate Students and a research fellow at the Free Market Institute at Texas Tech University. He is the author of more than 50 scholarly studies. He earned his Ph.D. at Emory University.

Acknowledgements

This book is part of a three-year research project undertaken by the Free Market Institute (FMI) at Texas Tech University investigating the "Origins of Economic Freedom and Prosperity." That research project involved scores of scholars at Texas Tech and many other universities. It is not practical to individually identify everyone who contributed to this research project overall, but I thank all of the scholars who conducted or assisted with research, attended our seminars, or were otherwise involved in this project. The Institute's associate director, Charles Long, does deserve special recognition. He was involved in managing every aspect of this project. Without his attention to detail and patience in managing our endless stream of visitors, the project would not have been possible.

The project also would not have been possible without the financial support of the John Templeton Foundation. I thank J.R. Clark for his guidance and suggestion to approach the Foundation with the idea for this research project. At the Templeton Foundation, I thank Daniel Green, who helped me through the grant approval process, and also Amy Proulx, who served as my liaison at the Foundation during the conclusion of this project.

Much of the research associated with this project was published as academic journal articles. A few of those studies are reprinted here, along with some original contributions that have not previously been published. I thank the Independent Institute, *Contemporary Economic Policy*, the *Journal of Institutional Economics*, the University of Chicago Press, and Springer for permission to reprint previously published material—although, in two cases, I do not appreciate the high fee that they required for their permission.

I thank Routledge's senior editor Andy Humphries and his anonymous reviewers for believing in this book, FMI's Amanda Smith and Estefania Lujan-Padilla, and Routledge's Anna Cuthbert, for assisting with manuscript preparation and other final production details necessary to bring it to print.

Finally, my greatest thanks are to the contributors to this volume. Their efforts have helped us to understand a little more about what factors lead countries to become freer.

Benjamin Powell
Lubbock, TX, 2018

Introduction

Benjamin Powell

There are strong reasons to believe that an institutional environment of economic freedom – an environment with strong protection of private property rights, predictable contract enforcement and the rule of law, and a large degree of freedom for individuals to negotiate mutually beneficial exchanges without third-party interference – is important for long-run prosperity. Peter Boettke (2012) recently argued that the main line of economic thought from Adam Smith to the present day lends strong theoretical support to the self-ordering property of markets to promote long-run prosperity. Since the creation of the Economic Freedom of the World (EFW) index in 1996 (Gwartney, Lawson and Block, 1996), there have been hundreds of papers measuring the empirical association between economic freedom and desirable social outcomes.[1]

Although a great deal of scholarship illustrates the theoretical and empirical benefits of an environment of economic freedom, how economic freedom is improved is much less understood.[2] This book begins to address this major gap in our knowledge. If private property and economic freedom are essential for achieving and maintaining a high standard of living, it is crucial to understand specifically how improvements in these areas have been achieved and whether there are lessons that can be replicated in less free areas of the world today.

In 2014, the Free Market Institute (FMI) at Texas Tech University began a three-year research project investigating the "Origins of Economic Freedom and Prosperity." That project commissioned new research papers, hosted visiting professors and guest research seminars, and supported academic conference presentations and a variety of other forms of scholarship, all aimed at achieving a better understanding of why some societies are more economically free than others and how changes in economic freedom come about.

There is no single appropriate methodology for investigating this research question. Some research was theoretical and some was empirical. Empirical methodologies varied from traditional cross-country regression analysis, through analytical narrative case studies and synthetic controls, to historical investigations and more.

This volume collects some of the studies that were part of this research project.[3] Taken together, the studies selected for inclusion in this volume provide a good overview of some of the most important areas of study undertaken in this research project and give a feel for the multiple methodologies that were used. Three of the following twelve chapters are theoretical, six are empirical and the final three are the keynote addresses that were delivered by prominent scholars at our concluding research conference.[4] Among the empirical chapters, the first two were selected to contrast our understanding of short-run changes in economic freedom compared to the role played by very long-run determinants. Chapters 6, 7 and 8 each serve as an example investigating a topic that multiple papers looked at – namely, democracy and movement, crisis and immigration. The final empirical example provides a case study of reform in China. China is an important case study because its improvement in economic freedom has been associated with the greatest number of people escaping extreme poverty in human history. The final three chapters consider how freedom can be promoted in economic development, international trade and an overall free society. Seven of these twelve chapters were recently published in academic journals; the other five appear here for the first time.

The book begins by considering three theoretical contributions. In Chapter 1, "Taming Leviathan," Peter Boettke and Liya Palagashvili argue that institutional reforms are necessary to constrain the growth of modern states in terms of both size and scope. They begin by documenting the growth of the U.S. government in the 20th century – although, as their discussion later reveals, the lessons they draw are equally applicable to European countries and other large welfare states. They argue that the nation state has grown because individual states have pushed much of their fiscal costs up to the federal government while decreasing competition between states. Meanwhile, central governments control monetary institutions, and have engaged in a "juggling trick" involving increased deficits and debt followed by debasement. To tame Leviathan, Boettke and Palagashvili argue that states need to become more polycentric, whereby each jurisdiction is responsible for financing its own spending, which would create greater competition between jurisdictions and lower the overall size of government. Meanwhile, they argue that rules are inadequate to constrain a central government's tendency to monetize debt, so that a complete separation of the state and money is also necessary to constrain government growth.

In Chapter 2, Alexander Salter complements the insights of Boettke and Palagashvili by building a theory of constitutional drift and political dysfunction that explains the transformation of governments in Europe and the United States. He argues that constitutional drift is the change in the de facto constitution governing a polity that results from the incentives facing people engaged in political bargaining processes. Those shifts have moved European states away from proprietary shareholder states and the United States away from a system of polycentric federalism, both toward monocentric nationalism. In the case of the United States, Salter argues that the original polycentric federalism – which entailed most spending at the local level, financed through property taxes, while only property owners voted – created powerful feedback mechanisms to help to guide politics to choose efficient policies. He argues that the constitutional drift that has resulted in greater national decision making, with a larger pool of voter decision makers, has created a fiscal commons, which provides insufficient informational feedback to decision makers and gets naturally depleted in a way that results in the Leviathan-like outcome described in Chapter 1.

In Chapter 3, Adam Martin shares an interest in polycentricity with the prior two chapters, but asks a more conceptual question: how might the right jurisdictional boundaries – both geographic and functional – be best determined? He argues that good boundaries are much like goods in the marketplace: their optimal form is not known in advance and, even when discovered, can change through time. Martin argues that jurisdictional boundary problems affect all sorts of governance arrangements and are subject to the same sorts of knowledge problems that make competition in the marketplace important for discovering the best arrangements. He contrasts *ex ante* consent forms of liberalism with *ex post* forms of exit-oriented liberalism. Exit-oriented liberalism can take multiple forms, including migration, secession and fragmentation of authority along functional lines. Martin argues that exit-oriented liberalism is underappreciated, especially because of its ability to enable the competitive discovery process to best find optimal jurisdictional boundaries.

Part II begins to empirically explore the determinants of economic freedom. Much of the empirical research in this book – and that associated with the research project more generally – employs the EFW index contained in the Economic Freedom of the World annual reports (Gwartney, Lawson and Hall, 2017). The index measures the consistency of a nation's policies and institutions with economic freedom. The report incorporates 43 variables across five broad areas:

1   Size of Government;
2   Legal Structure and Property Rights;
3   Access to Sound Money;
4   Freedom to Trade Internationally; and
5   Regulation of Credit, Labor, and Business.

At its most basic level, the EFW index measures the extent to which individuals and private groups are free to buy, sell, trade, invest and take risks without interference by the state. To score high on the EFW index, a nation must keep taxes and spending low, protect private property rights, maintain stable money, keep its borders open to trade and investment, and exercise regulatory restraint in the marketplace.

Chapter 4 begins our empirical examination of changes in economic freedom by looking broadly at how institutional change occurs. In the chapter, Russell Sobel makes three main findings. First, he finds that large improvements in economic freedom tend to take longer periods of time than large declines in economic freedom. Large improvements generally take about 25 years, while large declines happen within 10 years. However, his second important finding is that the speed of improvements in economic freedom seems unrelated to the durability of those improvements. Large improvements that occur quickly are as likely to persist as those that are more gradual. Finally, Sobel examines the sub-areas of the EFW index and finds that reforms in "Freedom to Trade Internationally" tend to be the first indicators of overall changes in economic freedom. Such reforms tend to occur first and are largely responsible for the overall magnitude of changes.

In Chapter 5, Steve Gohmann examines the very long-run determinants of current economic freedom. He builds on the "deep roots" of economic development literature by looking at how a country's geographic conditions (location, climate and biogeography) in 11,000 BC, level of technological adoption in AD 1,500 and history of experience with statehood from AD 1,500 onward impact on the country's economic freedom today. He argues that, of the five areas of economic freedom, the sub-areas of property rights and freedom to trade are more likely to be influenced by these deep roots than the other sub-areas of the index because the institutions of private property and free trade were developed to varying degrees thousands of years ago, while scientific monetary policy is a modern invention, and large welfare and regulatory states mostly developed after the Industrial Revolution. Gohmann finds that these deep roots can explain up to about 60 percent of the variation in countries' current property rights scores and roughly 40 percent of the variation in a countries' free trade scores, and that, as predicted, there is not a strong association between the deep roots and other areas of the index. Although Gohmann's findings indicate that a significant portion of two areas of the index are determined by factors beyond the control of today's reformers, they also indicate that most of the cross-country variation in economic freedom today is caused by more recent phenomena.

In Chapter 6, Joshua Hall examines the evolution of economic freedom across countries from 1980 to 2010. He finds that countries that had low initial levels of economic freedom tend to have improved their economic freedom more than countries that had high initial levels of freedom, leading countries to converge in their level of economic freedom over time. His chapter looks at what other initial conditions can lead to greater convergence in levels of freedom, finding that higher levels of education and a greater ability to exit a political jurisdiction lead to greater convergence. Importantly, Hall does not find various measures of democracy associated with greater convergence, leading him to speculate that the ability to vote with one's feet by leaving a jurisdiction might be more important in determining the evolution of economic freedom than voicing one's opinion through the political process.

Economists have long debated whether crises promote beneficial or harmful institutional change. Economic historian Robert Higgs (1987) argues that crises in the United States have generated a "ratcheting up" of the size and scope of government over the course of the 20th century. Meanwhile, other economists, such as Pitlik and Wirth (2003: 565), have maintained that it is "commonly shared wisdom among economists and political scientists . . . that crises promote the adoption of market-oriented reforms." In Chapter 7, Jamie Bologna and Andrew Young examine whether there is a general relationship between crisis and the evolution of the size and scope of government. They examine 70 countries from 1966 to 2010 using five different types of financial crisis (banking, currency, inflation, internal debt and external debt) to see how they impact on the size of government and on three other areas of the EFW index over 5-, 10- and 40-year time periods. Most of their results were statistically insignificant; when significant, they varied by type of crisis and measure of economic freedom. The authors' punchline is that the impacts of crises on the evolution of government in terms of size and scope are largely idiosyncratic and conditional on the particulars of time and country.[5]

The fear that immigrants from poorer countries will bring beliefs and social capital that are at odds with, and undermine, the institutions of destination countries is not new – but George Borjas (2015) touched off a new debate when he asserted that this impact could undermine the productivity of destination countries and erase the large gains that economists have estimated could be achieved in a world of unrestricted migration (Clemens, 2011). Borjas's claims are, however, purely speculative. In Chapter 8, several co-authors and I conduct the first new empirical investigation of how immigrants impact on destination countries' economic freedom.[6] Looking at both initial stocks of immigrants in 1990, which had been accumulated over decades, and subsequent 20-year flows of immigrants, we examine how each of 110 impacted countries changes in terms of its economic freedom between 1990 and 2011. Through multiple regressions, we find that immigration is generally associated with improvements in economic freedom, rather than deterioration. We also find that the magnitudes of improvement associated with greater economic freedom are economically meaningful in terms of enhanced growth. In our 32 regressions, we do not find a single statistically significant negative association between immigration and economic freedom.

Chapter 9 provides a case study of China – one of the most important countries to make large improvements in economic freedom. China's economic freedom has improved 57 percent since 1980. But even that large improvement understates the extent to which China has reformed because it measures national policies, while much of the reform in China has come at the local level, and special enterprise zones, where much of the growth has occurred, grant even greater economic freedoms. China has also experienced the greatest reduction in human history of sheer numbers of people living in extreme poverty. In this chapter, James Dorn explains how the reforms took place and what important areas remain to be liberalized. He argues that much of the reform was bottom-up, "spontaneous marketization." Much of this bottom-up reform, such as the household responsibility system, township and village enterprises, and urban private enterprises, came about through frustrated citizens trying to better themselves. Their experimentation, when successful, benefited from government leaders who cared about results and not only ideology. Although this spontaneous marketization has advanced economic freedom in China, much remains to be done. Dorn argues that the future of China will depend on the privatization of state-owned enterprises and financial institutions, and, importantly, on allowing a freer market in ideas.

The final part of the book considers where we might go from here. First, William Easterly explores the role of freedom compared to coercion in economic development and what can be done better to promote freedom. Then, Douglas Irwin considers the cases that can be made for free trade, as well as which cases resonate best with which audiences. Finally, we conclude with Deirdre McCloskey considering what a liberal society really is and how best to promote it.

In Chapter 10, William Easterly contrasts how freedom creates beneficial spontaneous orders that promote development with how the coercion employed by planners leads to detrimental spontaneous orders that undermine economic development. Yet what can development planners do if their advice is to simply leave people "free to choose" and observe the spontaneous order that emerges? Easterly suggests three ways in which development economists might give advice that would promote freedom and development. First, they might advise against giving aid to places such as weak and fragile states, whose economic systems are based on coercive spontaneous orders, because such aid can increase coercion while decreasing freedom. Second, they might advocate for reforms of bad coercive policies, such as those that lead to high black-market exchange-ratio premiums, high inflation, nominal interest rate controls and policies that repress international trade. Finally, he argues that economists need to argue more powerfully for the principle of consent rather than coercion and for respecting the rights of the poor. As he recognizes, the payoffs to these educational efforts are uncertain, but getting these ideas and ideals right would be a step in the right direction – and a worthy end in and of itself.

Economists have had their ideas right on the benefits of international trade for more than 200 years. Dating back to Adam Smith and David Ricardo's efforts, they have also been trying to influence policymakers. In Chapter 11, Douglass Irwin outlines the four basic cases for free trade – namely, theoretical, moral, political and empirical. He argues that, while powerful, the *theoretical* case for free trade is often too abstract for policymakers and the general public to understand, and it is vulnerable to challenges about whether all of its necessary assumptions hold. The *moral* case, either based on rights or religion, played a role in Richard Cobden's Anti-Corn Law League campaign to achieve free trade in 19th-century Britain, but it is not used by most economists today. The *political* case for free trade is based on how trade between nations improves international relations – particularly by improving prospects for peace. This idea has been around for hundreds of years, has recently gained empirical support in political science and might be better embraced by economists. The *empirical* case for free trade can be made on quantitative and historical grounds. Irwin argues that economists tend to be persuaded more by cross-country regression results that show that free trade improves incomes and growth, while policymakers and the general public are more persuaded by historical case studies, which illustrate how countries have improved their growth as they have changed policies away from protectionism and toward free trade. Each of these cases for free trade is important and Irwin's chapter encourages readers to think about "what type of ideas" are important for influencing policy formation in the direction of greater freedom to trade internationally.

The final chapter, by Deirdre McCloskey, broadens the discussion of what type of ideas matter and how they are communicated, to consider what a free society is and in what ways it might be better promoted. She makes the case for what she calls "Liberalism 1.0," or humane libertarianism, which is essentially a philosophy that values civil, social, religious and economic freedoms. It is a social system that relies on persuading others to cooperate rather than pushing them around with threats of violence – whether privately or through the government. For such a society to be promoted, first, those who understand it must keep making the intellectual case for it. A system that operates through persuasion must be brought about and maintained by persuasion. But humane liberals can do a better job than they have done to date. McCloskey argues that people must understand that humane liberalism is advocated, by many people, not out of selfish reasons, but because it is the best system for the poor and disadvantaged. She argues that humane liberals must not be confused with conservatives, and must criticize conservatives and not only progressives. Further, humane liberals should identify as radicals, much as their classical liberal brethren did in the 18th century. But while intellectual ideas are important, says McCloskey, they are not enough. She argues that energy, enthusiasm and emotion are as important for lasting ideological change as the ideas themselves, and that we need artists and storytellers in movies, novels and music lyrics to convey these ideas as well if we are to achieve and maintain a free society.

This book does not reach any definitive conclusion about how a free society is created or maintained. In fact, I suspect that there is no single answer or formula. But, hopefully, this volume will help scholars to better understand the role that some factors play in making a society more or less free and, hopefully, it will encourage scholars to pick up where the book leaves off, helping to develop a larger body of scholarship examining the origins of economic freedom and how such freedoms are best maintained.

Notes

1 For a recent survey, see Hall and Lawson (2013).
2 For a recent survey of the literature on the origins of economic freedom, see Lawson, Murphy and Powell (2017).
3 To see some of the other studies that were part of this project, see http://www.depts. ttu.edu/freemarketinstitute/research/research_origins.php
4 Chapter 12, by Deirdre McCloskey, was scheduled for presentation at the conference, but was subject to last-minute cancellation. Her written remarks that were to be presented are included here.
5 Another paper that was part of this larger research project (O'Reilly and Powell, 2015) found that war crisis resulted in long-run sustained increases in the scope of government regulation.
6 Other recent contributions to this literature that were associated with this grant include Powell, Clark and Nowrasteh (2017), and Padilla and Cachanosky (2018).

References

Boettke, P. 2012. *Living Economics: Yesterday, Today, and Tomorrow.* Oakland, CA: Independent Institute.

Borjas, G. 2015. Immigration and globalization: A review essay. *Journal of Economic Literature*, 53(4): 961–974.

Clemens, M. 2011. Economics and emigration: Trillion-dollar bills on the sidewalk? *Journal of Economics Perspectives*, 25(3): 83–106.

Gwartney, J., R. Lawson and W. Block. 1996. *Economic freedom of the world, 1975–1995.* Vancouver, BC: Fraser Institute.

Gwartney, J., R. Lawson and J. Hall. 2017. *Economic freedom of the world: 2017 annual report.* Vancouver, BC: Fraser Institute.

Hall, J., and R. Lawson. 2013. Economic freedom of the world: An accounting of the literature. *Contemporary Economic Policy*, 32(1): 1–19.

Higgs, R. 1987. *Crisis and Leviathan: Critical Episodes in the Growth of American Government.* New York: Oxford University Press.

Lawson, R., R. Murphy and B. Powell. 2017. *The Determinants of Economic Freedom: A Survey.* Working Paper.

O'Reilly, C., and B. Powell. 2015. War and the growth of government. *European Journal of Political Economy*, 40: 31–41.

Padilla, A., and N. Cachanosky. 2018. The Grecian horse: Does immigration lead to the deterioration of American institutions? *Public Choice*, 174(3): 351–405.

Pitlik, H., and S. Wirth. 2003. Do crises promote the extent of economic liberalization? An empirical test. *European Journal of Political Economy*, 19(3): 565–581.

Powell, B., J. Clark and A. Nowrasteh. 2017. Does mass immigration destroy institutions? 1990s Israel as a natural experiment. *Journal of Economic Behavior & Organization*, 141(Sept): 83–95.

Part I

Theory

1 Taming Leviathan

Peter J. Boettke and Liya Palagashvili

Introduction*

The public debt crisis in Greece seems to have reached an endgame. Prior to joining the European Union, Greece's government would have simply engaged in what Smith (1977 [1776]) had described as the "juggling trick"—namely, deficit increases, accumulation of debt, and debasement of currency—that all governments, ancient and modern, resort to when similarly confronted with public bankruptcy. But Greece (along with other countries in a similar situation) cannot engage in the debasement of currency to pay off debt because it operates under the common currency of the European Union. To pay off debt, it (and other countries like it) faces the following options: (1) exhibit fiscal discipline; (2) rely on European Union bailouts; or (3) exit the European Union so that it can engage in the debasement tactic. This is the drama unfolding in European democracies of the twenty-first century.

This situation in Europe simply highlights and brings to the forefront the public management of fiscal affairs and the embedded question for public management of the appropriate scale and scope of governmental activities. This problem also extends to the fiscal state of affairs in various U.S. states such as California, Illinois, Michigan, New York or Wisconsin, and to the U.S. federal debt and fiscal gap, as identified by Kotlikoff and Burns (2004, 2012). All of these examples serve to illustrate this new era of the "economics of illusion" (Hahn, 1949), whereby nations have embraced fully Smith's "juggling tricks" as the necessary approach to public sector management. Wagner (2014) explains that the essence of the peculiar business of politics is for citizens, interest groups, politicians, and bureaucrats to exchange votes for power, prestige, and privileges. Therefore, unless the public sector is constrained through constitutions and perhaps even more effectively by competition, the public sector will grow in terms of both scale and scope.[1]

The aim of this chapter is to utilize the discussion of public sector growth to illuminate the puzzle in political economy regarding effective government constraints and to provide an analysis of the institutional structures that can "tame Leviathan." We argue that altering the institutional structures to be more polycentric would contain important self-generating mechanisms to tame

Leviathan. Specifically, we point to the role of hard budget constraints and the role of competition in polycentric institutions for generating incentives compatible for reducing the size of government. Furthermore, we argue that one of the reasons why governments have grown expansively in the last century is because they are in a position to increase public debt and have the opportunity to monetize these debts. We discuss why a central bank's status as an "independent bank" is unable to effectively constrain government from monetizing its debt. As such, we contend that the decentralization of money would eliminate the federal government's option of monetizing its debt and thus be able to constrain the federal government in its natural quests to spend and grow.

In proceeding with our analysis, we taken as given that such growth of government is both undesirable and unsustainable. Thus, our title—"Taming Leviathan"—reflects both our starting point, (1) that public sector growth over the past seventy years has turned Western democracies into leviathans that threaten both continued economic progress and political freedom, and (2) that analytical efforts at taming such beasts deserve our full scholarly attention. In this sense, our chapter is not normative in nature, although it begins with what Schumpeter (1954) terms a "pre-analytic cognitive act" of vision about the appropriate functions of government in a society of free and responsible individuals. In other words, we taken as given that the appropriate functions of government should be limited to small, defined boundaries, and we proceed with a series of positive questions and analysis regarding the best means to achieve this end. Government in this vision should be prohibited from expanding its ranges of activities outside of its clearly delineated boundaries.[2] Our project follows in the footsteps of James Buchanan on what is referred to as "constitutional political economy." As Buchanan (1958: 5) put it when he founded the Thomas Jefferson Center for Studies in Political Economy at University of Virginia in the late 1950s:

> The Thomas Jefferson Center strives to carry on the honorable tradition of "political economy"—the study of what makes for a "good society." Political economists stress the technical economic principles that one must understand in order to assess alternative arrangements for promoting peaceful cooperation and productive specialization among free men. Yet political economists go further and frankly try to bring out into the open the philosophical issues that necessarily underlie all discussions of the appropriate functions of government and all proposed policy measures. They examine philosophical values for consistency among themselves and with the ideal of human freedom.

This chapter proceeds as follows. First, we will address the growth of government. We then introduce the concept of polycentricism, and we discuss the role of hard budget constraints and interjurisdictional competition in taming Leviathan. Next, we discuss how the decentralization of money can constrain the growth of government and, finally, we conclude.

The growth of government

Much of the discussion of the growth of government should begin with an understanding of the transformation of public administration in the early twentieth century. This period is referred to as the Progressive era, which started with U.S. President Woodrow Wilson seeking to relax the constraints that the U.S. Constitution imposed on government. Wilson (1956 [1885], 1887) argued that constitutional restrictions designed during an earlier age must be relaxed in the modern era. He explains:

> The "literary theory" of checks and balances is simply a consistent account of what our constitution makers tried to do; and those checks and balances have proved mischievous just to the extent to which they have succeeded in establishing themselves as realities. It is quite safe to say that were it possible to call together again the members of that wonderful Convention to view the work of their hands in the light of the century that has tested it, they would be the first to admit that the only fruit of dividing power had been to make it irresponsible.
>
> (Wilson, 1956 [1885]: 197)

According to the ideas of the Progressive era, constitutions must not be allowed to "pinch." The checks and balances of that earlier age are, in modernity, merely nuisances for good government. Epstein (2014: 7) summarizes the intellectual transformation when he states that, in the Progressive mindset:

> [T]he benevolent force of state power, exercised by dedicated and impartial administrative experts, can eliminate the chronic economic imbalances wrought by the unprecedented scale of industrialization that untamed market forces had driven . . . the traditional safeguards against excessive state power that animated early constitutional theory on both structural issues and property rights were perceived as pointless roadblocks that the modern technological state should overcome through a greater concentration and use of governmental power at all levels.

Because Progressive thought resulted in a transformation of public administration, it also resulted into a transformation of economics—since economics is an input into public administration. Economics, as a discipline, moved from a philosophical tool for social understanding and social criticism to a quasi-engineering tool for social control (Boettke, Coyne and Leeson, 2006). Samuelson (1948)—arguably the most influential economist of the twentieth century and also a product of the Progressive era—writes, in the first edition of *Economics*, that such older ideas of the classical liberal political economists and their individualist social philosophy must be rethought in the light of modernity. The vast interdependence of modern commercial society has made it impossible to continue to believe "that government governs best which governs least" (Samuelson, 1948: 153).

Unbridled capitalism, Samuelson argued, no doubt produced rapid economic growth in the eighteenth and nineteenth centuries, but it also resulted in business cycles, the wasteful exhaustion of resources, income inequality, monopoly power, and political corruption by moneyed interests. The complex economic conditions of modern life necessitate, for Samuelson, that "sensible men of good will be expected to invoke the authority and creativity of government" (Boettke, Coyne and Leeson, 2006: 551).

The growth of government, beginning in the early twentieth century, reflects a natural consequence of the changes in the intellectual ideas regarding the role of the state. These transformations happened not only in the United States, but also in Europe. In Table 1.1 and Figure 1.1, we present some measures of government expenditures as a percentage of gross domestic product (GDP) to illustrate the growth of government in Western democracies.

As Table 1.1 and Figure 1.1 show, government expenditures as a percentage of GDP during the period 1870–2013 have increased by 347 percent. This reflects a radical transformation of the scale and scope of government in the democratic West. Another common measure of the expansion of the scope of government is the regulation of economic activities. Figure 1.2 shows the growth of the number of pages published in the *Federal Register*, which is a document containing all U.S. government federal rules and regulations.

As shown, there has been a significant growth in federal regulations since 1936. And this increase in the quantity of regulations does not even capture the extent to which certain regulations have significantly increased the scope of government power.[3] The growth of government since the early 1900s and into

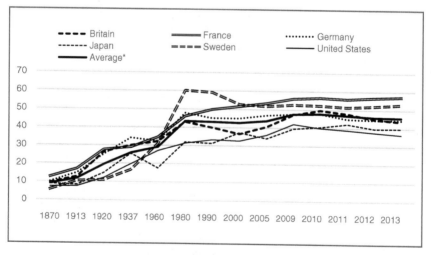

Figure 1.1 Government spending as a percentage of GDP

Table 1.1 Government spending as a percentage of GDP

	1870	1913	1920	1937	1960	1980	1990	2000	2005	2009	2010	2011	2012	2013
Austria	10.5	17	14.7	20.6	35.7	48.1	38.6	52.1	50.2	52.3	52.8	50.8	51.7	51.2
Belgium	n/a	13.8	22.1	21.8	30.3	58.6	54.8	49.1	52	54	52.6	53.5	55.1	54.5
Britain	9.4	12.7	26.2	30	32.2	43	39.9	36.6	40.6	47.2	49.7	47.9	45	43.8
Canada	n/a	n/a	16.7	25	28.6	38.8	46	40.6	39.2	43.8	47.3	45.8	44.8	44.5
France	12.6	17	27.6	29	34.6	46.1	49.8	51.6	53.4	56	56.6	55.9	56.7	57.2
Germany	10	14.8	25	34.1	32.4	47.9	45.1	45.1	46.8	47.6	47.7	45	44.7	44.5
Italy	13.7	17.1	30.1	31.1	30.1	42.1	53.4	46.2	48.2	51.9	50.4	49.9	54.4	54.5
Japan	8.8	8.3	14.8	25.4	17.5	32	31.3	37.3	34.2	39.7	40.6	42.3	40	39.9
Netherlands	9.1	9	13.5	19	33.7	55.8	54.1	44.2	44.8	50	51.3	50.1	47	46.7
Spain	n/a	11	8.3	13.2	18.8	32.2	42	39.1	38.4	45.8	46.4	45.9	47.8	44.9
Sweden	5.7	10.4	10.9	16.5	31	60.1	59.1	52.7	51.8	52.7	52.3	51.5	52	53
Switzerland	16.5	14	17	24.1	17.2	32.8	33.5	33.7	37.3	36.7	33.9	33.9	32.8	32.9
United States	7.3	7.5	12.1	19.7	27	31.4	33.3	32.8	36.1	42.2	40.1	39	37.8	36.6
Average	10.4	12.7	18.4	23.8	28.4	43.8	44.7	43.2	44.1	47.7	47.8	47	46.9	46.5

Sources: The Economist; International Monetary Fund (IMF); Organisation for Economic Co-operation and Development (OECD).

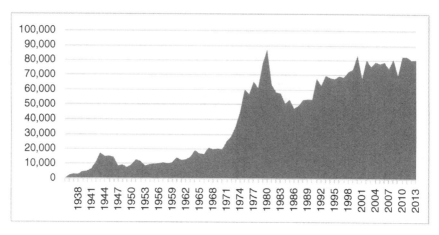

Figure 1.2 Total number of *Federal Register* pages published, 1936–2013

the twenty-first century has been thoroughly documented, and scholars have attributed this increase in the growth of government first to the Progressive era, and then the aftermath of World Wars I and II (Epstein, 2014; Ostrom, 1973; Holcombe, 1996; Higgs, 1987; Hamburger, 2014).

In the United States, for example, government expenditures as a percentage of GDP increased from 7.3 percent in 1870 to 7.5 percent on the eve of World War I in 1913, and from 12.1 percent after World War I to 19.7 percent during the Great Depression and the brink of World War II in 1937.[4] But, in 1980, just as the United States was about to embark on the Reagan revolution, that figure stood at 31.4 percent; in 2009, as the United States coped with the global financial crisis, that figure was 42.2 percent. Recent years have seen a decline, but nowhere near the figure of 32.8 percent that pre-dates the September 11, 2001 terrorist attacks (that is, "9/11"). This is, of course, a far different picture from that of before World War I and before the Progressive era, during which time government expenditures as a percentage of GDP were consistently low.

These numbers, by themselves, do not indicate causality between beliefs and massive expansion of government, but they do provide a description of the significant changes in government expenditures between the pre- and post-war eras, which should be understood in the light of the changes also occurring in the culture of public administration and the appropriate role of government.[5] The erosion of the constitutional checks and balances, and the transformation of the nature of government and its relationship to the economy, is fully institutionalized by the end of World War II.[6] How was this larger government financed? Taxes were not enough, and running deficits and debts became the norm. Hoover and Siegler (2000) analyze U.S. fiscal policy beginning in 1791 and find that taxes "caused" spending before World War I—that is, that increases in spending came from revenue generated through taxes. Hoover and Sheffrin

(1992) also find a distinct change occurring after the 1960s: before the 1960s, taxes also appear to be causing spending; after the 1960s, there is a decoupling of taxes and spending. These studies are providing evidence for this transformation in public administration and the nature of government. Government spending was dependent on the revenues it received. But this relationship changed throughout the twentieth century—and especially after World War II—during which government spending was now financed by something besides taxes: mainly, borrowing. The existing fiscal gap in the United States (obligations for future payments versus the ability to make those payments given current assumptions about administrative costs, real income growth, demographics, tax rates, and so on) has developed over the course of seventy years and not only over the past decade or two.[7]

James Buchanan once posed the following puzzle: if a fly that grows to nine times its current size can no longer fly, what does that say about fiscal dimensionality and the modern democratic state? Buchanan's question is an attempt to direct scholars toward the question of scalability and institutional architecture. From a certain perspective, governmental activities are scalable; from another perspective, governmental capacity has constraints that are independent of the philosophical case made for government activism. Administratively, the task simply overwhelms the apparatus of government as it grows in size and complexity. Friedman (1947) also addressed this concern and warned readers, in his review of Abba Lerner's *The Economics of Control*, that we cannot engage in public policy analysis as though the administration takes place in a vacuum.[8] There will always be incentive alignment issues, and information acquisition and utilization issues, even among men of good will who have received expert training. As the tasks of government grow exponentially, the administrative burden grows as well. It is true that the growth of government may represent an investment in improvements in our society, but we should also recognize that the problems of a lack of fiscal discipline that are evident throughout the democratic West are also causing problems for long-term economic growth and vitality in these societies. Thus it is important to consider Buchanan's question about fiscal dimensionality and the architectural design of the modern state.[9]

The great puzzle in political economy, and the puzzle in our theme of taming Leviathan, revolves around the issue of defining and constraining governmental activity. Buchanan (1975, 1977) distinguishes between what he refers to as the *protective* state (providing secure property rights and enforcing contracts), the *productive* state (providing essential public goods), and the *redistributive* state (providing special privileges to groups). The puzzle is how to simultaneously empower the protective and productive states without unleashing a redistributive state that threatens governmental capacity. Implicit in Buchanan's puzzle is the understanding that governments have a natural tendency to grow and expand. If the incentives were not aligned to encourage government growth, perhaps the puzzle would not be that difficult to address.

One solution is for government to pre-commit to a set of policies and a set of promises to abide by these policies. However, the problem with this solution is that, during times of crises, government breaks these promises and expands under the justification of an "emergency." This was the case in the growth of government after World War II. Higgs (1987) documents how the growth of government during World War II was thought of as a necessary response to the emergency nature of the war. However, even after the war ended, he discusses how there was a ratchet effect—meaning that governments did not roll back the huge bureaucratic organizations that they had formed for their initially "temporary" needs. Thus, when the emergency ended, the emergency government programs did not. These times of crises are an opportunity to call for short-run relief from the vagaries of the disruptions of economic change, and they are normally justified because the trade-off with long-term economic growth is either muted by offsetting factors or hidden through some combination of monetary and fiscal illusion. Calls on the fiscal side for a balanced budget proposal or a tax limitation proposal are not sufficient to bind the political authority because they can break any such promises when needed. In the context of our discussion, taming Leviathan requires institutional solutions that have self-generating incentives to constrain government even in crisis. In the following sections, we address how altering the institutional structures to be more polycentric and how decentralizing money can effectively constrain governments during these moments of temptation.

Taming Leviathan with polycentricity

A polycentric organization of government describes a system with many centers of decision-making units that are formally independent of each other and it involves multiple, overlapping systems of autonomous governments (Ostrom, Tiebout and Warren, 1961). This idea is similar to Bruno Frey's (2001, 2005) analysis of functional, overlapping, competing jurisdictions.

The organization of a society can be understood as being "more" or "less" polycentric. The more autonomy and competition there is among localities, the more polycentric a given country or society is. If many activities are organized at the level of the central government, then we can classify the U.S. system, for example, as "less" polycentric. If U.S. states and localities have significant autonomy and are more independent from the central (federal) government, then the organizational structure is "more" polycentric.[10] The significance of a polycentric system of governance is that it has important features that create self-generating mechanisms to incentivize governments to be more accountable to their citizens, and which force citizens and political actors to internalize the costs of a more expansive government. It is our contention that Leviathan can be tamed through polycentric institutions. Specifically, we point to the role of hard budget constraints and of competition in polycentric institutions for generating incentives compatible with reducing the size of government.

The role of hard budget constraints

An important feature of what makes an institutional structure "more" or "less" polycentric is the degree of autonomy of the states, localities, or subunits in the society. This also refers to the fiscal independence of localities, which means that each locality faces a hard budget constraint when financing its activities. When the subunits of government are more autonomous, then each unit of government finances its spending either through increasing taxation in its jurisdiction or by borrowing money. The budget of this local government can "soften" when it receives external money. This is called intergovernmental fiscal transfer—or "federal aid," as it is referred to in the United States. Greve (2012) documents how there was a radical shift in the institutional structures of a federalist system in the United States after the advent of intergovernmental fiscal transfers and federal aid programs. The number of grants-in-aid programs in the United States rose from 15 in 1930 to 530 by 1970 and to 1,122 in 2010 (Edwards, 2013). Federal aid going to states and localities totaled US$607 billion in 2011, and it is now the third largest item in the federal budget after social security and national defense (Congressional Budget Office, 2013).

Intergovernmental fiscal transfers lead to a growth of government in scope and scale through two mechanisms. First, because they soften the budget constraint of state governments, states become less sensitive to the desires of taxpayers and these additional funds allow state governments to increase their activities in all areas. Second, intergovernmental fiscal transfers transform state and local governments into special interest groups who engage in lobbying the central government to give them money—that is, state and local political actors want to bring back the "bacon" to their home states. In this way, intergovernmental fiscal transfers transform the subunits of governments into special interest groups that lobby for more funds and consequently increase overall *federal* government spending.

In the first mechanism, when the federal government gives states and localities such things as block grants, this means that states now have an additional source of income for financing their activities. Prior to the grants, states could finance their activities either through increasing the taxes of their citizens or by borrowing money. The additional source of income from the federal government allows states to expand their activities more than they would have been able to otherwise. However, it is possible that, when states receive these grants, they actually maintain their original level of activity and thus are able to return tax money to their citizens. This is called the substitution effect with federal aid. But this is unlikely to occur because financing more activities through aid is beneficial to the political actors, since it allows political actors at each level of government to receive the "praise" for spending, while shifting the blame for high tax burdens to other levels of government. Also, many of these grant programs have promoted the growth of state bureaucracies to administer the program, and these bureaucracies have an incentive to continue asking for more and more money year after year. This is the logic of bureaucracies and the reason why we almost never see bureaucratic downsizing (Tullock, 2005).

Furthermore, the few empirical studies available on this question also suggest that federal grants and aid *do not* result in a reduced tax burden for the citizens in that jurisdiction (substitution effect), but instead result in greater expenditures in the particular area toward which aid was directed, as well as in other areas of government activities. For example, Jack Osman (1966: 362, 367) found that each dollar of federal aid was associated with an increase in total expenditures for the state and that there is a "highly significant positive impact of federal aid to all [other] functions."[11] The Advisory Commission on Intergovernmental Relations (1977) also found no substitution pattern with federal aid; rather, it found that federal grants tend to *stimulate* expenditures by the state in other areas. The Commission (1977: 2) concludes: "Total state and local expenditures for all jurisdictions increased more than proportionally per dollar of Federal aid." In both studies, there is a "stimulating" effect of intergovernmental fiscal transfers—that is, fiscal transfers result in greater expenditures in the state and localities. Thus, instead of political actors returning tax money to citizens when they receive fiscal transfers from the federal government, they instead use that money to finance more activities and increase the extent of their powers and domain.

In terms of a slightly different, but pressing, example, consider how federal government transfers through military equipment and police funds have allowed local police to move beyond the scope of their original domains and into such things as drug raids, war-on-terror raids, SWAT raids, and a number of other activities.[12] The "we have a police state" sentiment reflects the notion that state and local police have vastly expanded into areas in which citizens do not desire them to be. But these activities were enabled through fiscal transfers from the federal government.

One of the other reasons why state and local government activity expands through intergovernmental fiscal transfers is because some federal grant programs require matching—that is, for every x amount a state spends on a program, the federal government will contribute y amount. This incentive has stimulated state spending, and has led to the continuous program expansion and creation of bureaucracies to supervise spending and to continue applying for these various grants (Edwards, 2013).

Eliminating the current institutional structure of intergovernmental fiscal transfers, and thereby giving the government subunits more autonomy and independence from the central government, would better constrain the growth of these state and local governments. This is because it forces the state and local government budget constraint to be more binding because the state and local government can finance government programs only through (1) increasing taxes or (2) borrowing money. The third option of fiscal transfers has been eliminated.[13] In other words, government becomes more constrained in its ability to spend and grow. When we alter the institutional structures of our society to be more polycentric by eliminating these intergovernmental fiscal transfers, we can significantly constrain overall growth of government by constraining the expansions of state and local governments.

In the second mechanism, intergovernmental fiscal transfers increase *federal* government spending. This occurs because, when state and local governments are tied to the central government fiscally, a new avenue is created for state and local governments to demand *more* grants from federal governments in a political bargain exchange. Just as special interest groups lobby the government to enact certain polices, to receive subsidies, or to obtain other special privileges, state governments now essentially turn into special interest groups lobbying the federal government to increase the amount that they can bring back to their home states, or lobbying for certain policies that would benefit their states or the companies in their states. As states and localities lobby for more and more grants from the federal government, this increases federal government spending and adds to the growing problem of public debt that has motivated this chapter. It is no surprise that, when we open up this avenue for states to lobby for more and more Medicaid funding, for example, this leads to skyrocketing national spending on Medicaid.

Furthermore, opening up this avenue of intergovernmental fiscal transfers creates a moral hazard problem for the states, which leads to even more federal government spending. Because the states now face a soft budget constraint, they can run deficits in anticipation of the federal government subsidizing them and bailing them out. States can now act more "carelessly" with their finances. This is analogous to the moral hazard problems created when the government gives firms an implicit or explicit guarantee of bailouts or financial assistance in the event of difficulty. Kornai (1986: 3, 22) describes how this idea can be applied to government: "If a local government gets additional funds from a higher-level government budget, then a soft budget constraint situation may evolve," and just as a soft budget constraint incentivizes firms to act carelessly, it also incentivizes local governments to act carelessly. Consider, for example, California asking for $6.9 billion in federal aid in 2010 when it was on the brink of a budget crisis (Woo and Carlton, 2010). California and states such as New Jersey, New York, Illinois, Massachusetts, and Kentucky were ranked among the worst-off fiscally in 2013 (Norcross, 2015). Thus, by creating an avenue for states to become special interest groups lobbying the government, intergovernmental fiscal transfers have allowed for and led to a massive growth of *federal* government spending.

Altering the institutional structures of the U.S. government to be more polycentric by creating more autonomous state and local subunits would eliminate the problems caused by intergovernmental fiscal transfers. This is because, when we eliminate the intergovernmental fiscal transfers, we also eliminate the two channels we identified that allow for massive public debt problems and the growth of state, local, and federal governments.

The role of competition

The central feature of polycentricism is that it allows for competition among localities for citizens. In this type of setting, there is a high degree of competition that can effectively act as a check on governments because citizens "vote with their feet" and this generates incentives for localities to compete for citizens—that is, the Tiebout (1956) model. In other words, because citizens have the ability to leave jurisdictions, this gives them the power to incentivize government officials to provide governance services that are better suited for their needs or else they will relocate their "payments" (taxes) to other suppliers of governance.[14] The possibility of exit power in a polycentric organization mimics (to a lesser degree) market competition whereby consumers "vote" with their dollars for the products or services that meet their desires and needs. The competition for the consumer dollar incentivizes firms to provide better products and services.

This type of competition thus creates self-generating mechanisms to align the incentives of government closer with the desires of their people and thereby creates a more responsive government. Localities that heavily burden their citizens with taxes and provide bad services will, in exchange, see their citizens migrate to other jurisdictions. If a particular locality chooses to cater more to special interest groups and less to their citizens, these citizens (taxpayers) can punish government actors by moving elsewhere. The competition among localities for citizens on the whole creates subgovernments that cater less to special interest group and, as result, we see fewer things like large farm bills benefiting only big farmer owners.

It is true that some citizens would prefer to live in areas in which there are "larger" governments and in which governments provide more services, such as transfer programs. In this case, citizens would move to localities that have more government programs. However, these citizens would be forced to internalize the costs of having a large government because the cost of government programs is now spread among a smaller population. This is one important self-generating mechanism in polycentric institutions that would help to minimize the growth of government. In polycentric institutions, citizens who prefer to have "large" governments could live in that world, but they would have to pay for their own large government. In other words, you can have your welfare state, but it's going to cost you. Because polycentric institutions force citizens to internalize the cost of large government programs, this leads to pressure for "demanding" a smaller government. Furthermore, political actors also internalize the costs of spending because citizens have the ability to exit and vote with their feet. If one state or locality provides a large welfare state and because the costs of the welfare state are spread among a smaller population, making it more costly per person, then citizens who choose to leave because it is too expensive to live in that area are putting pressure on government leaders to internalize their natural proclivities to expand.

This idea that competition between localities can constrain is also discussed by Scott Gordon (1999: 361), who argues that "efficient government and constrained government are not incompatible," and that the critical institutional discovery over time and place (from ancient Athens to modern Britain) is that, in those instances in which this was achieved, there was a pluralistic distribution of political power and the principle of countervailance was embedded in the constitutional construction. When these principles are absent in the institutional configuration, or are allowed to be eroded, then efficient government and constrained government are in conflict: Leviathan gets tamed by competition, rather than unleashed through the suppression of the competitive forces that nudge decision makers to pursue prudent fiscal policy. Good governance—that is, the quest for efficient and constrained government—results as a byproduct of the competitive forces at work in the political economy.

The importance of a polycentric system of government in constraining government power here is that it has self-generating incentives to keep government small even in the face of a crisis. If we want political leaders to abide by certain principles, it should be in their best interests to do so. Polycentric institutions align the incentives of government with their citizens, so that "not overstepping its boundaries" is in the government's best interests. These self-generating incentives are present because localities face hard budget constraints (no intergovernmental fiscal transfers) and this is coupled with interjurisdictional competition.

The decentralization of money

The narrative in taming Leviathan must also begin with the recognition that the federal government can raise revenue in only three ways: taxing, borrowing, or printing money. In *The Wealth of Nations*, Adam Smith (1977 [1776]) expounded on the idea of the "juggling trick" whereby governments hide the extent of their public debt through "pretend payments." Smith's idea was that government spending in the name of the public interest often leads to significant increases in the public debt. This public debt is sustainable for a period of time and can be serviced through pretend payments, such as subsequent borrowing or the printing of money. As he explains:

> When national debts have once been accumulated to a certain degree, there is scarce, I believe, a single instance of their having been fairly and completely paid . . . public bankruptcy has been disguised under the appearance of a pretend payment. . . . When it becomes necessary for a state to declare itself bankrupt, in the same manner as when it becomes necessary for an individual to do so, a fair, open, and avowed bankruptcy is always the measure which is both least dishonorable to the debtor, and least hurtful to the creditor. The honour of a state is surely very poorly provided for, when in order to cover the disgrace of real bankruptcy, it has recourse to a juggling trick of this kind. . . Almost all states, however, ancient as well as modern, when reduced to this necessity, have upon some occasions, played this very juggling trick.
>
> (Smith, 1977 [1776]: 466–68)

The reason why Smith argued that governments resort to borrowing and printing money is that there are real problems and limits to financing spending by taxing. First, it creates political backlash and is political suicide for those politicians who advocate burdening citizens with increases in taxes. Second, increasing tax rates may actually result in less revenue (the Laffer curve) because citizens are incentivized to work less. Third, it creates an underground economy and tax-evading responses. Lastly, it incentivizes citizens to move their work to areas with more favorable tax climates.

Borrowing money and inflating are the remaining choices, and this is what politicians tend to do. Buchanan and Wagner (1999) argue that, because present taxpayers are not burdened by debt-financing expenditures and because present taxpayers are the ones voting for politicians, politicians have an incentive to keep tax rates low (so as to not burden the present generation) and to pay for public expenditures with debt. Governments can finance spending by borrowing money, and then they have the ability to inflate and pay it back in a cheaper currency. Thus, when the federal government is not constrained in its borrowing and inflating abilities, it will continue to use those methods. In this light, the public debt crisis should not come as a surprise.

One way of preventing this natural growth in public debt that has been proposed is a rule that would stipulate independence between the federal government and the Federal Reserve (known as the Fed). Further, scholars have also advocated that the Fed should follow a set of guidelines when practicing monetary policy so that it is not acting as an arm of the federal government. There are a variety of ways in which this argument has been presented, from Friedman's (1953) long and variable lag, through Kydland and Prescott's (1977) time inconsistency, to Epstein's (1995) simple rules for a complex world. But our concern with this traces back to what Hayek (1976a, 1976b) saw as the critical contribution of Smith and his contemporaries: the establishment of an institutional regime of governance that minimized the downside risk of bad men in power doing harm. In *Capitalism and Freedom*, Friedman (1962: 50) captured this point when he argued that:

> It may be that these mistakes were excusable on the basis of the knowledge available to men at the time—though I happen to think not. But that is really beside the point. Any system which gives so much power and so much discretion to a few men that mistakes—excusable or not—can have such far-reaching effects is a bad system. It is a bad system to believers in freedom just because it gives a few men such power without any effective check by the body politic—this is the key political argument against an "independent" central bank. But it is a bad system even to those who set security higher than freedom. Mistakes, excusable or not, cannot be avoided in a system which disperses responsibility yet gives a few men great power, and which thereby makes important policy actions highly dependent on accidents of personality. This is the key technical argument against an "independent" bank. To paraphrase Clemenceau, *money is much too serious a matter to be left to the Central Bankers.*

The manipulation of money and credit, as well as deficit financing, is simply too seductive a set of tools for earning short-run political "profit" to be easily bound by rules. This is evident from the history of the Fed's relationship with political leaders. Even though the Fed is technically supposed to be independent, the reality is that it regularly accommodates debt and succumbs to political pressures (Smith and Boettke, 2015). Smith and Boettke (2015) document the relationship between each Federal Reserve chairman (beginning in the 1950s) with the U.S. President and Treasury Department. For example, in November 1955, the Treasury was having a difficult time issuing securities on the market. As a response, the Federal Open Market Committee supported the debt issue (Smith and Boettke, 2015). Describing the events of this time, Clifford (1965: 321) noted:

> Such quick and strong cooperative action showed that there was indeed a "revolving door" in the "fence" between the independent agencies, the Treasury and the Federal Reserve. Perhaps it could be said that really the fence was invisible and that the neighbors cultivated a common garden, but each with his own tools.

Smith and Boettke (2015) also document how U.S. President Dwight Eisenhower constantly put pressure on then Fed chairman William Martin to provide accommodating monetary policy throughout the 1950s. This passage from Eisenhower's diary illustrates this point:

> [T]alked to the secretary of the Treasury in order to develop real pressure on the Federal Reserve Board for loosening credit still further. . . . Secretary Humphrey promised to put the utmost pressure on Chairman Martin of the Federal Reserve Board in order to get a greater money supply throughout the country.
>
> (Quoted in Smith and Boettke, 2015: 5)

When U.S. President Lyndon Johnson took office in 1963, he also utilized the Fed as he vastly expanded spending to begin his Great Society programs and to finance the Vietnam War (Smith and Boettke, 2015). Another well-documented event is the pressure that was put on then Fed chairman Paul Volcker in the 1980s, of which Smith and Boettke (2015: 18) write, "thus, under the pressure to accommodate deficit spending, and under the pressure from the executive and legislative branch, Volcker delivered easy monetary policy."

What these examples illustrate is that the Fed is often used as a tool for politicians, which reality stands in stark opposition to Bernanke's (2010: 13) statement that we need an independent Fed to "make monetary policy independently of short-term political influence." In fact, it seems as though the Fed's monetary policy is used precisely *for* the purposes of short-term political needs.

In monetary policy, the three leading classical liberal political economists of the second half of the twentieth century—Hayek, Friedman, and Buchanan—all sought ways of binding the monetary authority by rules and tried to think through additional ways of establishing effective constraints, only to be frustrated in their efforts. In consequence, they all decided in one way or another that monetary policy should be taken out of the hands of state decision makers (Boettke and Smith, 2014). Hayek (1976a, 1976b), who originally advocated for central banks, became disillusioned with this idea. He most famously called for the denationalization of money and for the abolition of a state monopoly supplier of the currency, stating:

> I do not want to question that a very intelligent and wholly independent national or international monetary authority might do better than an international gold standard, or any other sort of automatic system. But I see not the slightest hope that any government, or any institution subject to political pressure, will ever be able to act in such a manner.
>
> (Hayek, 1976a: 14)

Later, Hayek (1976a: 16) expanded on the idea: "Money is certainly too dangerous an instrument to leave to the fortuitous expediency of politicians—or, it seems, economists."

One of the beneficial effects of taking monetary policy out of the hands of the government is the immunization of money from the influence of democratic politics. There are other institutional immunizations, such as currency boards—and, in fact, the European Central Bank (ECB) was one such attempt to eliminate the ability of the member nations to monetize their fiscal irresponsibility and, in this way, to impose on them a need for fiscal discipline that otherwise they never could have pursued. Sound money may be possible only under a competitive note issue system, as advanced and argued by Lawrence White (1984, 1992, 1999). Political pressures aside, sound money requires a matching of supply and demand to both provide the "needs of trade" and approximate, as best as is humanly possible, a "neutral" money.[15] Selgin (1988) has argued that a free banking system best accomplishes this task because of the incentives and information provided through the competitive process of note issue, whereas a monopoly supplier of the currency has to attempt to match the supply and demand for money without such guiding signals.

Thus, to tame Leviathan, we need to complement polycentricism with the decentralization of money. Since the Fed acts as an arm of the Treasury and is not constrained by its "independence" rule, the U.S. federal government does not face a budget constraint. Recall that a hard budget constraint is necessary to induce a government to act carefully with its finances. This ability to monetize debt basically tells the federal government that it can "go crazy" with spending. Taking money out of the hands of the federal government would harden the budget constraint of the government such that if it were to want to increase spending, it would have only two options: (1) to increase taxes; or

(2) to borrow. But, this time, borrowing would have an enormous cost because the government would have to behave as other borrowers do in the market for loanable funds. Taking money out of the hands of government would thus constraint government in its growth and spending habits.

Conclusion

One of the reasons why governments have grown expansively in the last century is because they are in a position to increase public debt and they have the opportunity to monetize those debts. The second half of the twentieth century was a long march away from the governing principles of classical liberal political economy. And the twenty-first century has continued that trend, rather than reversed it, despite the evidence of the failure of the communist alternative in Eastern and Central Europe and the former Soviet Union, and the problems identified with the social democratic welfare states of the Western democracies. The public debt crisis that is identified with Portugal, Ireland, Italy, Greece, and Spain (known as the PIIGS countries) could easily be applied to the situation in various U.S. states such as California, Illinois, Michigan, New York, and Wisconsin.

Adam Smith long ago identified the natural proclivities of governments to engage in the tactics of deficits, debts, and debasement. Left unconstrained, this method will lead to a breakdown in economies and economic well-being. Rather than Smith's text serving as a warning, as it had for roughly the first 150 years of U.S. history, the last seventy years have seen this tactic intellectually justified and it has, in fact, become institutionalized. The unleashing of Leviathan that results from the ability to run deficits, debts, and debasement has resulted in an extraordinary expansion of the scale and scope of government. The problem is that this method is unstable and, in terms of long-run economic vitality, it is disastrous.

The taming of this Leviathan cannot rely on asking politicians to cut down on spending. We propose that the only way of effectively constraining government is by altering the institutional structures to be more polycentric and by eliminating the government monopoly on currency. While we acknowledge that these institutional fixes are not perfect, we believe they are the best available options, since they have important self-generating mechanisms to constrain government even in the face of temptations to expand. The features of a polycentric institution complemented by the decentralization of money would move us closer to the reality of a constrained government.

Notes

* "Taming Leviathan" was originally published in the *Supreme Court Economic Review*, 2015, vol. 23, no.1, pp. 279–303. It is reprinted here with permission from the University of Chicago Press.
1 See also Greve (2012: 257), who explains that the founding architects of the U.S. Constitution were not oblivious to the prospects of fiscal end-runs, but thought that the prohibitions against paper money and unapportioned direct taxes would serve

as a constraint. Furthermore, they operated under the assumption that the central government functioned under a hard budget constraint.

2 We will not go into specific details of what these activities are, but we believe that the ongoing public debt crises occurring in Western democracies is one important indication of governments that have massively expanded beyond their delineated boundaries.

3 See, e.g., Anderson and Hill (1980).

4 We are referring to the numbers in Table 1.1.

5 See Epstein (2006, 2014), who provides evidence and an examination of how the Progressives rewrote the U.S. Constitution.

6 Consider, for example, the emergence of Keynesian economics after the Progressive era. The Keynesian hegemony and, in fact, the neoclassical synthesis of macroeconomic demand management aiming to eradicate economic fluctuations and mass unemployment with microeconomic regulation aiming to address the inefficiencies of market failures, including, but not limited to, monopoly power, was established in the economics profession to fit the new institutional reality of government. There has been a long "clash of economic ideas," as White (2012), details, in which this post-World War II consensus in economics gets challenged on a theoretical and empirical level at every turn. Although ideas are important and can serve as constraints, it is important also to analyze the institutional structures and the ways in which they can constrain government growth.

7 See Kotlikoff and Burns (2004). See also Wagner (2013: 13): "Once it is recognized that budgets arise through a political process, we can use the pattern of budgetary outcomes over some sequence of years to draw inferences about the central operating properties of the budgetary regime out of which that pattern has emerged. During the first 150 years or so of the American republic, that pattern conformed largely to the budgetary principles of sound finance. Deficits were acquired during wars and depressions, while surpluses were accumulated during normal times to reduce the debt. In contrast, the past fifty or so years of budgetary experience shows a starkly different budgetary pattern, one that conforms pretty much to the principle of functional finance, where little significance is attached to the condition of the budget per se. With functional finance, the condition of the budget, whether in deficit or surplus, should be whatever is necessary to promote full employment, however this might be defined. To be sure, it could be argued that a proper application of functional finance over the past half-century would have seen more than five years of surplus. Nevertheless, a regime of functional finance is the alternative to a regime of sound finance in that the budget balance is no longer a standard against which fiscal responsibility can be judged." As Wagner goes on to explain in this book, institutional constraints that were in place under a regime of sound finance were relaxed under functional finance; the ability to wrestle with the fiscal commons is jeopardized, and the peculiar business of politics exacerbates the deterioration of fiscal discipline and fiscal responsibility.

8 Friedman (1947: 415): "Lerner writes as if it were possible to base conclusions about appropriate institutional arrangements almost exclusively on analysis of the formal conditions for an optimum. Unfortunately, this cannot be done. It has been long known that there are alternative institutional arrangements that would enable the formal conditions for an optimum to be attained."

9 Aspects of government growth, such as through scale and scope, are conceptually different. However, for the purposes of this chapter, scope is tied to scale and thus they are treated as interrelated.

10 For the purposes of this chapter, we will use states and local governments interchangeably as a way of referring to subgovernments or subunits of government.

11 Osman here is describing how, when aid was directed to education, expenditures on government activities other than education increased. He also finds similar results when analyzing aid to other areas, such as health.

12 See Balko (2006, 2014); Hall and Coyne (2013).

13 Unlike the federal government, states do not have the ability to print money.

14 One structure of a polycentric order is federalism. We use "polycentricism" in this chapter because it is a broader concept and encompasses the structure of federalism. Thus our analysis here can be extended to include federal structures and fiscal federalism. "Federalism" refers to a hierarchic structure of government that allows for considerable autonomy and competition between lower levels of government. Polycentric systems of government organization do not necessarily have this direct hierarchic structure.

15 See Selgin and White (1994). See also Selgin, Lastrapes and White (2012), who explain macroeconomic performance under the Federal Reserve System in the United States and argue that it has not outperformed earlier systems.

References

Advisory Commission on Intergovernmental Relations (ACIR). 1977. *Federal grants: Their effects on state-local expenditures, employment levels, wage rates.* Report, February. Available at http://www.library.unt.edu/gpo/acir/Reports/policy/A-61.pdf

Anderson, T. L., and P. J. Hill. 1980. *The birth of a transfer society.* Stanford, CA: Hoover Institution Press.

Balko, R. 2006. *Overkill: The rise of paramilitary police raids in America.* Washington, DC: Cato Institute.

Balko. R. 2014. *Rise of the warrior cop: The militarization of America's police forces.* New York: Public Affairs.

Bernanke, B. 2010. *Central bank independence, transparency, and accountability.* Speech, November. Available at http://www.federalreserve.gov/newsevents/speech/bernanke20100525a.htm

Boettke, P. J., and D. J. Smith. 2014. *Monetary policy and the quest for robust political economy.* Working paper.

Boettke, P. J., C. Coyne and P. Leeson. 2006. High priests and lowly philosophers: The battle for the soul of economics. *Case Western Reserve Law Review, 56*(3), 551–568.

Buchanan, J. M. 1958. The Thomas Jefferson Center. *University of Virginia News Letter,* 35.

Buchanan, J. M. 1975. *The limits of liberty.* Indianapolis, IN: Liberty Fund.

Buchanan, J. M. 1977. *Freedom in constitutional contract: Perspectives of a political economist.* College Station, TX: Texas A&M University Press.

Buchanan, J. M., and R. Wagner. 1999. *Democracy in deficit.* Indianapolis, IN: Liberty Fund.

Clifford, J. 1965. *The independence of the Federal Reserve System.* Philadelphia, PA: University of Pennsylvania Press.

Congressional Budget Office (CBO). 2013. *Federal grants to state and local governments.* Report, March. Available at https://www.cbo.gov/publication/43967

Edwards, C. 2013. Fiscal federalism. *Web page,* June 1. Available at https://www.downsizinggovernment.org/fiscal-federalism

Epstein, R. 1995. *Simple rules for a complex world.* Cambridge, MA: Harvard University Press.

Epstein, R. 2006. *How the progressives rewrote the constitution.* Washington, DC: Cato Institute.

Epstein, R. 2014. *The classical liberal constitution: The uncertain quest for limited government.* Cambridge, MA: Harvard University Press.

Frey, B. 2001. A utopia? Government without territorial monopoly. *Journal of Institutional & Theoretical Economics, 157*(2), 162–175.

Frey, B. 2005. Functional overlapping, competing jurisdictions: Redrawing the geographic borders of administration. *European Journal of Law Reform, 5*(3/4), 643–555.

Friedman, M. 1947. Lerner on the economics of control. *Journal of Political Economy, 55*(5), 405–416.

Friedman, M. 1953. *A monetary and fiscal framework for economic stability in essays in positive economics.* Chicago, IL: University of Chicago Press.

Friedman, M. 1962. *Capitalism and freedom.* Chicago, IL: University of Chicago Press.

Gordon, S. 1999. *Controlling the state.* Cambridge, MA: Harvard University Press.

Greve, M. 2012. *The upside-down constitution.* Cambridge, MA: Harvard University Press.

Hahn, L. A. 1949. *The economics of illusion: A critical analysis of contemporary economic theory and policy.* New York: Squier.

Hall, A., and C. Coyne. 2013. The militarization of U.S. domestic policing. *The Independent Review, 17*(4), 485–504.

Hamburger, P. 2014. *Is administrative law unlawful?* Chicago, IL: University of Chicago Press.

Hayek, F. A. 1976a. *Choice in currency: A way to stop inflation.* Occasional paper. Available at https://iea.org.uk/publications/research/choice-in-currency-a-way-to-stop-inflation

Hayek, F. A. 1976b. *Denationalisation of money.* London: Institute for Economic Affairs.

Higgs, R. 1987. *Crisis and Leviathan: Critical episodes in the growth of American government.* New York: Oxford University Press.

Holcombe, R. 1996. Growth of the federal government in the 1920s. *Cato Journal, 16*(2), 175–199.

Hoover, K., and S. Sheffrin, 1992. Causation, spending, and taxes: Sand in the sandbox or tax collector for the welfare state? *The American Economic Review, 82*(1), 225–248.

Hoover, K., and M. Siegler. 2000. Taxing and spending in the long view: The causal structure of U.S. fiscal policy. *Oxford Economic Papers, 52*(4), 745–773.

Kornai, J. 1986. The soft budget constraint. *Kyklos, 39*(1), 3–30.

Kotlikoff, L., and S. Burns. 2004. *The coming generational storm.* Cambridge, MA: MIT Press.

Kotlikoff, L., and S. Burns. 2012. *The clash of generations.* Cambridge, MA: MIT Press.

Kydland, F., and E. Prescott. 1977. Rules rather than discretion: The inconsistency of optimal plans. *Journal of Political Economy, 85*(3), 473–492.

Norcross, E. 2015. *Ranking the states by fiscal condition.* Report, July. Available at https://www.mercatus.org/statefiscalrankings-2015-edition

Osman, J. 1966. The dual impact of federal aid on state and local government expenditures. *National Tax Journal, 19*(4), 362–372.

Ostrom, V. 1973. *The intellectual crisis in American public administration.* Tuscaloosa, AL: University of Alabama Press.

Ostrom, V., C. Tiebout and R. Warren. 1961. The organization of government in metropolitan areas: A theoretical inquiry. *American Political Science Review, 55*(4), 831–842.

Samuelson, P. 1948. *Economics.* New York: McGraw-Hill.

Schumpeter, J. 1954. *History of economic analysis.* London: Allen & Unwin.

Selgin, G. A. 1988. *A theory of free banking.* Lanham, MD: Rowman & Littlefield.

Selgin, G. A., and L. White. 1994. How would the invisible hand handle money? *Journal of Economic Literature*, *32*(4), 1718–1749.

Selgin, G. A., W. Lastrapes and L. White. 2012. Has the Fed been a failure? *Journal of Macroeconomics*, *34*(3), 569–596.

Smith, A. 1977 [1776]. *An inquiry into the nature and causes of the wealth of nations*. Chicago, IL: University of Chicago Press.

Smith, D. J., and P. J. Boettke. 2015. An episodic history of modern Fed independence. *Independent Review*, *20*(1), 99–120.

Tiebout, C. 1956. A pure theory of local expenditures. *Journal of Political Economy*, *64*(5), 416–424.

Tullock, G. 2005. *Bureaucracy*. Indianapolis, IN: Liberty Fund.

Wagner, R. 2013. *Deficits, debt and democracy: Wrestling with tragedy on the fiscal commons*. Cheltenham: Edward Elgar.

Wagner, R. 2014. *Politics as peculiar business: Insights from a theory of entangled political economy*. Cheltenham: Edward Elgar.

White, L. 1984. *Free banking in Britain*. Cambridge: Cambridge University Press.

White, L. 1992. *Competition and currency*. New York: New York University Press.

White, L. 1999. *The theory of monetary institutions*. Hoboken, NJ: Wiley-Blackwell.

White, L. 2012. *The clash of economics ideas*. New York: Cambridge University Press.

Wilson, W. 1887. The study of administration. *Political Science Quarterly*, *2*(2), 197–222.

Wilson, W. 1956 [1885]. *Congressional government*. New York: Meridian Books.

Woo, S., and J. Carlton. 2010. California requests billions from the U.S. *Wall Street Journal*, January 9.

2 Constitutional drift and political dysfunction

Underappreciated maladies of the political commons

Alexander William Salter

Introduction*

My purpose in this chapter is to develop a theory of political dysfunction as it relates to constitutional drift—the tendency of *de facto* political procedures to change when these procedures are no longer incentive-compatible for wielders of political power. Importantly, constitutional drift will refer to informal constitutions—that is, the actual decision procedure of the state—with drift the unintended result of political bargains among political elites. As such, formal "constitutional moments" or revisions are not covered under this category. My exploration will be theoretical, using tools of economic and political theory to explain how, in the ordinary course of governing, the institutions of governance may undergo organizational change such that the governors no longer have access to the knowledge necessary to govern in a generally beneficial manner, even assuming that they wished to do so.

The term "political dysfunction" may be normatively charged, but I believe it is capable of doing positive analytical work in helping us to understand the state of currently existing governance institutions in the Western constitutional democracies. For clarification, by "political dysfunction," I do not simply mean "outcomes we do not like," although this certainly is a part of it; instead, I will argue that political dysfunction is best understood as an institutional malady. In particular, political dysfunction describes constitutional drift resulting in a particular structure of governance institutions that lack important self-correcting (negative feedback) mechanisms. Alternatively, political dysfunction lies in the failure of political institutions to cope with the "knowledge problem" (e.g. Hayek 1960, 1978–81; see also Oakeshott 1991) as applied to the political process. It is thus complementary to, but conceptually distinct from, schools of thought that emphasize "incentive problems" in politics—namely, the Virginia School of political economy (e.g. Buchanan and Tullock 1962; Buchanan 1987). A concrete way of conceptualizing the distinction is to recognize that constitutional drift frequently has its roots in incentive problems—namely, incentive incompatibility between the welfare of political elites and the welfare of those subject to their rule (Salter 2015). This in turn leads to a reordering of political structures such that these structures are less capable of coping with the knowledge problem. Political dysfunction is the conjunction of the two. I will take the former as my point of departure and focus analytical efforts on the latter, showing the nature and importance of political dysfunction in the context of the American republic.[1]

Political dysfunction so conceived will be concerning for those continuing Buchanan's (1975) project: enabling the protective state and the productive state, while enfeebling the predatory state. Political dysfunction culminates in political institutions' increasing difficulty in generating reliable informational feedback and hence the erosion of mechanisms for correcting errors. This means that effective means for enforcing property rights, upholding the rule of law, and providing public goods—all abstract *desiderata* that require institutional context for navigating the trade-offs involved—will increasingly be difficult to discover, while political processes fall prey to intergroup expropriation and rent seeking. Errors in the political process will not only be difficult to correct, but also difficult to identify in the first place. The sense in which I use terms such as "mistake" or "error" should be thought of in terms of this means–ends framework, rather than as relating directly to normative goals. In this sense, I am building on the foundation laid by Austrian political economy (Mises 1951; see also Ikeda 1997, 2003), to which means–ends analysis of political process, from the perspective of information compatibility, is essential.

Seminal theories of political dysfunction (although this exact terminology was not employed by their authors) are those of Madison and Tocqueville. Madison worried about the tyranny of the majority; Tocqueville, about a paternalistic mild despotism. These are arguments concerning the erosion of political institutions—a version of what I have called constitutional drift. In addition, these authors worried that the political forces that bring them about would not subsequently relent. This is clearly a vision of undesirable end-states that are not self-correcting. However, it is sometimes difficult to ascertain whether these are, in essence, problems of outcome or problems of process. In other words, it is unclear whether the end-state is inherent in the initial setting of the meta-rules, as opposed to constitutional novelty arising from bargains in an environment of genuine uncertainty. In reality, both play a role, but the relationship between process and outcome in a theory of political dysfunction could be more fully specified. Furthermore, these processes implicitly contain a mixture of incentive problems and knowledge problems. It is not problematic that these frictions are entangled—in political dynamics, they are necessarily so—but we could benefit from a more rigorous theoretical paradigm that (a) places a conceptual boundary on these two kinds of problems, and (b) specifies the properties and implications of each. My theory of political dysfunction will identify the boundary between information and incentive problems. It will also highlight the difficulties associated with political institutions whose information feedback is diluted.[2]

Before proceeding, I want to state clearly that I will not treat political dysfunction attributable to conscious constitutional change, such as the 17th

Amendment to the U.S. Constitution, which provided for the direct election of senators (Zywicki 1994). Instead, I focus on the morphing interpretation of existing constitutional restraints, akin to Warren's (1932) treatment of Congress and the General Welfare Clause. Also, I will not argue that all constitutional drift has injurious consequences. Counterexamples abound. For example, the transformation of Great Britain under the Stuarts, from an absolutist state to one of *de facto* limited government that credibly committed to protecting property rights and upholding the rule of law, was a constitutional change that many look upon favorably (North and Weingast 1989). I am limiting myself to constitutional drift that results in deleterious consequences for the purpose of building a theory of political dysfunction. That the former can result in the latter does not mean that it must.

I organize the remainder of the chapter as follows: In the next section, I provide an overview of constitutional drift as rooted in constitutional bargains among political elites. Understanding this bargaining process is necessary to set the stage for analyzing currently existing governance institutions and hence political dysfunction. I then focus on developing the theory of political dysfunction proper, showing its necessary relation to feedback erosion that follows from the "tragedy of the commons" in governance. As an illustration of the theory, I consider the case of fiscal imbalances in the American republic, showing how these imbalances are simply one way in which political dysfunction manifests. I conclude by discussing some implications of my theory, as well as the costs and benefits of some possible remedies.

Constitutional bargains and constitutional drift

Constitutional drift is the necessary starting point of my theory. In the United States, it is almost self-evident that there has been a significant amount of constitutional drift since 1789. The resemblance between the existing *de facto* constitution and the original *de jure* Constitution is tenuous at best (Epstein 2014; Greve 2012). This is explained by a series of constitutional modifications that took place outside the official procedures for Constitutional (note the capital) amendment, the most notable being the New Deal. While it would be a mistake to reify the New Deal as a complete break with the previous constitutional tradition, it nonetheless remains the singular event that characterized the restructuring of U.S. political institutions. What had previously been, in an ideal-typical sense, best characterized as a system of polycentric federalism (Ostrom 1997, 2008 [1971], 2008 [1973]; see also Buchanan and Tullock 1962) has since evolved into a system of monocentric nationalism. In the language of Greve (2012), "competitive" federalism has been replaced by "cartel" federalism: genuine competition between jurisdictions in the provision of governance services and other collective goods has ceased, and local administrative bodies are largely implementation bureaucracies for plans devised in Washington.

I want to emphasize that, for the purposes of this chapter, I attach no primary normative significance to constitutional drift. There were, and continue to be, powerful arguments justifying the drift and the final state of affairs; there were, and continue to be, powerful arguments against them. I do not wish to engage this issue here. I take as my starting point that constitutional drift—both in the United States and in political regimes throughout history—exists as an important phenomenon for study, and I will focus on drawing out its implications.

As hinted above, constitutional drift always centers around the *de facto* constitution—that is, the actual balance of power, reflected in political structures and procedures, between the One, the Few, and the Many. *De jure* constitutions—that is, formal or written constitutions—can reflect this actual balance, but do not necessarily do so. *De jure* constitutions can be binding only if the structure they elucidate is self-enforcing (de Lara, Grief, and Jha 2008; Leeson 2011; Mittal and Weingast 2011). This does not mean that *de jure* constitutions are superfluous. They can be extremely useful as coordinating devices. For example, since there are frequently many, many possible political structures that have some legitimacy within a given population, the creation of *de jure* constitutions can help holders of political power to coordinate on one particular political equilibrium, when many such equilibria are possible (Hardin 1982, 1989; Ordeshook 1992). However, if the *de jure* structures and procedures do not accurately reflect the *de facto* relationships among relevant wielders of political power, the *de jure* constitution may obscure, rather than illuminate, the actual operations of the political sector (Salter 2014).

Constitutional drift is best understood as flux in *de facto* political structures and procedures. In the United States, the result is the wedge between the Constitution and the constitution. In polities without formal constitutions, such as Great Britain, the distinction is less obvious, but no less real. Constitutional drift must be understood as a result of the political bargaining process. The final distribution of political power, at any given point, is the outcome of bargains between holders of political power. To the extent that these bargains change the actual operating procedures of the political process, they can properly be classified as constitutional bargains.

Briefly broadening our perspective will help us to understand the importance of constitutional bargains. Congleton (2011) explores a series of constitutional bargains in Western polities dating back to the Middle Ages. His analysis focuses on bargains between kings and their councils/parliaments. The overall narrative documents the transition from medieval "shareholder states," in which holders of political power were literally owners of the realm, to modern constitutional democracy. In his narrative, these bargains were beneficial for the One, the Few, and the Many—originally, the king, the nobility, and the commoners. That the bargains were beneficial for kings and nobles is not surprising, given that they themselves were parties to the bargain. What is interesting is that, although commoners did not begin with a "seat at the table," constitutional bargains up to and including the reforms that formalized and expanded the franchise nonetheless increased their welfare.

It cannot be taken for granted that constitutional bargains will necessarily improve the welfare for all those who are subject to a given polity's structures and procedures. Whereas Congleton (2011) sees the rise of political modernity as a series of welfare-enhancing bargains, an alternative perspective is offered by Jouvenel (1993 [1945]). Jouvenel examines the same history as Congleton, finding instead a series of welfare-enhancing bargains between kings and the commoners, at the expense of nobles. This is only temporarily beneficial for kings: eventually, commoners recognize that the king, in their attempt to build a sufficiently powerful coalition against nobles, has granted commoners so much *de facto* power that commoners seize power, taking over an already-existing bureaucratic administrative apparatus. Whereas Congleton sees a monotonic increase in welfare, Jouvenel sees rises and falls, and, in some cases, cycles. In this sense, Jouvenel's analysis harks back to the cyclical political theories of classical antiquity, whereas Congleton's analysis is distinctly Whiggish.

For the theory of political dysfunction I develop here, it is unimportant whether Congleton's or Jouvenel's is ultimately the "correct" interpretation of Western political history.[3] What matters is the juxtaposition of the narratives, which highlights the *contingent* nature of welfare improvements for subjects as a result of constitutional bargains. This reminds us that when political bargains are struck between holders of political power and are also binding on those without political power, these bargains will not necessarily be in subjects' interests. (And, following Jouvenel's logic, they are not necessarily even in the interests of those party to the bargains!) We can use the perspective offered by Congleton and Jouvenel to analyze the properties of governance institutions as they existed, and as they currently exist, to see how they cope with information feedback in the context of political processes. Issues of feedback and error correction will follow from issues of incentive alignment (rulers exercising power in the interests of the ruled), which is why constitutional bargains and constitutional drift matter in the first place, but are conceptually distinct and merit their own discussion.

Political institutions and political dysfunction

The evolution of governance structures in Western polities (excepting the American republic) culminated in modern liberal democracy, from a form of government that we may call shareholder states. The crucial difference between these two forms, for the purposes of this chapter, is the structure of political property rights—what privileges are attached to those who hold and exercise political power. European shareholder states were a consociation of sometimes cooperating and frequently competing powers: kings contended with nobles, with the Church, with free cities and trade associations, etc. In these polities, significant political action could not be undertaken without near-unanimous support of the (representatives of) these corporate bodies, resulting in a *de facto* "generality norm" (Buchanan and Congleton 1998). In addition, each party to the political bargaining process was a *residual claimant*—they were owners of property and the income derived therefrom, the value of which would fluctuate in response to the conditions of governance. Governance arrangements that were in the interests of one party, presumably, would increase the value of their property and their income; governance arrangements contrary to these interests would do the opposite. Since each party to political bargains was concerned with the effects of politics on their property and income, and little could be done without near-unanimous consent, governance tended to be in the pecuniary interests of these groups and also had the (unintended) consequence of improving the economic value of the realm.

Ownership of the realm, in the form of residual claimancy attached to political property rights, is the bridge linking issues of incentive alignment to information alignment and knowledge generation. The story above contains an implicit reliance on the knowledge-generating properties of market processes made famous by Hayek (1948). We do not need to postulate an overly strong version of *homo economicus* to justify this narrative; instead, rationality among the actors resides in the fact that they operated within an environment that gave them information feedback to correct errors through time (Smith 2009). If the "owners of the realm" agreed to political action that they mistakenly believed would be beneficial, but which was in fact harmful, the reduction in the value of their property and income provided them with the signal needed to identify the error and correct it. Again, this was privately beneficial, but was also conducive to the stewardship of the economic value of the polity, since the polity itself was privately owned. These governance arrangements were obviously not intended to benefit those not party to political bargains, but frequently did so as a result of the particular institutional context, much as does ordinary market exchange as described in any textbook on the principles of economics. This is why several notable authors insist that the remarkable story of economic growth in the West is incomplete without reference to the *de facto* polycentricity, in an environment of political residual claimancy, that characterized the Middle Ages (e.g. Anderson 1991; Baechler 1975; Berman 1983; Raico 1994; Stark 2011: chs. 14–16).

Obviously, these governance structures no longer exist. Liberal democracy in the West is characterized by a very different structure of political property rights. The realm (now the state) is no longer private property; instead, the state is a *commons*, entrusted to representatives of the people (and the representatives' appointees) whose private benefit from exercising governance rights is significantly less tightly attached to their success in stewarding the polity's resources.[4] Political agents control the current use value of governance structures, but not their future (or market-capitalized) value. That this arrangement results in regrettable incentives for stewardship is well known (Hardin 1968). As seen above, it also has crucial implications for knowledge generation and error correction.

Without residual claimancy to the governance of the state, the aforementioned information feedback mechanism breaks down. For simplicity, assume a political agent in this environment whose only desire is to promote the "productive state"—that is, to provide the mixture of state-supplied goods and services that contributes to the public welfare (Buchanan 1975). How should she go about doing this? The most promising way seems to be to rely on the knowledge-generating features of the market process. Her shorthand decision rule is: provide the mixture of goods and services that maximize the value of the resources used in the provision.[5] In this sense, she can use profits derived from her activity purely as an informational crutch, abstracting from the admittedly powerful incentives that profits provide. However, this solution is not actually possible. Profits are the surplus of revenues over costs. The political agent can keep track of costs well enough, but since she is a public supplier in an environment of the state-as-commons, her output cannot be priced via market processes (supply and demand). She thus has no way of actually calculating revenue and hence half of the necessary information for calculating profits is unavailable. Without profitability (the analogue of income in a privately owned shareholder state), she has no access to a feedback mechanism to guide her in adjusting, over time, the mixture of state-supplied goods and services that the public most values (Mises 1944; Niskanen 1994 [1971]; Tullock 2005).

Thus an important information feedback mechanism, resulting from the transition from private to public governance, is no longer available. The dominant alternative, electoral feedback, which is ultimately supposed to structure bureaucratic activity, is inadequate under a range of plausible scenarios (e.g. Brennan 2014; Gunn 2014; see also Caplan 2007; Somin 2013).[6] The most obvious solution to the problem—to allow the political agent to supply her goods and services in the market, and hence allow them to be priced—would be a return to *de facto* private governance and thus solves the problem only by sidestepping it completely.[7] This impels us to search for an institutional arrangement that retains a powerful information feedback mechanism for governance, but avoids the abuses of private governance—sufficiently well known that, in the interests of space, I do not recount them—throughout history. With the above in mind, we can return to the specific example of the American republic, both as it was and as it is, to see what solutions it offers, if any.

The American republic and the fiscal commons

It is widely recognized that the American republic finds itself in a fiscal situation that is, at minimum, troubling. At time of writing, the national debt stands at approximately US$18 trillion, which is 107% of current gross domestic product (GDP). However, the national debt greatly understates the degree of the American republic's fiscal problems because it does not take account of unfunded liabilities. Unfunded liabilities are obligations that the central government has undertaken, but which have not yet come due. The largest sources of unfunded liabilities include expected future payments for social programs such as Medicare, Medicaid, and Social Security. There is no precise figure for unfunded liabilities as there is for the national debt, since the magnitude of unfunded liabilities depends on future claims, which itself depends on factors such as population growth, labor force participation, etc., which are probabilistic. As such, it is unclear for how much taxpayers are liable. Some (e.g. Wagner 2015) suggest $100 trillion as a reasonable estimate for the magnitude of unfunded liabilities, but Kotlikoff (2013: 6) argues that it may be as high as $205 trillion, or 10.3% of the estimated present discounted value of all future GDP.

The constitutional drift that resulted in the transformation of the American republic from a system of polycentric federalism to a system of monocentric nationalism created the environment out of which the current fiscal situation grew. In 1930, total government expenditure was 9.4% of GDP, of which 3% was central and 6.4% was state and local. In 2010, total government expenditure had grown to 38% of GDP, of which 24% was central and 14% was state and local. Constitutional drift resulted in not only an absolute growth in the size of government, but also a transference of activity away from state and local governments to the central government. Indeed, it is unlikely that, without the constitutional drift that resulted in an increase in the activities of the central government relative to state and local governments, such an absolute growth in size would not have been possible. When the *de facto* constitution limits government financing of state-supplied goods to smaller and more local governance units, they are incapable of imposing sufficient economic burden to finance this spending without driving the populace away to a less economically burdensome locality. This is the well-known Tiebout (1956) model: citizens "vote with their feet" to select the locality that provides their most-preferred mixture of state-supplied goods for a given tax bill. By relocating the locus of state-supplied goods provision from state and local to the central government, constitutional drift inadvertently resulted in significantly higher exit costs—it is more costly for individuals to leave their country, than to leave their city, county, or state—so, all else being equal, a larger fiscal burden becomes practicable.[8]

The fiscal situation is a predictable result of the creation of a fiscal commons (Wagner 2007, 2012a). The fiscal unit of government, or *fisc*, is stocked via taxation and depleted via ordinary expenditure. Political agents possess current control rights to the fisc, but not future value rights—these rights are inalienable and inseparable into negotiable shares, as opposed to more familiar private corporate enterprises.[9] The obvious result is that the fisc is understocked and overdepleted, as is any common pool resource in an environment without institutions that effectively check privately beneficial, but socially costly, behavior. This lack of institutional oversight in aligning incentives also explains why, from the perspective of holders of political power, public debt and unfunded liabilities are relied upon more than taxation (Wagner 2015).

But incentive misalignment, a result of constitutional drift, is only part of the story; we also need to consider the information feedback properties of such a system. Abstracting from whether the massive increase in state-supplied goods and services by the central government was justified or desirable, we notice that, in such a system, there is only weak informational feedback for whether such a system improves governance from the perspective of the governed. How can honest and well-intentioned political agents tell whether the current tax bill, along with present and future indebtedness, is "worth it" to consumers of state-supplied goods and services? Emigration may be one measure, but it is inherently noisy. Individuals may emigrate for a number of reasons only tangentially related to the quality of governance. Given that many other polities are wrestling with their own commons problems in governance and hence leaving one polity for an unambiguously preferred polity is highly unlikely, the informational content of emigration statistics is weak. Gross domestic product is also unsatisfactory, since while today's GDP can be increased by significant borrowing and spending by the public sector, is this worth the future costs? Nor is electoral feedback sufficient, given the voting public's well-known political and economic ignorance (Caplan 2007; Somin 2013). Since each voter has essentially no chance of casting the decisive vote, voters rationally abstain from acquiring political-economic information that would improve the quality of their decisions. This seriously undermines what is popularly, but mistakenly, believed to be the sufficient guarantee of error correction in political processes.

Furthermore, even if it were decided that the present fiscal situation is undesirable—that is, that it was reached in error—the lack of an information feedback system precludes the possibility of negative feedback dictating when the quality of fiscal decisions has improved. How do we "get out" of the current fiscal situation? "Raise taxes and cut spending" is a purely formal answer, which is to say not an answer at all. It is the same kind of statement as advising a private business to maximize profits "by setting marginal revenue equal to marginal cost": it describes the properties of a specific set of decisions, but provides no guidance for what the content of those decisions should be. It is unclear what information, if any, can be consulted to let political agents know how the mixture of state-supplied goods and services, and their accompanying financing methods, should be adjusted to restore fiscal balance, while still governing in the interests of the governed.

The American republic was previously structured in a manner that provided much more useful informational feedback concerning the mixture of state-supplied goods and services and their financing methods. Unlike the European polities, the American republic was never a privately owned realm. That model was explicitly rejected at the "constitutional moments" that produced both the Articles of Confederation and the Constitution. Instead, the model chosen was one that maintained many of the favorable properties of European-style private governance, but also left room for genuine self-governance. Consider an ideal-typical governance arrangement in the early days of the American republic, especially before the election of President Andrew Jackson. Constitutional rules focused the majority of public activity at the local level. The local fisc was stocked via property taxes, and the franchise was restricted to property owners. In such a system, raising taxes to increase the provision of goods by local government would be balanced against how these taxes would affect property values. If providing additional collective goods via collective action ultimately made the locality a more desirable place to live, from the perspective of current and potential residents, property values would increase. If, instead, the additional provision of collective goods was not worth the expense, in the eyes of current and potential residents, property values would decrease. Combined with the standard Tiebout (1956) mechanism, changes in property values provided those in a position to influence political decisions with reliable information as to the quality of those decisions at a moment in time, as well as guidance as to whether changes in the provision of collective goods by public means was improving throughout time. Thus polycentric federalism, with norms of localism and subsidiarity, combined with the particular public finance and franchise arrangements described above, were able to approximate the market mechanisms, in the form of negative feedback loops, which made European shareholder states effective governance providers (Olson 1982, 1993; Salter and Young 2016). But they did so in a way that preserved republican "liberty under law." The American experiment is thus illuminating for implementing a blueprint for governance that was effective and adaptive, in that it created the means for, and made effective use of, information feedback systems, but did not come with the baggage of the formalized sociopolitical hierarchy that was prevalent in Europe.

It was this negative feedback system that constitutional drift ultimately destroyed. We thus have a complete theory of political dysfunction: Beginning with bargains among holders of political power (an issue of incentives), constitutional drift results in a state of affairs in which the *de facto* political structure is no longer capable of generating information conducive to diagnosing political error (an issue of information) nor correcting error even if, perhaps as a result of a prior agreement on normative theory, holders of political power were to so desire. Since there is no feedback for error correction, there is no clear way in which the political process could revert to a more favorable arrangement for generating governance outcomes in the interests of both governors and governed.

Conclusion: pathways towards a constitution of functional politics

I chose the fiscal commons as the example to illustrate political dysfunction in the American republic because of the inherent link between extensive goods and services provision by the central government and the fiscal arrangements that make such provision possible. While it is a salient example, fiscal crisis is not the only example that the theory of political dysfunction can explicate. In the interests of brevity, I will not explore others, but it does appear that considering modern political issues by those features that they have in common—the existence of problems long decried by both the right and left, combined with their puzzling persistence—yields patterns rendered intelligible by political dysfunction. Importantly, these patterns cannot be understood without a unified conception of how information problems relate to incentive problems. My theory provides this link, and while it is obviously not the sole explanation of political maladies, it is one that is particularly timely.

While I do not want to link my theory too closely to any particular normative framework, I should state that the reality of political dysfunction via constitutional drift does not unambiguously support classical liberalism, although this is frequently the normative prior of many scholars interested in promoting productive and protective governance, while preventing predatory governance. Governance institutions in the West were, for a time, approximately classically liberal and proved unable to maintain themselves. While they were not then dysfunctional, they fell prey to the constitutional drift that eventually resulted in political dysfunction. As such, it is reasonable to conclude that no school of thought currently has a "solution" to the problem of political dysfunction. Nonetheless, in closing, I feel it appropriate to make some brief remarks as to some potential avenues for undoing political dysfunction.

The overall process of political dysfunction is emergent. It is not reducible to the intentions of any one person or group acting within the political process; instead, it is a result of the interaction between them. There is no direct and simple relationship between the "macro" phenomenon of political dysfunction and the "micro" phenomenon of individual or group decision-making (Wagner 2012a, 2012b). Since constitutional drift began the process, it may appear as though sub-constitutional "tweaks" to political processes will be insufficient to reverse it. Does this mean that constitutional problems require constitutional solutions? It does appear that only by "getting the meta-rules right" can the framework be laid for within-institutions political action that may be resistant to political dysfunction (Buchanan and Brennan 2000 [1985]).

Importantly, constitutional solutions do not have to be formal constitutional revisions. Any change in the actual decision process of the state qualifies. Following Buchanan (1959), proposing large-scale change within existing formal meta-rules, while securing the consent of all interested parties, is one possibility for informal-without-formal constitutional change. Consider the following thought experiment: immediately close all U.S. government departments except the Departments of Defense, Interior, Justice, and Treasury. Continue to pay all former employees full salary and benefits, irrespective of their future employment status. In addition, spin off and continue to make transfer payments formerly made under now-defunct departments, such as Medicare and Medicaid, into independently administered agencies, as is done with Social Security. Such a proposal would—if the theory I have sketched is accurate—entail large wealth gains for the polity. Given existing political dysfunction, it follows that lack of access to knowledge-generating governance mechanisms is resulting in significant waste. But this waste lies in the mobilization of resources in an inefficient manner, not in the salaries and benefits paid to public employees and transfer recipients per se. As such, the real resources previously mobilized that were almost certainly inefficiently employed can now be put to use in processes with sufficient knowledge-generating mechanisms at least to tend towards efficiency. At the same time, former employees of these departments and transfer recipients do not lose, since continuing to pay their salaries and benefits ensures that their command over resources is unchanged. This proposal obviously would change the actual decision procedure of the state—surely these organizations do not operate in isolation, but interact with each other in ways that influence not only the content, but also the process of public decisions—without formal constitutional revision. It thus qualifies as *de facto* constitutional amendment, in a similar manner (albeit in the opposite direction) as the New Deal.

My theory also draws attention to the merits of "designed" versus "grown" constitutions, suggesting a healthy degree of skepticism towards the former (e.g. Devins et al. 2015). The competitive federalism of the early American republic was perhaps the best-designed attempt to enable profitable collective action, while preventing the predatory possibilities of the political commons, yet devised. As we have seen, it proved quite vulnerable to cartel federalism when the ideological climate, and the payoffs associated with particular political bargains, shifted. Cartel federalism was not the result of usurpation by national political actors at the expense of local political actors; rather, it was the result of voluntary bargains between these actors, whose private payoff came at the expense of political institutions capable of resisting dysfunction. This impels the question of how constitutional solutions can be reached when there is no guarantee that the constitutional structure in question will be self-enforcing? The question is merely a rephrasing of Hamilton's dilemma from *Federalist No. 1*, but the framework from which the question arises may also suggest the beginnings of an answer, which can reinvigorate the designed constitutions project by reorienting it.

Securing the benefits of the productive state, while also restraining the predatory state, requires (in part) setting the demarcation between supplying goods and services by private contract versus collective action. If political meta-rules begin with a list of what specific prerogatives are permitted to collective action, then these meta-rules also embody an implicit assumption about where this demarcation lies. Using constitutions to coordinate around this kind of an equilibrium will be largely ineffective if that political equilibrium quickly becomes pressured by constitutional drift; instead, if we treat the demarcation as something that must be *discovered* as part of the operation of the political process, rather than decided upon *ex ante*, the imperative becomes setting the meta-rules such that they are most conducive to this discovery procedure. The political question shifts from, "Ought the government to supply Good X?" to "What political structure will result in the government supplying Good X if it is productive or protective, and not if it entails predation?" Interestingly, the latter question is easier to answer, since it limits itself to questions of procedures, which are more definite than questions of specific collective action. This is because the particulars of time and place can plausibly be both conducive and unconducive to collective action concerning Good X. Constitutions that de-emphasize specific rights permitted to collective action, or reserved to private contract, and emphasize procedures for discovering which rights are best allocated to which provision method in a given context may be more compatible with the requirement that constitutions must be self-enforcing. Political operatives probably have less incentive to deviate on procedures than specific outcomes, because outcomes are more likely to draw the support, or hostility, of interest groups. Procedural focus at the constitutional level thus affords a degree of flexibility that constitutions mandating specific outcomes lack. If formal constitutions can facilitate coordination around a set of political meta-rules that are conducive to this discovery process, they can be significantly more helpful in securing lasting protective and productive, and avoiding predatory, outcomes.

Thinking of the problem in this way switches the focus from the incentive-aligning features of constitutions (preventing political predation), which traditionally receive the lion's share of attention in political economy and philosophy, to the information-generating feature of constitutions (discovering the demarcation between private contract and collective action). Preventing undesirable constitutional drift, and hence political dysfunction, requires that constitutions be robust in both of these senses. If the *epistemic* feature of constitutions is sufficiently favorable, political agents are more likely to receive a sufficiently high payoff from directing their entrepreneurial activities toward productive uses that they refrain from predatory procedural changes. Ascertaining which procedures create the most favorable epistemic environment, while also remaining incentive-compatible for holders of political power, would be the focus of a research program oriented toward resisting political dysfunction. There is obviously no final solution to this problem—at some level, everything is endogenous, so everything can change—but there are almost certainly political orders more resistant to dysfunction than others. This will almost certainly involve some institutional arrangement that curbs the effects of the political commons from which political dysfunction proceeds.

Notes

* "Constitutional Drift and Political Dysfunction: Underappreciated Maladies of the Political Commons." Author: Alexander Salter. Sections of this article are reprinted with permission from the publisher of *The Independent Review: A Journal of Political Economy* (Spring 2017, Volume 21, no 4, pp. 569–585). Copyright 2017, Independent Institute, 100 Swan Way, Oakland, CA 94621-1428 USA; info@independent.org; www.independent.org

1 Very similar arguments could be made for other Western constitutional democracies. I use the American republic as my case study because it is the example with which I am most familiar.

2 The process vs. outcome distinction itself is trickier. Martin (2010) focuses more specifically on this aspect of the problem.

3 I am not denigrating either Congleton's or Jouvenel's analysis; in fact, I find Jouvenel's account of the importance of ideology particularly persuasive. Instead, I want to emphasize that, with respect to these theories, my focus will be on constitutional bargains per se.

4 For the purposes of this paper, *commons* is shorthand for a property rights arrangement characterized by current use value, but not future capitalized value. I do not claim that there are not control rights over political procedures; such an assertion would fly in the face of reality and would do violence to the spectrum of institutional arrangements on the state–market spectrum that emerge to facilitate interpersonal cooperation (E. Ostrom 2010). I simply want to convey that those in the position to wield the means of governance reap current benefits from their activities, but because these means are non-alienable property, they do not internalize fully the capitalization effects of their decisions.

5 This is not a "materialistic" or "reductionist" account of human welfare. It simply recognizes that if the value of society's resources is not maximized, mutually beneficial exchange between two parties is still possible, meaning that their self-perceived well-being can be increased, without damage to another's.

6 *The Critical Review*, 2014, 26(1–2), recently ran a symposium on political epistemology, which treats this issue in far more detail.
7 By "return," I mean "more closely mimicking past arrangements." Normatively, whether one views this as an improvement or not depends on one's definition of self-governance and whether one views such governance as a desirable end, apart from whatever means it may serve.
8 Space constraints prevent me from detailing additional examples. See Greve (2012), Epstein (2014), Higgs (2013 [1987]), Holcombe (2002), and Wagner (2007, 2012a) for analyses of other cases of constitutional drift.
9 It may be strange to think of governance in the same terms as a for-profit corporation, but the development of Western polities in an environment of realm ownership, as discussed in previous sections, shows that governance can be extremely profitable for holders of political property rights and that, with the "correct" structure of political property rights, profit-accruing governance can also be in the interests of non-holders of political property rights.

References

Anderson, J. L. 1991. *Explaining long-term economic change*. London: Macmillan.

Baechler, J. 1975. *The origins of capitalism*. B. Cooper, trans. Oxford: Basil Blackwell.

Berman, H. J. 1983. *Law and revolution: The formation of the Western political tradition.* Cambridge, MA: Harvard University Press.

Brennan, J. 2014. How smart is democracy? You can't answer that question *a priori*. *Critical Review*, 26(1–2): 33–58.

Buchanan, J. M. 1959. Positive economics, welfare economics, and political economy. *Journal of Law and Economics*, 2(Oct): 124–138.

Buchanan, J. M. 1975. *The limits of liberty: Between anarchy and Leviathan*. Chicago, IL: University of Chicago Press.

Buchanan, J. M. 1987. The constitution of economic policy. *American Economic Review*, 77(3): 243–250.

Buchanan, J. M., and G. Brennan. 2000 [1985]. *The reason of rules: Constitutional political economy*. Indianapolis, IN: Liberty Fund.

Buchanan, J. M., and R. D. Congleton. 1998. *Politics by principle, not interest: Towards nondiscriminatory democracy*. Cambridge: Cambridge University Press.

Buchanan, J. M., and G. Tullock. 1962. *The calculus of consent: Logical foundations of constitutional democracy*. Ann Arbor, MI: University of Michigan Press.

Caplan, B. 2007. *The myth of the rational voter: Why democracies choose bad policies*. New Haven, CT: Yale University Press.

Congleton, R. D. 2011. *Perfecting parliament: Constitutional reform, liberalism, and the rise of Western democracy*. Cambridge: Cambridge University Press.

de Lara, Y. G., A. Grief, and S. Jha. 2008. The administrative foundations of self-enforcing constitutions. *American Economic Review*, 98(2): 105–109.

Devins, C., R. Koppl, S. Kauffman, and T. Felin. 2015. Against design. *Arizona State Law Journal*, 47(3): 609–681.

Epstein, R. A. 2014. *The classically liberal constitution: The uncertain quest for limited government*. Cambridge, MA: Harvard University Press.

Greve, M. S. 2012. *The upside-down constitution*. Cambridge, MA: Harvard University Press.

Gunn, P. 2014. Democracy and epistocracy. *Critical Review*, 26(1–2): 59–79.

Hardin, G. 1968. The tragedy of the commons. *Science*, 162(3859): 1243–1248.

Hardin, R. 1982. *Collective action*. Baltimore, MD: Johns Hopkins University Press.

Hardin, R. 1989. Why a constitution? In B. Groffman and B. Wittman, eds., *The Federalist Papers and the new institutionalism*. New York: Agathon Press.

Hayek, F. A. 1948. *Individualism and economic order*. Chicago, IL: University of Chicago Press.

Hayek, F. A. 1960. *The constitution of liberty*. Chicago, IL: University of Chicago Press.

Hayek, F. A. 1978–81. *Law, legislation, and liberty*. Three volumes. Chicago, IL: University of Chicago Press.

Higgs, R. 2013 [1987]. *Crisis and Leviathan: Critical episodes in the growth of American government*. Oakland, CA: Independent Institute.

Holcombe, R. G. 2002. *From liberty to democracy: The transformation of American government*. Ann Arbor, MI: University of Michigan Press.

Ikeda, S. 1997. *Dynamics of the mixed economy: Towards a theory of interventionism*. London: Routledge.

Ikeda, S. 2003. How compatible are public choice and Austrian political economy? *Review of Austrian Economics*, 16(1): 63–75.

Jouvenel, B. de. 1993 [1945]. *On power: The natural history of its growth*. Indianapolis, IN: Liberty Fund.

Kotlikoff, L. 2013. *Assessing fiscal sustainability*. Mercatus Center research paper. Available at http://mercatus.org/publication/assessing-fiscal-sustainability

Leeson, P. 2011. Governments, clubs, and constitutions. *Journal of Economic Behavior and Organization*, 80(2): 301–308.

Martin, A. 2010. Emergent politics and the power of ideas. *Studies in Emergent Order*, 3: 212–245.

Mises, L. von. 1944. *Bureaucracy*. New Haven, CT: Yale University Press.

Mises, L. von. 1951. *Socialism: An economic and sociological analysis*. New Haven, CT: Yale University Press.

Mittal, S., and B. R. Weingast. 2011. Self-enforcing constitutions: With an application to democratic stability in America's first century. *Journal of Law, Economics, and Organization*, 29(2): 278–302.

Niskanen, W. A. 1994 [1971]. *Bureaucracy and public economics*. Cheltenham: Edward Elgar.

North, D. C., and B. R Weingast. 1989. Constitutions and commitment: The evolution of institutions governing public choice in seventeenth-century England. *Journal of Economic History*, 49(4): 803–832.

Oakeshott, M. 1991. *Rationalism in politics and other essays*. Indianapolis, IN: Liberty Fund.

Olson, M. 1982. *The rise and decline of nations: Economic growth, stagflation, and social rigidities*. New Haven, CT: Yale University Press.

Olson, M. 1993. Dictatorship, democracy, and development. *American Political Science Review*, 87(3): 567–576.

Ordeshook, P. C. 1992. Constitutional stability. *Constitutional Political Economy*, 3(2): 137–175.

Ostrom, E. 2010. Beyond markets and states: Polycentric governance of complex economic systems. *American Economic Review*, 100(3): 641–672.

Ostrom, V. 1997. *The meaning of democracy and the vulnerability of democracy: A response to Tocqueville's challenge*. Ann Arbor, MI: University of Michigan Press.

Ostrom, V. 2008 [1971]. *The political theory of a compound republic: Designing the American experiment*. Plymouth: Lexington Books.

Ostrom, V. 2008 [1973]. *The intellectual crisis in American public administration.* Tuscaloosa, AL: University of Alabama Press.

Raico, R. 1994. The theory of economic development and the "European miracle." In P. J. Boettke, ed., *The collapse of development planning.* New York: New York University Press.

Salter, A. W. 2014. *Sovereignty as exchange of political property rights.* Working paper.

Salter, A. W. 2015. Rights to the realm: Reconsidering Western political development. *American Political Science Review,* 109(4): 725–734.

Salter, A. W., and Young, A. T. 2016. *Market-preserving federalism as polycentric sovereignty.* Working paper.

Smith, V. 2009. *Rationality in economics: Constructivist and ecological.* Cambridge: Cambridge University Press.

Somin, I. 2013. *Democracy and political ignorance: Why smaller government is smarter.* Redwood City, CA: Stanford University Press.

Stark, R. 2011. *The triumph of Christianity: How the Jesus movement became the world's largest religion.* New York: HarperCollins.

Tiebout, C. 1956. A pure theory of local expenditure. *Journal of Political Economy,* 64(5): 416–424.

Tullock, G. 2005. *Bureaucracy: Selected works of G. Tullock,* vol. 6, C. K. Rowley, ed. Indianapolis, IN: Liberty Fund.

Wagner, R. E. 2007. *Fiscal sociology and the theory of public finance.* Cheltenham: Edward Elgar.

Wagner, R. E. 2012a. *Deficits, debt, and democracy.* Cheltenham: Edward Elgar.

Wagner, R. E. 2012b. A macro economy as an ecology of plans. *Journal of Economic Behavior and Organization,* 82(2–3): 433–444.

Wagner, R. E. 2015. *Fiscal crisis as failure of progressivist democracy.* Working paper. Available at http://www.depts.ttu.edu/freemarketinstitute/research/research_crisis_papers/FiscalCrisisasFailureofProgressivistDemocracy.pdf

Warren, C. 1932. *Congress as Santa Claus—or, national donations and the General Welfare Clause of the Constitution.* Charlottesville, VA: Michie.

Zywicki, T. 1994. Senators and special interests: A public choice analysis of the Seventeenth Amendment. *Oregon Law Review,* 73: 1007–1055.

3 The limits of liberalism
Good boundaries must be discovered

Adam Martin

Introduction*

Competition is an indispensable tool for dealing with human ignorance. Individuals are not born with knowledge of the lowest cost means of achieving their goals, the best theories with which to explain the world around us, or the best way of governing human interaction so as to avoid conflict and promote cooperation. We can err. And, in a world of scarcity, errors crowd out alternatives. Societies thrive when individuals are free to undertake many experiments in cooperation, and failed experiments are shut down in a peaceful and orderly manner. Hayek (1978 [1968]) refers to this sort of process as competition. Both the freedom to experiment and responsibility for failure are necessary for innovation and progress. Experimentation allows us to discover new ways of doing things, but we must also stand ready to abandon existing approaches.

Competition also enables adaptation. Even if a static state were desirable, it is simply not achievable given that environmental conditions, preferences, and ideas can always change. This is why Hayek (1960) always focused on the struggle between the forces of progress and the forces of decline. Stasis is not a viable option, even if we do not value progress for its own sake. We can dispense with peaceful forms of competition only when we already know the best way of doing things, and the best way of doing things often changes.

While Hayek developed his theory of competition with regard to the production and exchange of goods and services, he later came to apply it to the rules that govern market exchange (Stringham and Zywicki 2011). Following Leoni (1961), Hayek (1973) argues that a long process of legal evolution allowed the West to stumble into a set of legal principles and practices that secured extensive spheres of individual control within which individuals are free to choose. Judges tried out different legal principles as methods for resolving disputes, learning from one another in a decentralized fashion. This accidental emergence of liberal institutions made individuals free to act on their own knowledge and ideas—especially those that were at odds with existing practices—and thus allowed for the West to thrive. Later, Hayek (1988) made competition over rules a centerpiece of his theory of social evolution more generally. Societies that adopted rules of private property and freedom of contract prospered and grew, supplanting societies that relied on rules of common property.

This chapter extends Hayek's analysis of institutions by focusing on a particular aspect of rules: jurisdictional boundaries. To whom should a given set of rules apply? I focus on why this question matters for classical liberals, although many of the arguments below are relevant for a wide range of political theories. Good boundaries—those that enable innovation and adaptation—are, in important respects, like good methods of production or good scientific theories: they are best discovered through a competitive process. The next section introduces the concept of jurisdictional boundary problems, arguing that such problems are (a) ubiquitous, afflicting all sorts of governance arrangements, and (b) subject to the same sorts of knowledge problems that make competition so valuable for directing economic activity.

Edward Stringham's book *Private Governance* (2015) is especially relevant for raising the issue of how to effectively draw boundaries. Stringham (2015) focuses not on the boundaries of government authority, but on the formation of private clubs as a source of governance. Clubs too have boundaries, depending both on who is admitted into membership and on what being a member entails. Although he is not primarily concerned with boundary problems, Stringham explores a variety of historical cases in which club governance proved to be an effective and peaceful method for adjusting boundaries on the margin. Clubs work well primarily because individuals consent to join and cheaters can be expelled.

But chapter 13 of *Private Governance* takes a different turn, in two respects: its subject and its mechanism. Based on Stringham's work with Zywicki (Stringham and Zywicki 2011), it offers a Hayekian argument for market-made law. Stringham and Zywicki (2011) utilize the Hayekian idea of competition as a discovery procedure to put forward a case for Hayekian anarchism. So, rather than relying on the mechanisms of consent and exclusion, Stringham (2015, ch. 13) relies on a decentralized process of social learning. This is at least a difference in emphasis on what mechanisms make private law work well. As far as subject goes, the sort of law that Stringham (2015, ch. 13) discusses is different from the governance provided by clubs that the rest of the book discusses in at least one important respect: it is meant to adjudicate boundaries themselves and not merely to establish or renegotiate them. As a result, it more directly addresses the problem of boundary conditions.

While both parts of Stringham's work offer important insights, I argue that the competitive approach taken in Stringham (2015, ch. 13) is especially underappreciated. In the third section of this chapter, I distinguish between two criteria that classical liberals have traditionally used for evaluating boundaries: *ex ante* consent to jurisdictional boundaries or the ability to exit from them *ex post*. Both criteria emphasize individual choice, but they come at it from opposite directions. The consent approach evaluates institutional arrangements according to whether individuals have agreed to them *ex ante*, while the exit approach evaluates institutions according to whether individuals have an exit option. I then make a case that exit-oriented liberalism is underappreciated, especially in its capacity to deal with boundary problems by enabling a competitive discovery procedure.

Boundary problems and the irreducible commons

James Buchanan (1975, p. 5) argues that anarchy is ideal, but unworkable. Anarchists fail to adequately address a fundamental question: "What are to be the *defining limits* on individual freedom of behavior?" (Buchanan 1975, p. 5, emphasis added). While "ordered anarchy" (Buchanan 1975, p. 9) governs most human interaction, it operates only to the extent that boundary problems about the allocation of decision rights—especially property rights—are settled in an acceptable fashion: "The logical foundation of property lies precisely in this universal need for boundaries between 'mine and thine'" (Buchanan 1975, p. 13). It should be noted Buchanan has an extensive definition of property rights in mind. Property includes not only concerns bare possession, but also the uses to which individuals may put the claims that they have. Buchanan even extends the definition to include legal personhood, from slaves with minimal legal standing to masters with expansive personal spheres that include extensive claims on others. While recognizing that there is wide scope for reciprocal, spontaneous recognition of such boundaries, Buchanan contends that the state is necessary to prevent marginal defections from those accepted limits from unraveling such a tenuous social contract.

Buchanan expresses sympathy for the market anarchist theories of both Murray Rothbard (1973) and David Friedman (1973), but he argues that neither successfully addresses these boundary problems (Buchanan 1974, 1975, p. 9, fn. 2). Rothbard (1973, pp. 37–53) assumes, for instance, that a libertarian legal code predicated on a radical Lockean approach to natural rights is firmly in place before arguing that competing firms could provide effective law and order. What he fails to explain is the process by which such a departure from existing property practices can initially gain a foothold in either his preferred system or the present one. Friedman (1973, ch. 31) admits more readily that market-based law is not necessarily libertarian law, because individual beliefs and preferences matter a great deal in determining what sorts of rights will ultimately get enforced.

Wagner (2007) develops a framework that helps to extend Buchanan's point. He argues that private property and common property are two different grammars by which human beings relate to one another. The language of private property—"mine and thine"—takes hold to the extent that we take others' decision rights as given. But the grammar of private property can never fully encapsulate all social interaction, for two reasons. First, the boundaries of private property are always contestable (Wagner 2007, p. 47). Private property only ever extends to the limits of others' forbearance. At any given point in time, some property claims will be fixed, but individuals often seek to limit or compel the uses to which others may put their property, or to engage in redistribution of decision rights. All of these activities either shift private property into the commons or change who has a given property claim. These activities necessarily invoke the grammar of common property—of "we together." Second, interaction structured by the grammar of private property always occurs through a medium of common property. To approach you with an offer to exchange privately held decision rights, I must be able to initiate contact. Gaining your permission requires that, at some level, the right to seek your permission is held in common.

The boundaries of private property are always worked out in common property, and the rules of common property denote a group of individuals who share governance arrangements. Classical liberals are well versed in the challenges confronting common property arrangements. They often entail a lack of incentives to use resources effectively, and since they are non-severable, they do not enable economic calculation. Theoretically and historically, clubs have offered at least a partial solution to both of these problems (Buchanan 1965). Stringham (2015) documents a number of examples of clubs that have effectively provided governance services for their members, including early financial and insurance markets. Clubs function by extending the scope of private property, providing effective and voluntary means for alleviating commons problems when fully individual claims are not functional. But fencing in common property only alleviates commons problems for that which has been fenced in. Clubs push out the boundaries of common property, but do not eliminate boundaries altogether. Whether between individual property owners or club providers of governance problems, any non-monolithic society confronts some irreducible legal commons. So while clubs play an important role in dealing with boundary problems, there are still boundary problems between clubs.

The existence of an irreducible legal commons means that "privatize everything" is not a viable approach to securing a liberal order. But this does not mean that we should uncritically accept Buchanan's preferred approach of a constitutionally constrained state. Even if the best option for dealing with boundary problems is to establish a monopoly referee with incentives to be productive and protective, but not predatory, this option is too abstract to be of any real help. This strictly formal condition is like saying that we want goods created through low-cost methods of production: it tells us nothing about what those methods of production are.

One important consideration that Buchanan's formal proposal does not tell us is: what are the appropriate boundaries for a governance jurisdiction itself? The reason why a system of club governance does not completely eliminate commons problems is that there are forms of activity that fall outside of its jurisdiction. But the same is true of any liberal form of public governance as well. Only a totalitarian, socialist state completely insulated from other jurisdictions would not confront its own boundary problems.

Discovering good jurisdictional boundaries is a problem of overcoming ignorance that confronts both public and private forms of governance. Many factors determine whether a boundary is well drawn. Most importantly, a good boundary is liable to be different for different sorts of governance problems. Governance problems are shaped by technological, organizational, and social factors. Technologically, collective goods have different economies of scale.

Spillover effects vary radically in size. Organizational and decision-making costs vary both from one community to the next and for different collective goods problems. Socially, an area with a heterogeneous population is likely better served by smaller jurisdictions than one with a homogenous population. As a consequence of these sources of variation, the efficient jurisdictional boundary for, say, the provision of police services is unlikely to be the same as that for governing groundwater usage. Even within the narrower domain of police services, different neighborhoods, industries, and law enforcement functions have varying needs and varying economies of scale. Ostrom (1976), for example, notes that forensic services are liable to have much larger-scale economies than regular police patrols. The effective provision of governance is a multidimensional problem of balancing conflicting means and ends no less than the effective provision of private goods and services.

Moreover, boundaries themselves are multidimensional and varied. Some boundaries are best defined geographically, such as those governing a clearly defined common pool resource. Others may best be defined by function, such as the merchant law governing contracts among medieval traders (Benson 1989, 1990). Boundaries may be more or less porous to entry and exit. The right level of exclusion or inclusion will vary from one governance problem to the next. And some boundaries may need to be redrawn more frequently, while others can work only to the extent that they are stable. This leads to the most important feature of boundaries from a Hayekian point of view: change.

"Economic problems arises always and only in consequence of change," says Hayek (1945, p. 523). All of the features that make for effective boundaries are liable to shift through time with both technological and social changes (Foldvary and Klein 2002). Safer fertilizers, for example, may decrease the area that needs to be monitored to protect a groundwater basin. More effective information technology, by contrast, may increase the efficient scale of police dispatch services. Communities may grow more or less homogenous, changing the costs of collective decision making. Hayek argues that market socialist proposals are flawed because they fail to grapple with the omnipresent reality of change. Similarly, it would be strange if there were a once-and-for-all solution to boundary problems.

Providing effective governance requires more than thinking about abstract issues such as externalities, collective action problems, and boundary problems, just as effectively coping with the economic problem requires more than thinking through the implications of a perfect competition model or economies of scale. In both cases, not only scientific knowledge, but also the more ephemeral knowledge of time and place are important. And, in both cases, we can assess the relevance and validity of such knowledge only through some experimental process. In the provision of governance, just as in the provision of goods and services or the generation of scientific knowledge, societies prosper to the extent that there is wide scope for experimentation and a mechanism for peacefully shutting down failing experiments. Hayek uses a single word to sum up these two conditions: competition.

My aim here is not to outline a specific model of what competition over jurisdictional boundaries might look like. At a minimum, competition would entail a form of competitive federalism. More radical proposals might look like Bruno Frey's "functional overlapping competing jurisdictions" (Eichenberger and Frey 2006), a system of small city states, or full-blown private governance as imagined by thinkers such as Murray Rothbard and David Friedman. My aim is more modest: to establish that a commitment to such competition is a likely (if not necessary) concomitant of recognizing the existence of boundary problems. To the extent that boundary problems are a binding constraint, providing effective governance may require a commitment to a peaceful method for determining jurisdictional boundaries.

Competition over jurisdictional boundaries may sound utopian, especially among those whose fundamental vision of the world is Hobbesian. Peaceful competition among governance providers could, after all, readily cease to be peaceful. Indeed, this is always a possibility. But there is, in the end, only one alternative to peaceful competition: some combination of conflict and poorly defined jurisdictions. The prospects for peaceful competition over jurisdictional boundaries may be grim, but this would not be a rebuttal of my argument so much as a counsel of pessimism.

Consent and exit: finding good boundaries

Classical liberals advocate widespread reliance on private property as a method for reducing commons problems, settling conflicts, and incentivizing cooperation. Whether they ground private property rights in natural law or social convention, there is more agreement than disagreement about what such property rights should entail. Different strands of liberalism, however, emphasize different ways of dealing with the establishment and maintenance of boundaries. Some liberals argue that what makes for a good boundary is that individuals have consented to it *ex ante*. Others argue that what matters is whether individuals can exit *ex post*.

Drawing a distinction between consent-focused and exit-focused classical liberals makes sense only if a few qualifications are kept in mind. The two orientations overlap to a very large extent, tending to differ in emphasis rather than in substantive judgments. Figure 3.1 depicts a range of positions from the most consent-focused to the most exit-focused. All of the positions in the middle are likely uncontroversial among most classical liberals. These judgments reflect the ordinary morality of market activity, which, in most forms, gives wide scope for both *ex ante* consent and *ex post* exit. Synchronic agreements, such as transactions over hamburgers and haircuts, can be justified in terms of either consent or exit. Most liberals would also allow that some intertemporal exchanges that contain safeguards against reneging are also allowable, such as contracts involving an escrow account. Going in the other direction, most would also likely rebut the enforcement of specific performance of labor contracts: one can make a laborer pay damages for reneging on a deal, but forcing them to do specific

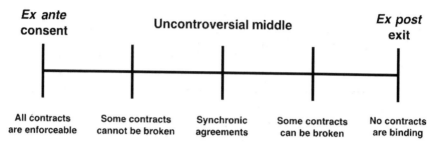

Figure 3.1 Ex ante consent/*Ex post* exit

work amounts to servitude. But few classical liberals would hold the positions on either extreme of this continuum: that no contracts are binding or that all contracts (e.g. voluntary slave contracts) should be binding. So, rather than two wholly separate approaches we have two tilts—one *ex ante* and one *ex post*—for how we understand what it means to be free to choose.

But where the middle positions are largely uncontroversial among those who advocate robust private property rights, differences in tilt become more pronounced in addressing boundary problems. Thinkers with a consent tilt argue that good boundaries are those to which we have consented *ex ante*. Thinkers with an exit tilt argue that good boundaries are those that individuals can opt out of *ex post*. These two positions can be quite different when it comes to analyzing how good rules might come about and to whom they should apply.

Figure 3.2 divides some prominent classical liberal thinkers into those with a consent tilt and those with an exit tilt. The classification is not meant to offer a nuanced reading of each thinker's position, because my aim is not to elaborate on the history of liberal thought; rather, my goal is merely to illustrate consent- and exit-oriented arguments by appealing to salient examples. Every thinker listed values both *ex ante* consent and *ex post* exit to a large extent, but iconic arguments from these thinkers tend to lean in one direction or the other. Figure 3.2 pairs thinkers who otherwise have similar commitments to

Consent-tilt	Exit-tilt
James Buchanan social contract	Chandran Kukathas liberal archipelago
John Stuart Mill autonomy	F.A. Hayek true individualism
Murray Rothbard voluntarism	Randy Barnett competition principle
Gary Becker rational choice	Israel Kirzner discovery and error

Figure 3.2 Consent tilt/Exit tilt

some aspect or subset of the liberal program to illustrate that this distinction cuts across traditional boundaries, such as consequentialism vs. deontology or minarchism vs. anarchism, and across different academic disciplines.

Consider the differences between Buchanan's (1975) model of a unanimous social contract and Kukathas's (2007) model of a diverse liberal archipelago. For Buchanan (1962), the only statements of value that count are those expressed in voluntary choices. Economics becomes a tool of moral philosophy by allowing the economist to propose changes in the rules of the political game by which boundaries are set. Proposals are justified to the extent that they approach unanimous approval. For Kukathas (2007), the fundamental freedom is freedom of conscience, which is cashed out in social life by freedom of association and, especially, freedom of disassociation. All associations are partial, so none can claim the absolute allegiance of an individual. Life under existing rules is only sometimes a matter of consent and more often a matter of mere acquiescence: we do not try to leave or are willing to bear only so much cost to change the rules. But acquiescence is acceptable as long as individuals have robust exit rights. Kukathas goes so far as to claim that a society of competing, but restrictive, monastic orders is freer than a unified polis governed by those concerned with engendering individual autonomy. But also note that neither thinker is single-minded: Buchanan recognizes the importance of federalism and club governance, implying an appreciation for exit; Kukathas, likewise, values both rights of association and disassociation. But, when considering tough cases about the essence of liberty, Buchanan's argument leans towards *ex ante* consent, while Kukathas's approach leans towards *ex post* exit.

Jacob Levy (2015) offers an alternative, but in some ways overlapping, distinction between strains of the liberal tradition, which he dubs rationalism and pluralism. Rationalist liberals believe in the importance of a uniform legal code administered by a centralized state aimed at protecting individual liberty. Pluralist liberals place a heavier emphasis on the importance of intermediate associations, including both private clubs and local government jurisdictions. Obviously, this latter approach has much in common with an exit-focused approach to liberalism, since both entail a commitment to polycentric governance. But since both centralized states and local groups can be sources of domination or tyranny, Levy argues that we should not try to purge one or the other strand of liberalism and must learn to live with the tension between the two. He also argues that the pluralist strand of liberalism is relatively neglected. Exit-tilt liberalism, I argue, is likewise unduly neglected, especially when it comes to dealing with boundary problems.

Exit may take a variety of forms, and it is not my goal to identify when one or another form is most appropriate. Migration changes who is subject to a law, as does geographic secession or the fragmentation of existing authority along functional lines. But exit need not take such radical forms. Benson (1999) argues that contracting provides an important mechanism for bypassing existing default rules. The forms of exit are also affected by the available forms of entry into the provision of governance. What mix of these forms of exit is most conducive to solving particular governance problems is part of what we want a competitive process to discover. Again, accepting an exit-tilt version of liberalism is not the same as arguing for an absolute right of exit. The optimal porousness of a jurisdictional boundary is one of the very things we wish to discover. So the right of exit may not be uniform from one jurisdiction to the next.

Exit is undervalued because, when it comes to dealing with boundary problems, it facilitates social learning to a greater extent than does *ex ante* consent. Both innovation and adaptation require dissent from existing ways of doing things. The fact that a jurisdictional boundary is agreed to at time *t* will not make it appropriate at time *t*+1. Institutional entrepreneurs may discover better ways of carving up the social world, or technological conditions may make existing arrangements less functional or just. Exit has several advantages over *ex ante* consent in dealing with these issues. First, exit lowers the costs of agreement by allowing those with distinct preferences to go their own way. Lower-cost dissent means more experimentation with rules, including jurisdictional boundaries.

Second, exit works from within the status quo. The world we inhabit is not governed by institutions founded on consistently liberal principles or consented to by all parties. Consent-focused accounts, to genuinely endorse institutional change, either have to use unanimity as a yardstick or must imagine that rights are distributed correctly to begin with (Buchanan 1962). Consent-tilt liberals thus have a difficult time dealing with objections to pro-liberty proposals rooted in the reality of historical injustice (Lomasky 2005). Exit has the advantage of being empowering from the present, not only if it was applied in the past. The overwhelming barrier to human liberty and flourishing in the modern world is defunct institutional arrangements that were founded upon, and continue to facilitate, predation (Acemoglu and Robinson 2012). The dead hand of the past mostly impairs life prospects through the endurance of bad rules. So while exit does not address all distributive concerns of past injustice, the ability to leave is the most valuable for precisely those most afflicted by oppressive institutions (Martin 2015). Placing more emphasis on exit gives liberals an important tool in addressing historical injustice. At the same time, an exit tilt allows classical liberals to maintain a strong stance against existing government transfer programs, because the right to opt out can take normative priority over the expectations that such programs have established for their beneficiaries.

Third, exit-tilt liberalism avoids reliance on hypothetical consent. Since unanimous agreement is not forthcoming regarding most real-world institutional changes, a standard philosophical move for consent-tilt liberals is to argue about what individuals would agree to under certain idealized conditions. At the same time, a standard complaint about exit as a mechanism for allowing individuals to choose rules is that it can be very costly, especially when it involves migration. Certain forms of exit are costly, but this can in fact be an advantage for certain sorts of choices. Individuals who can engage in cheap talk can easily hold up beneficial changes in governance arrangements (Kuran 1995; Buchanan and Tullock 1962). Making choice costly elicits genuine preferences. On the other hand, many forms of exit—such as the sort of contracting around default rules that Benson (2011) describes—not only are much less costly than collective choices, but also generate genuine unanimity among the contracting parties.

Finally, an exit tilt allows liberals to more effectively counter stock charges of atomism that various thinkers level against liberalism. Communities can matter a great deal—even unchosen communities, such as families and religious groups. Many social practices are not exactly coercively imposed, but neither are they actively consented to. An exit-tilt liberalism does not need to posit humans that arrive to the social world as pre-made, autonomous individuals and to affirm only governance arrangements that such individuals would choose; rather, it needs only to insist that groups have value only insofar as individuals are willing to stay a part of them. Exit-tilt liberalism can thus allow classical liberals to make an important contribution to debates about multiculturalism that are typically carried between competing camps of progressives (Tebble 2016).

Conclusion

In an address to a Cambridge University conference commemorating the 75th anniversary of the publication of Keynes' *General Theory*, Paul Krugman (2011) distinguishes between "Chapter 12ers" and "Book 1ers." The former are those who like Keynes' philosophical ruminations regarding expectations about the future and beauty contests; the latter are those who have more appreciation for the formal models meant to demonstrate the possibility of a shortfall in aggregate demand. We might similarly distinguish two readers of Stringham's *Private Governance* (2015): "Part 1ers" would find the work on club governance—which takes a consent-tilt approach focused on contracts and exclusion—most compelling; "Chapter 13ers" would find the arguments about Hayekian anarchism—taking an exit-tilt approach focusing on competition and social learning—most compelling. And while there is a great deal of insight in both, I find myself drawn to Stringham (2015, ch. 13).

Boundary problems are among the most difficult for any political philosophy to deal with. Buchanan (1975) builds an entire book on them, and it is among his most pessimistic works. Nozick (1974, ch. 4), even after assuming a robust set of individual rights at the outset of *Anarchy, State, and Utopia*, dedicates a long and technical chapter to the problem of "border crossings." And Kukathas (2007, p. 37), who offers what is arguably the seminal defense of the right of exit, leaves open the question of what I get to take with me when I leave a group. I have argued that these may be better thought of as matters of institutional design than as universal philosophical principles.

The answer to the question "what makes a good boundary?" is contingent on the circumstances of time and place. The best boundaries, then, are those that have been discovered through a competitive process and which are subject to some degree of challenge to ensure that they continue working.

Classical liberals have often emphasized the role of consent in evaluating the institutional processes that generate boundaries. I have argued that an alternative strain of classical liberalism—one that emphasizes *ex post* exit—offers more promise. Most importantly, exit does a better job of facilitating and capitalizing on social learning, allowing for both adaptation and innovation of jurisdictional boundaries.

Despite these advantages, however, it is worth keeping in mind that a tilt towards *ex post* exit should remain just that: a tilt. There are some disadvantages from an exit-focused approach to evaluating institutions. First, there remains the thorny issue of when individuals should be able to enter into binding agreements, including those involving jurisdictional boundaries. The optimal number of such binding agreements is far from zero. A social order in which criminals can exit from a jurisdiction's authority after committing a crime is simply not functional. But these qualifications are no different than the general recognition that no moral principle or right is absolute and unconditional, especially when it comes to questions of institutional design and evaluation. Second, exit-tilt liberalism leaves ambiguous the dividing line between voluntary association and local government. The ability to exit a small municipality may be no less than the ability to exit a neighborhood association, even if one resulted from conquest and another through contract.

Exit does not tell us everything about whether a state of affairs counts as voluntary or not. Exit-tilt liberals tend to be more concerned with whether present governance arrangements are polycentric and competitive than with the history of how they came about, which will leave some questions unanswered. Just as we must live with a tension between rationalism and pluralism, then, classical liberals must learn to live with conflicting commitments to *ex ante* consent and *ex post* exit, even though I contend that the advantages of exit have typically gone underappreciated. Exit should play a more central role in the body of liberal thought.

Note

* Reprinted by permission from Springer: *Review of Austrian Economics*, "The Limits of Liberalism: Good Boundaries Must Be Discovered," Adam Martin. Copyright 2018.

References

Acemoglu, D., & Robinson, J. A. 2012. *Why nations fail: The origins of power, prosperity, and poverty*. New York: Crown.

Benson, B. L. 1989. The spontaneous evolution of commercial law. *Southern Economic Journal, 55*(3), 644–661.

Benson, B. L. 1990. *The enterprise of law: Justice without the state*. San Francisco, CA: Pacific Research Institute.

Benson, B. L. 1999. To arbitrate or litigate: That is the question. *European Journal of Law and Economics, 8*(2), 91–151.

Benson, B. L. 2011. The law merchant's story: How romantic is it? In: P. Zumbansen & G.-P. Calliess (Eds.), *Law, economics and evolutionary theory* (pp. 68–87). Cheltenham: Edward Elgar.

Buchanan, J. M. 1962. Politics, policy, and the pigovian margins. *Economica, 29*(113), 17–28.

Buchanan, J. M. 1965. An economic theory of clubs. *Economica, 32*(125), 1–14.

Buchanan, J. M. 1974. Review of *The machinery of freedom: Guide to a radical capitalism. Journal of Economic Literature, 12*(3), 914–915.

Buchanan, J. M. 1975. *The limits of liberty: Between anarchy and Leviathan.* Chicago, IL: University of Chicago Press.

Buchanan, J. M., & G. Tullock. 1962. *The calculus of consent: Logical foundations of constitutional democracy.* Ann Arbor, MI: University of Michigan Press.

Eichenberger, R., & B. Frey. 2006. Functional, overlapping, competing jurisdictions. In: E. Ahmad & G. Brosio (Eds.), *Handbook of fiscal federalism* (pp. 154–181). Cheltenham: Edward Elgar.

Foldvary, F. E., & D. B. Klein. 2002. The half-life of policy rationales: How new technology affects old policy issues. *Knowledge, Technology and Policy, 15*(3), 82–92.

Friedman, D. 1973. *The machinery of freedom: Guide to a radical capitalism.* New York: Harper.

Hayek, F. A. 1945. The use of knowledge in society. *American Economic Review, 35*(4), 519–530.

Hayek, F. A. 1960. *The constitution of liberty.* Chicago, IL: University of Chicago Press.

Hayek, F. A. 1973. *Law, legislation, and liberty, vol. I: Rules and order.* Chicago, IL: University of Chicago Press.

Hayek, F. A. 1978 [1968]. Competition as a discovery procedure. *New Studies in Philosophy, Politics, and Economics* (pp. 179–190). Chicago, IL: University of Chicago Press.

Hayek, F. A. 1988. *The fatal conceit: The errors of socialism.* Chicago, IL: University of Chicago Press.

Krugman, P. 2011. *Mr. Keynes and moderns.* Address to the Cambridge conference commemorating the 75th anniversary of the publication of *The general theory of employment, interest, and money,* June. Available at https://www.princeton.edu/~pkrugman/keynes_and_the_moderns.pdf

Kukathas, C. 2007. *The liberal archipelago: A theory of diversity and freedom.* New York: Oxford University Press.

Kuran, T. 1995. *Private truths, public lies: The social consequences of preference falsification.* Cambridge, MA: Harvard University Press.

Leoni, B. 1961. *Freedom and the law.* Los Angeles, CA: Nash.

Levy, J. 2015. *Rationalism, pluralism, and freedom.* New York: Oxford University Press.

Lomasky, L. 2005. Libertarianism at twin Harvard. *Social Philosophy and Policy, 22*(1), 178–199.

Martin, A. 2015. Degenerate cosmopolitanism. *Social Philosophy and Policy, 32*(1), 74–100.

Nozick, R. 1974. *Anarchy, state and utopia.* New York: Basic Books.

Ostrom, E. 1976. *Police consolidation and economies-of-scale: Do they go together?* Police Service Study technical reports, Indiana University Workshop in Political Theory and Policy Analysis.

Rothbard, M. N. 1973. *For a new liberty: The libertarian manifesto.* London: Macmillan.

Stringham, E. P. 2015. *Private governance: Creating order in economic and social life*. New York: Oxford University Press.

Stringham, E. P., & T. J. Zywicki. 2011. Hayekian anarchism. *Journal of Economic Behavior and Organization*, 78(3), 290–301.

Tebble, A. J. 2016. *Epistemic liberalism*. New York: Routledge.

Wagner, R. 2007. *Fiscal sociology and the theory of public finance: An exploratory essay*. Cheltenham: Edward Elgar.

Part II

Empirical explorations and case studies

4 The rise and decline of nations

The dynamic properties of institutional reform

Russell S. Sobel

Introduction*

Economic growth and prosperity is a function of both the resources available and the institutions under which these resources are put to productive use. Institutions are the formal and informal rules governing human interactions (North 1990, 1991). The link between these institutions and economic growth has been recognized since the time of Adam Smith (1976 [1776]), and major theoretical contributions that furthered our knowledge in this area have been advanced by many authors including Hayek (1994 [1944], 1945), North (1990, 1991), Easterly (2001), Olson (1982), and Baumol (1990).

Only more recently has this literature expanded into the empirical arena, with a robust modern literature confirming this hypothesis empirically using different institutional measures, frequently including the *Economic Freedom of the World* (EFW) index by Gwartney, Lawson, and Hall (2015). Evidence that higher levels of economic freedom lead to a number of improved societal outcomes is now abundant.[1] For example, higher levels of economic freedom have been shown to lead to higher levels of income, economic growth, entrepreneurship, investment productivity, happiness, and longevity. At the other end of the spectrum, those countries with the worst institutions not only stagnate, but also are often better off stateless or with private governance mechanisms (Leeson 2007; Leeson and Coyne 2012).

While the literature is clear on the importance of good institutions, we understand little about how and why countries transition from poor institutions to good ones, and vice versa. There has been only sparse and unrelated work on these transitions, leaving a major gap in our understanding of the process of economic and institutional reform.

This chapter attempts to contribute to our understanding of these institutional changes by empirically analyzing the dynamic properties present in the EFW data for countries undergoing major transitions. I pose several questions of interest. For example, are there similarities between institutional declines and institutional improvements, or are these different processes? Is the process of transition generally a single large, abrupt change, or does it occur over a longer time period? Are there particular areas of policy that tend to move first, being "leading indicators," so to speak, of institutional change?

My empirical analysis finds that institutional improvements and declines do indeed share many similarities, including the policy areas that tend to move first. However, they differ in terms of the time span, with declines happening much more abruptly. Institutional improvements appear to be a process of sustained gradual reforms. In addition, the permanence of the changes does not appear to be systematically related to whether they happened quickly or slowly. I use these empirical regularities to attempt to link the separate, but equally applicable, areas of literature on institutional changes, including the work regarding the U.S. government growth in the 20th century, and the transition process of the post-socialist economies.

Literature review

As was mentioned in the introduction to this chapter, while generations of scholars have contributed to our understanding of what makes for "good" institutions, only recently has this literature expanded into the empirical arena, with a more robust modern literature confirming this hypothesis empirically using different institutional measures. While some authors have used measures of the colonial or legal origins of countries,[2] by far the most predominant statistical measure employed in the recent literature is the EFW index (Gwartney, Lawson, and Hall 2015), which has been published annually since 1996 and ranks the institutional quality of countries on a 0–10 scale. The data span 1970–2013 in the most recent report at time of writing, at five-year intervals from 1970 to 2000 and annually thereafter.

While the literature is clear on the importance of good institutions, we understand little about how and why countries transition from poor institutions to good ones, and vice versa. There is a strand of literature that attempts to explain why some countries have poor institutions while others have good institutions, examining everything from the colonial and legal origins of countries to ethnolinguistic fractionalization, resource endowments, and religious homogeneity.[3] However, there has been only sparse and unrelated work on the transitions and changes, leaving a major gap in our understanding of the process of economic and institutional reform.

Some studies have examined how foreign aid impacts the institutions of the recipient countries, generally finding that it causes deterioration or no change.[4] However, changes in foreign aid do not explain any of the major transitions, such as the collapse of socialism in the Soviet Union, the Arab Spring movements, or the socialist swings in Cuba or Venezuela. Quite simply the foreign aid explanations for institutional change in practice probably explain only small downward movements in the institutional quality of already weak nations and yields little insight into major institutional reforms.

Other studies examine how "crisis"-type events tend to lead to expansions in the size and scope of government. With respect to institutional changes that decrease economic freedom, perhaps the largest such literature is the seemingly stand-alone body of research on the transition to growth of the U.S. Federal Government during the early 1900s. After over 100 years of remaining relatively small as a percentage of the economy, both in terms of spending and regulation, the U.S. Federal Government began a transition to rapid growth in many areas of the economy at that time.[5] Obviously, the economic freedom level of the United States fell significantly between the late 1800s and the mid-1900s, but this pre-dates measures of economic freedom. While Anderson and Hill (1980) trace the origin to an increase in regulatory power allowed by the U.S. Supreme Court in *Munn v. Illinois* 94 U.S. 113 (1877), Holcombe (1992, 1999, 2002) discusses many other factors, such as the rise of Union Civil War veterans as an interest group pushing for increased government transfers. Higgs (1987) attributes the growth to a change in political ideology in the Progressive era and many larger "shock"-type events (such as the Great Depression, World War II, and the terrorist attacks of September 11, 2001, known as 9/11) that created "ratchets" in the size and scope of government. This literature seems to suggest that expansions in the scope of government (that is, declines in economic freedom) happen quickly and abruptly as the result of single major crisis events or court rulings. Some recent work in this area considers whether financial or inflationary crises result in the initiation of economic reforms, with mixed results.[6] Olson (1982) argued that institutional declines happen through time as interest groups become more entrenched and argued that shocks were one of the few ways of dislodging these entrenched interests. Various other "single-event" factors that may (or may not) explain institutional changes are present in the literature, including theories about transformational leaders, political-party control changes, expansions in the voting franchise, and military interventions.[7]

There is evidence that institutional reforms do spill over between neighboring countries (Sobel and Leeson 2007; Leeson, Sobel, and Dean 2012), as well as evidence that the EFW institutional measure is non-stationary (that is, not "mean-reverting"), suggesting that reforms do indeed have permanent effects rather than decaying away through time (Sobel and Coyne 2011; Coyne and Sobel 2010).

Perhaps the largest body of stand-alone literature related to this topic regards the transition process in the post-communist countries that emerged in the 1990s after the collapse of the Soviet Union. In most cases, these are performed as case studies and illustrate a deep divide among scholars in that literature about whether the speed or sequence of reforms mattered for the effectiveness of the transition. While many authors argued for quick "shock"-type transitions, others argued for a more gradual approach, and, despite almost two decades of post-collapse transition data, this debate still persists.[8]

As should be evident from the preceding discussion, there are several strands of literature that have developed independently, with little cohesion or cross-citation between them. This leaves a lot to be desired in terms of developing a unified understanding of the process of intuitional change and leaves many unanswered questions as to how these processes relate.

How big is "big"?

When one speaks of major institutional changes, this obviously means a degree of reform that is significantly larger than normal policy variation. So what does normal variation look like, and how large do the changes need to be to be significantly different from normal? Figure 4.1 shows the relative frequency distribution of the annual changes in the EFW index, using 16 equal-width intervals from the minimum to maximum value of the annual changes. While the entire dataset goes back to 1970, it is at five-year intervals until 2000, so the data depicted are for the annual changes in the chain-linked index for all 123 countries in the data from 2000 to 2013.[9]

In Figure 4.1, the distribution appears very narrow, with over 70 percent of observations lying in the two groupings closest to the center of the distribution. While the visual perspective will be highly important for the comparison that follows, the statistics presented at the bottom of Figure 4.1 are the initial point to discuss. The proper interpretation of these values is as follows: because the value corresponding to "Bottom 1%" is −0.489, this means that if we pick a random country in a randomly selected one-year interval, the probability that the EFW index will show a decline of 0.489 or more is only 1 percent. Thus

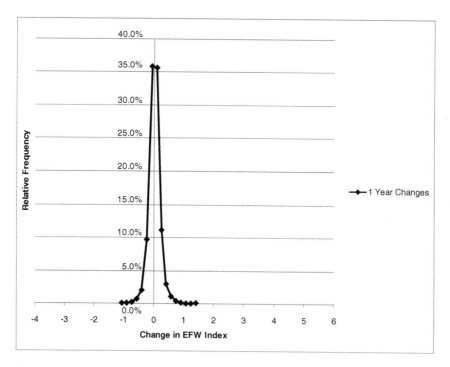

Figure 4.1 Relative frequency distribution of one-year changes in economic freedom, 2000–13

a country declining by a half a point in the index in one year would place it in the 1 percent lower tail of the distribution. Similarly, an annual increase of 0.568 or more happens in only 1 percent of the cases. Thus, based on the numbers shown in Figure 4.1, if we use a standard 90 percent confidence interval around the mean in both directions, a "significant" annual change in economic freedom is a change that is *outside* of the range −0.261 to 0.328.[10] Bear in mind that "significant" in this context is not "statistically significant," as per the result of a statistical test procedure, but simply out of the ordinary in comparison with the large bulk of countries and how they are changing from year to year.

This relative frequency and percentile data, when performed at varying time intervals, yields some interesting insights. Figure 4.2 shows how the relative frequency distribution changes as the time-length horizon expands, while Table 4.1 shows the percentile data and descriptive statistics for these periods of time.[11]

The most striking aspect of Figure 4.2 is how the distribution widens as the time interval considered lengthens. Normally, for a "mean-reverting" stationary series, the variation collapses with expanded lengths of time, because random year-to-year fluctuations tend to cancel each other out over longer periods of time. As the findings of Sobel and Coyne (2011)

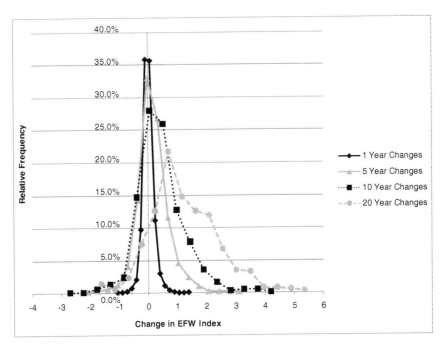

Figure 4.2 Relative frequency distributions changes in economic freedom by period, 2000–13

supported, the EFW series is indeed non-stationary and therefore is not mean-reverting. This means that changes are more permanent and build upon one another, rather than cancel each other out. In other words, the policy reforms stick. This is particularly true of the right-hand tail of the distribution, as can be seen in Figure 4.2.

The fact that the right-hand tail of the distribution grows through time, while the left-hand tail does not, is of great importance. It suggests that when there are declines in institutional quality, the full declines happen fairly rapidly to their full extent. We tend not to see the decline process stretch out as long as the process of positive institutional reform. The full extents of institutional improvements appear to take longer to unfold. For example, while we see almost no cases of countries jumping by 2 points in the EFW index in a single year, there are a substantial number of cases of a 2-point increase over longer periods of time, as is shown by the growing height of the relative frequency distribution curve at a value of +2.0. At this point, the lack of symmetry with which the distribution expands seems to be evidence against increases and decreases following the same pattern.

Turning to the data shown in Table 4.1 allows for a more precise discussion. Consider, for example, the rows showing the percentile cut-off values for the bottom 1% and top 1%. Moving to the right in the columns shows how those values change as the time horizon considered changes. Note that, looking across the row for the bottom 1%, there is little change moving out from the 10-year to 20-year periods. Contrast this with the row for

Table 4.1 Descriptive statistics for changes in economic freedom by time length

	1-year changes	5-year changes	10-year changes	20-year changes
Percentiles				
Bottom 1%	−0.489	−1.229	−1.522	−1.583
Bottom 5%	−0.261	−0.597	−0.602	−0.384
Bottom 10%	−0.184	−0.370	−0.399	−0.058
Top 10%	0.223	0.780	1.412	2.685
Top 5%	0.328	1.091	1.828	3.287
Top 1%	0.568	1.760	3.131	4.515
Other descriptive statistics				
Maximum	1.318	2.956	3.981	5.114
Minimum	−1.140	−2.280	−2.933	−1.851
Average	0.018	0.168	0.430	1.223
No. of countries	123	123	123	113
No. of data points	1599	1677	1062	447
Years included	2000–13	1970–2013	1970–2013	1970–2010

Note: Underlying data is annual, beginning in 2000, prior in five-year intervals back to 1970.

the top 1%, in which the values continue to climb by large amounts even between the 10- and 20-year periods. The interpretation is straightforward: the declines that happen, in the abundance of cases, seem to be fully concluded by 10 years after the transition begins, while for the improvements in institutional quality, a substantial number of cases continue to climb in the second decade of reform.

The skewness of the distribution also means that what is a "big," or significant, change differs for declines and increases in the data. Over 20-year periods, only 1 percent of cases show declines of more than 1.583, while the similar statistic for improvers is 4.515. Thus a country falling 2 points in economic freedom over two decades would be rare, while a country rising 2 points in economic freedom over two decades does not even make it into the top 10 percent tail of the upper distribution (which begins at 2.685). Again, I shall conclude by pointing out the 90 percent "confidence intervals," which are 5-year changes outside the range −0.597 to 1.091, 10-year changes outside the range −0.602 to 1.828, and 20-year changes in EFW outside the range −0.384 to 3.287. Countries rising (or falling) by more than these values have experienced what one may consider a "significant" change in institutional quality relative to the other countries of the world.

How long does "significant institutional change" take?

The data in the previous section took specific time intervals and then computed the changes in EFW index over those specified intervals. This section basically does the opposite by computing the time lengths for the changes seen in the underlying index data.

The EFW data presents some hurdles when considered in this way. To capture the time length it required for a country to "reform" in a positive direction, one would, in theory, find the minimum value prior to the improvement and the ending maximum, then compute the difference in the year values from the minimum to maximum values of EFW. While easy in theory, there are the following issues in the practical data:

(1) how to handle cases in which there are multiple years that take on the same minimum (or maximum) values;
(2) how to handle cases whose first year in the data (or last year) are the maximums and minimums, such that a full time length for the reform cannot be computed within sample; and
(3) how to handle cases in which a country has two maximums (or minimums) with a minimum (maximum) occurring between them (such as V-shaped patterns).

While there are no perfect solutions, as a first step the following procedures were used to arrive at a statistically useful sample of countries undergoing transitions.

(1) For a county that improves, I employ the most recent year of the EFW minimum (that largest year value among minimum EFW years) and the earliest EFW maximum year (the smallest year value among maximum EFW years). Thus, for example, if a country had EFW values of 4, 4, 4, 5, 6, 7, 8, 8, 8, the third year would be used as the year of the minimum, while the seventh year would be used as the year of the maximum, so the time length of reform would be Year 7 minus Year 3, or four years taken to fully reform.

(2) For now, I exclude any country whose maximum or minimums occur at the endpoints because the full time length for the reform cannot be calculated, but I will reintroduce and reconsider the specific countries with ending maximum or minimum in a later section.

(3) For now, I proceed by excluding any country that has a minimum value between two maximum values, or vice versa (for example V-shapes), to focus on countries that clearly reformed upward or downward through time.

Table 4.2 Years in transition from minimum to maximum EFW values (or vice versa)

Rank	Change in EFW	Years in transition	Rank	Change in EFW	Years in transition
1	5.34	27	36	2.22	10
2	4.89	25	37	2.11	30
3	4.74	25	38	2.07	27
4	4.65	25	39	2.06	31
5	4.58	20	40	2.03	28
6	4.43	32	41	2.00	25
7	3.97	29	42	1.88	16
8	3.89	25	43	1.88	25
9	3.80	16	44	1.84	25
10	3.71	30	45	1.83	22
11	3.68	22	46	1.81	16
12	3.54	15	47	1.72	18
13	3.38	32	48	1.67	31
14	3.38	21	49	1.63	32
15	3.30	26	50	1.57	25
16	3.23	26	51	1.53	25
17	3.22	25	52	1.49	20
18	3.15	20	53	1.47	19
19	3.12	25	54	1.46	16
20	2.81	21	55	1.44	21
21	2.80	26	56	1.43	17
22	2.70	22	57	1.38	26
23	2.68	25	58	1.28	20
24	2.61	30	59	1.25	25

25	2.48	36	60	1.17	20
26	2.45	22	61	1.15	11
27	2.43	30	62	1.04	25
28	2.41	30	63	1.03	25
29	2.38	25	64	1.00	6
30	2.38	25	65	0.92	17
31	2.25	32	66	0.90	24
32	2.24	27	67	0.62	24
33	2.24	18	68	0.55	5
34	2.23	21	69	−0.88	10
35	2.22	32	70	−2.93	10

Note: Maximum possible is 43 years given the length of the data in the EFW index.

Table 4.2 shows the results, using the beginning useful sample of 70 countries that have transitioned fully from their maximum to minimum EFW values (or vice versa) within the years covered in the EFW index data. Names have been omitted *intentionally*. Prior literature has treated each of these changes as special individual cases; the entire point of this undertaking is to look for *systematic* patterns in the data that apply across all countries. Examining the first column of Table 4.2, the largest minimum-to-maximum positive changes are listed at the top. Strikingly, the period of time it took to undergo change is surprisingly similar across most of the countries in the top half of the first column of countries. Three of the top five all took 25 years, with the other two narrowly surrounding that value, at 20 and 27 years. Looking down the first column, it seems clear that the overwhelming majority of upward reformers took somewhere between 20 and 30 years to complete the process of institutional reform.

At the other end of the list, there are only two countries in this smaller sample of clean data that declined, both taking 10 years. While one would normally be skeptical of drawing conclusions from only two data points, recall the relative frequency distributions presented earlier, which included all data from all countries. Those figures have already demonstrated that the process of decline was finalized more rapidly than the process of improvement. There are now several aspects of the EFW data that seem to point toward declines occurring more rapidly than upward reforms. It is worthwhile to now revisit the literature with respect to this data-driven conclusion. The "crisis," or "ratchet," theory of single events driving expansions in the size and scope of government seems to be entirely consistent with the data. These would obviously be declines in economic freedom and, if caused by abrupt changes, would play out more quickly. Events such as the 9/11 terrorist attacks causing a large abrupt change in airline and other types of security spending and regulations, or the 1929 stock market crash (and that of 2008) leading to large government responses, are examples of this phenomenon. This does not mean that declines in EFW are always caused by shocks or abrupt ratchet-type changes; only that these crisis events, which result in expansions in government, are consistent with this view.

However, this theory seems to not explain movements in the opposite direction (that is, large positive EFW movements) very well. There apparently are no analogous "shock"-type events that drive significant and quick reforms in the upward direction; instead, significant increases in economic freedom seem to involve a long-run process of smaller changes that accumulate through time. Creating an environment of enhanced economic freedom seems to be a longer, but effective, battle; destroying an environment of economic freedom seems (unfortunately) to be accomplished more rapidly.

Speed of reform versus permanence: does "shock" work as well as "gradual" transition?

As was cited earlier in this chapter, what was, and is, a lively and hotly contested debate in the post-socialist countries is whether reforms should be accomplished quickly or slowly. While those debates have focused on those specific set of countries, the data at hand allow an exploration of this at a meta level across all countries. The question is simple: does the "years in transition" variable from Table 4.2 correlate with whether the final ending value persisted into the future, meaning that the reform "stuck"?

The difference between the maximum EFW value at the end of transition and the EFW value at the end of the sample (2013) is employed as the measure of the amount of "erosion" in the reforms post-transition. More precisely, I compute an "erosion" variable equal to 1 minus the ratio of the ending EFW to the maximum post-transition value. In simpler terms, this number reflects the percentage of the maximum EFW score that the country obtained that decayed away. If gradual reforms work better than "shock" reforms, for example, then it should be the case that the longer the time of transition, the less erosion that follows. Figure 4.3 shows the data for all countries that improved by more than 2 points in the EFW index, as set out in Table 4.2.

As is clear in Figure 4.3, there is no relationship. The degree of erosion does differ across countries, but it neither grows systematically nor shrinks with the duration taken to complete the reform process. At face value, this implies that shock transitions work equally well as gradual transitions when all countries are considered.

However, given the clear importance of this finding for the large literature on post-socialist transition policy, it is worth looking at a few underlying cases. From Table 4.2, beginning at the top of the left-hand column of countries, of those with the largest positive changes two near the top stand out as accomplishing change faster than the rest. The 9th and 12th data points listed took 16 and 15 years, respectively, to complete their transitions, while other countries in the list that experienced similar changes in EFW took slightly longer than average (the 10th and 13th data points). Thus, while the 9th and 10th data points from Table 4.2 experienced almost identical changes in EFW, they took drastically different time periods to complete the change, and a similar logic applies for the 12th and 13th data points. Would a comparison

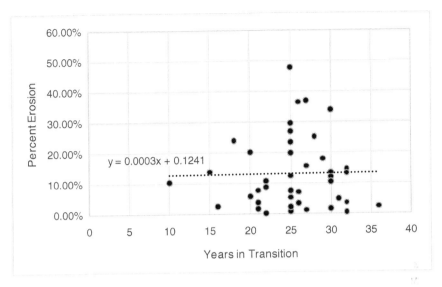

Figure 4.3 Does transition process length matter for permanence?

of these countries allow additional insights into whether the changes remained in place (or deteriorated) differently for fast versus slow reformers? Figure 4.4 reveals these countries and their end results as of the 2015 EFW index (which includes data up to 2013).

First, consider Iceland. This country experienced a minimum-to-maximum change that began in 1975, with an EFW value of 4.40, and reached its maximum (a value of 8.11) in 2005. Thus, in Table 4.2, Iceland was shown to have a 3.71 EFW improvement over a period of 30 years. Since 2005, however, the country has gone backward, with its EFW ending at a value of 6.85 in 2013. In other words, Iceland improved substantially over a long gradual transition, but its reforms have recently decayed, eroding almost half of the improvement. However, while Mauritius demonstrates a similar improvement (a 3.38 increase in EFW over 32 years), its reforms have not decayed and seem to have "stuck." Thus, for two of the longer gradual transitions, we see that one remained, while another decayed. A similar split is evident in the two faster reformers, Rwanda and Bolivia: Rwanda experienced a 3.8 improvement in EFW over 16 years, and this reform has seemingly stuck in place, while Bolivia underwent a 3.54 improvement in EFW over 15 years that has partially decayed by 1 point. Again, this split demonstrates opposite experiences with permanence. These four cases seem to illustrate the general finding from Figure 4.3 of little correlation between the time length and durability of the changes. What this implies for the literature is that factors other than time duration must be the primary determinants of whether reforms stick or erode.

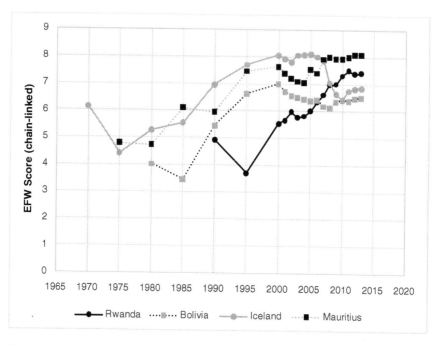

Figure 4.4 Fast versus gradual transitions: some examples

Simon says: which areas lead, and which follow?

I now examine the areas of the EFW index. In particular, I wish to see whether countries that underwent major reforms showed any similarities in terms of which EFW areas moved first in the process. This could be important information because it may indicate that, if we wish to begin the reform process in a country, we should first initiate reform of a particular set of policies to get the process rolling more broadly.[12] For those countries that decline, an analogous question would be which areas decline first. If a country wishes to maintain a high level of economic freedom, this knowledge may indicate which areas of policy change are most important to preserve and thereby prevent broader decline.

There are five "areas" of the EFW index, as follows.

- Area 1 measures the size of government (in terms of government consumption expenditures, transfers and subsidies, taxes, and government-run enterprises).
- Area 2 measures the legal structure and security of property rights (impartial courts, protection of property rights, contract enforcement, etc.).
- Area 3 measures access to sound money (inflation and currency control measures).

- Area 4 measures the freedom to trade internationally (tariff and non-tariff barriers, as well as capital movement controls).
- Area 5 measures regulation of credit, labor, and business (interest rate controls, workplace regulations and minimum wages, and "ease of doing business" measures).

It is unfair to ask which area moves as an early warning signal precisely because the areas are components of the overall index and hence movement in any one area will move the entire index value for the country. Thus a better measure of leading reform policies is which moved "first" among the five areas. So, for example, if Area 1 begins to trend upward in 1980, while the other areas do not begin their upward trend until a later year, then I consider Area 1 to be a "first mover." If two areas both begin their upward trend earliest, I consider that a tied result and count both.

I begin with those countries that moved up in the index by computing the percentage of the cases of upward EFW reform in which that particular area moved first. I do this separately for the countries improving by 3 or more points (23 countries) and also for those moving up by 2 or more points (53 countries). Included here are countries that completed their transitions within the sample (Table 4.2) and those that are still rising (that is, those that have maximum values at the final year of data) because the length of the reform process is not relevant; only what areas moved first. The results are presented in Table 4.3. Because there are ties in the data when two areas move first, the percentages presented in Table 4.3 may total more than 100 percent.

In roughly two-thirds or more of the cases of large reforms, Area 4 (freedom to trade internationally in capital and goods) seemed to be the clear first mover in cases of institutional reforms toward greater economic freedom. Areas 2 (legal structure and security of property rights) and 1 (size of government) moved early in roughly a quarter of the cases. On the opposite end of the spectrum, Areas 3 (access to sound money) and 5 (regulation of credit, labor, and business) rarely moved early in the process, tending to lag behind the other areas in the upward process, especially for the larger (>3.0 point) movements in the index.

Table 4.3 First-mover analysis of EFW areas: institutional improvements

Change in EFW index	Area 1 (Size of govt.)	Area 2 (Legal system & property rights)	Area 3 (Monetary stability)	Area 4 (Free trade)	Area 5 (Regulation)
Percentage of countries in which the area moved first (ties allowed)					
> +3.0	30.4%	26.1%	13.0%	65.2%	13.0%
> +2.0	20.8%	18.9%	15.1%	64.2%	30.2%

Taken at face value, this suggests that the single most important area of policy to target early to trigger reforms in a country is policies regarding restrictions on international trade and capital movements. Constraining the size of government (and/or cutting government spending, taxes, and ownership of enterprises), as well as improving the legal structure and security of property rights, come in as second-tier targets in early stages of reform. But the data suggest that widespread EFW reforms generally are not initiated by changes in policies that target monetary stability or reducing government regulations. The idea that free trade can be a precursor to widespread economic reform is also consistent with the view that free trade is a foundational value for a society. In fact, the economists of the Enlightenment, including Adam Smith, argued for free trade, and this was a primary first-mover policy argument in the entire classical liberal movement.

The two countries with clear declines in the sample, Venezuela and Zimbabwe, do not present a clear picture with regard to the first-mover areas and whether they differ for declining nations. Venezuela was already declining at the start of the EFW index in 1970, as were its Areas 1, 3, and 4. Zimbabwe's Areas 2 and 4 were the two areas that moved first in their process of decline. Area 4 does appear in both cases, however, which is one of the few instances of consistency between risers and decliners. However, with such a small sample of decliners, it is difficult to draw any conclusions about them specifically; to the contrary, they also present no evidence conflicting with the conclusion that Area 4 (freedom to trade internationally in capital and goods) is a key first mover in the process of institutional reform.

The foregoing analysis simply asked which area moved first in terms of timing. However, there are other ways of approaching this issue of first movers. For example, while a particular area may have moved first, it may not have moved much and therefore may not have contributed much to the overall improvement (or decline). An alternative question would be to ask what areas contributed most to the overall change in EFW and whether there were particular areas dominant in the early versus late years of the reform process.

Again, for the big movers (that is, those moving by more than 2 or 3 points in the index), I estimate the percentage of the overall EFW improvement that is attributable to the changes in each EFW area. I then repeat the calculation for only the first five years of the overall institutional improvement. By comparing these numbers, we can see what areas drive overall reforms and what areas tend to matter most at the beginning. The results are presented in Table 4.4.

In Table 4.4, we see that, for those countries improving by more than 3 points in the EFW index, the single largest area contributing to the reforms is Area 4 (free trade), which accounts for 29.4 percent of the entire EFW change for the average country in this group. Similarly, for the larger group of countries improving by 2 or more points, Area 4 (free trade) is also the largest contributor, at 25.2 percent. The area contributing the second most

Table 4.4 Percentage contribution of EFW areas to overall reform: institutional improvements

Change in EFW index	Area 1 (Size of govt.)	Area 2 (Legal system & property rights)	Area 3 (Monetary stability)	Area 4 (Free trade)	Area 5 (Regulation)
Relative contribution over full reform					
> +3.0	15.1%	14.7%	27.3%	29.4%	13.5%
> +2.0	16.8%	19.4%	25.1%	25.2%	13.5%
Relative contribution over first five years of reform					
> +3.0	39.1%	5.3%	10.6%	28.4%	16.7%
> +2.0	14.7%	32.9%	16.0%	23.6%	12.8%

heavily over the entire sample is Area 3 (monetary stability). However, when one examines the next rows in the table, showing the percentages only for the first five years of reform, the picture changes slightly. While free trade is still a major contributor (28.4 percent and 23.6 percent), Areas 1 (size of government) and 2 (legal system and property rights) seem to play a major role. Interestingly, Area 1 (size of government) is the largest contributor in the case of countries moving by more than 3 points, while it is way down the list even for the first five years once we move to all countries improving by 2 or more points. Similarly, Area 2 (legal system and property rights) appears to have a sizeable impact during the initial years for countries rising by more than 2 points, but not for those that move more than 3 points. In summary, what Table 4.4 seems to suggest is that improvements in Area 4 (free trade) are critical to reforms and are, again, an important first-mover area. Areas 1 (size of government) and 2 (legal system and property rights) are the two other areas important to monitor in the early stages of major institutional change.

I now examine the two countries suffering the largest declines in EFW, Venezuela and Zimbabwe, as shown in Table 4.5. For these two countries, over the full period, worsening monetary stability (Area 3) and free trade (Area 4) were the dominant areas over the entire period. Because Venezuela was already moving in a downward direction prior to the first year of data, I cannot compute what occurred in the first five years for Venezuela. For Zimbabwe, however, Area 4 (free trade) was the first mover. This, again, suggests a striking similarity with countries that improved and an early strong change in international free trade policies. For Zimbabwe, Area 3 (monetary stability) also seems to be more important in contributing to the overall decline. As prior literature has argued, financial or fiscal crisis are sometimes factors that cause dramatic declines in government policy and high rates of inflation. These data are consistent with the literature.

Table 4.5 Percentage contribution of EFW areas to overall reform: institutional
decliners

Country	Area 1 (Size of govt.)	Area 2 (Legal system & property rights)	Area 3 (Monetary stability)	Area 4 (Free trade)	Area 5 (Regulation)
Relative contribution over full reform					
Venezuela	19.5%	15.0%	33.0%	26.0%	6.4%
Zimbabwe	16.3%	18.0%	33.2%	24.5%	8.1%
Relative contribution over first five years of reform					
Venezuela	N/A	N/A	N/A	N/A	N/A
Zimbabwe	18.5%	8.2%	32.5%	43.6%	0.0%

A final method of approaching this question is to compute, for each EFW area, what percentage of the improvement in that specific area occurred within the first five years of reform (versus what percentage of the change in the area happened in the remainder of the reform years). This data is given in Table 4.6.

This final approach to looking at the issue of areas that lead the reform process seeks to understand what percentage improvements in each area occur early and late in the reform process. According to Table 4.6, for example, for countries rising 3 or more points in EFW index, of the total movement in the Area 1 score, 43.5 percent of the Area 1 improvement occurs in the first five years (implying that the remaining 56.5 percent occurs in the rest of the later reform period). The two areas in which movements seem to be the most heavily weighted toward the early years are, again, Areas 4 (free trade) and 1 (size of government).

A closer examination of free trade policy

Focusing on trade liberalization as a first step in promoting reform seems to be a promising conclusion driven by this data analysis. In virtually every way

Table 4.6 Percentage of reforms in first five years by EFW area: institutional
improvements

Change in EFW index	Area 1 (Size of govt.)	Area 2 (Legal system & property rights)	Area 3 (Monetary stability)	Area 4 (Free trade)	Area 5 (Regulation)
Percentage of area movement occurring in first five years					
> +3.0	43.5%	27.6%	16.5%	37.9%	20.3%
> +2.0	30.3%	18.3%	18.5%	30.1%	14.6%

of analyzing the data, this one area (Area 4) dominates the discussion. It is the single area contributing most to the overall changes and the clear robust first mover across measures, both for countries improving and for those declining. This section takes a closer look at this EFW area in terms of both theory and the data. But, before discussing these issues, it is important to note that this area of the EFW index is based on several variables. The area includes measures of tariff rates and revenue, non-tariff trade barriers (such as quotas), currency controls (measured by black-market exchange rates), the freedom of foreigners to visit, capital controls, and restrictions on foreign investment and ownership.

A focus on trade policy as a first step has theoretical merit drawn from the previous literature on institutional reform. In particular, Christopher Coyne's book *After War: The Political Economy of Exporting Democracy* (2008) examines cases of targeted military interventions that have been undertaken in the name of "nation building," aiming to improve institutions. His book concludes that these have generally been failures and argues that the best strategy is to promote a policy of free trade with these nations instead. Similarly, Leeson, Sobel, and Dean (2012), and Sobel and Leeson (2007), explore how institutional improvements spread between nations using spatial econometric modelling, and concluded that one obvious common factor between those countries that "catch" better institutions from each other is their linkage in trade volume. However, what appears to be important is not only opening domestic trade toward these nations, but also getting them to open their policies in return (as in a trade agreement). The implications for the current situation with Cuba are clear: negotiating free-trade policies that cause improvements in Cuba's trade openness may well be the best first target in attempting to promote larger and broader economic and institutional reforms in that country. Given that the data for this area include restrictions on foreign ownership and investment, and freedom of travel, both of which are problem areas for Cuba, these seem to be logical first steps in any trade negotiations aimed at long-run reform in that country.

At the risk of pushing this conclusion too far, but with the reward of possibly linking two strands of literature, it is worth discussing how the timing of restrictions on international trade correlate with clear decline in what would have been the measured EFW index score for the United States in the early 1900s. As discussed earlier, scholars have differentially attributed this to a variety of factors, such as an 1877 ruling of the Supreme Court, successful interest group evolution in the 1890s, the "Progressive era" ideology evolving from the 1890s to 1920s, the ratchet/crisis response to the 1920 stock market crash, the 1933–38 enactment of New Deal programs, and expanded government control and the withholding of income tax during World War II. Arguably, if the EFW index were measured then, the largest changes would have occurred under the New Deal from 1933 to 1938, caused by higher levels of government spending and greater regulatory controls on banking and labor. However, one of the factors most often blamed for the severity of the Great Depression, which preceded the onset of the New Deal programs and was caused by this "crisis"-induced ratchet in the size and scope of government, was the Smoot-Hawley Tariff Act of 1930, which raised tariffs by more than 50 percent on approximately 3,200 imported products (to the highest levels in U.S. history).[13] This would have caused a decline in Area 4 of the index in 1930 that preceded the declines in the size of government (Area 1) and increased regulation (Area 5) during the 1933–38 New Deal period. Thus, had economic freedom been measured then, Area 4 (restrictions on free trade) may have very well moved first for the United States in the process of the institutional erosion in economic freedom that occurred in the early 20th century. While most authors point to other factors and an earlier gradual start, clearly the decline in U.S. economic freedom during the New Deal, if measured, would have been correlated with a preceding change in trade policy. This correlation with the Smoot-Hawley Tariff Act is perhaps a fruitful avenue of research that could meld two islands of research on institutional change in the literature.[14]

Also interestingly, one area of concern is the recent decline in economic freedom in the United States. After maintaining a rank of third in the EFW index for years, the United States fell fairly dramatically into the teens in the EFW rankings, experiencing a decline of almost 1 point in the chain-linked EFW score between 2000 and 2011. Figure 4.5 shows the EFW overall score, along with the two areas of the index that moved first in the overall decline, Areas 2 and 4.

Consistent with what we have found in general, Area 4 (freedom to trade internationally in capital and goods) and Area 2 (legal structure and security of property rights) were the two first movers in the recent decline in EFW for the

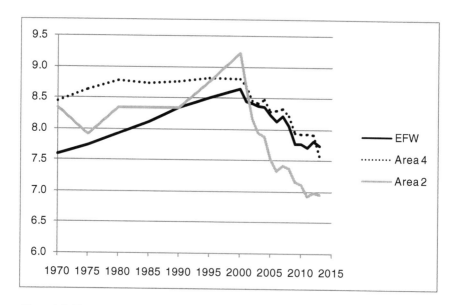

Figure 4.5 First-mover areas in the recent EFW decline for the United States

United States. U.S. trade policy moved away from free trade through increases in tariffs that were sometimes large, such as the tariffs on Chinese steel and tires. Quite ironically, these are the same two areas that were first movers in Zimbabwe's EFW decline as well. While these are anecdotal conjectures, they do appear to be consistent with the idea that expanding or adopting restrictions on free trade tend to be precursor events for larger changes to come in institutional quality. It is also suggestive that future research will be better able to integrate these separate strands of research on institutional decline and transitions.

Are the post-socialist transition economies special cases?

Up to this point, I have treated all countries the same: data is data. A country moving from an EFW index score of 4 to 7, a change of 3 points, is examined similarly to one moving from 6 to 9. However, a common comment on early drafts of this paper was that the post-socialist transition countries are somehow different. They are, after all, moving from socialism to capitalism, not only changing their level of capitalism. Also, given the stand-alone nature of the transition literature and my desire to move toward an integration of these various areas of literature, it is worth examining this question in more detail.

The most common list of such countries includes Estonia, Latvia, Lithuania, Poland, Czech Republic, Slovak Republic, Hungary, Romania, Bulgaria, and Slovenia. All ten of these countries are covered in the EFW data, although with differing first years of coverage. The earliest coverage begins for Hungary in 1980, with Bulgaria, Poland, and Romania joining in 1985, and the remainder, in 1995. In this section, I simply ask: do the general conclusions found earlier across all countries still hold up when examining only the post-socialist transition economies?

First, let us consider the question of the speed of reforms vs. their permanence—that is, the topic of the "shock" vs. gradual transition arguments prevalent in the literature on these countries. Figure 4.6 shows the overall EFW index scores for all ten countries. Obviously, there is no way, in black-and-white print, to label ten different lines so that they are discernable—but this is part of the point: if we examine them as a group, what do we see?

One of the most striking features of Figure 4.6 is that while the countries varied substantially in terms of how quickly their upward reforms began, and how long they took, all of them end up within a very narrow band at the end, ranging from 6.43 to 7.59. Slovenia is the lowest at the end of the sample, the clear single line trending down in the final few years of data. For the other nine, the band is even narrower, with a range of only 7.17 to 7.59. Clearly, the differences in the processes yielded very similar long-run outcomes. Two countries show significant decay in terms their advancements, Slovenia and Estonia, both of which have fallen from their maximum scores. But, again, there appears to be no clear link between speed of transition and erosion: Slovenia had rapid improvements, but decayed, while Estonia's reform took longer and decayed. Similarly, Romania started slowly, rose quickly, and

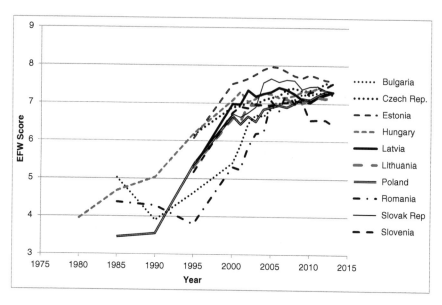

Figure 4.6 The post-socialist transition economies

shows no decay, while Hungary followed a longer process and shows no decay. Just as with the evidence from all countries, there is no clear link between speed of reform and permanence in this data: they are the same as those of other countries who reformed by similar magnitudes.

I now turn to the question of which areas move first or account for the largest percentage of overall EFW movement. Again, what is important is whether these countries are different or similar from the entire sample shown earlier. Table 4.7 shows the data.

Because the question is one of early movers, Table 4.7 shows the data for the only four countries whose data pre-dates 1995, and thus we have data on the early years. However, even using all of them, the results are similar. Again, just like for the overall sample, Areas 3 (monetary stability) and 4 (free trade) carry most of the weight of the reform over the full sample and are the early movers as well. Quite simply, there is nothing here to discuss that is different from the overall sample. I find no evidence that these countries are somehow different in their data. The dynamics of their EFW changes is not significantly different from the dynamics experienced by other countries. To put it more bluntly, there is no reason why the transition economy literature cannot be intertwined with the other literatures on institutional declines and institutional improvements. Indeed, integrating these various areas of the literature may help to drive major advances in our understanding of the process of institutional change more generally.

Table 4.7 Percentage contribution of EFW areas to overall reform: post-socialist countries

Country	Area 1 (Size of govt.)	Area 2 (Legal system & property rights)	Area 3 (Monetary stability)	Area 4 (Free trade)	Area 5 (Regulation)
Relative contribution over full reform (minimum to maximum)					
Bulgaria	21.3%	6.0%	31.8%	24.7%	16.2%
Hungary	20.5%	6.7%	20.6%	33.6%	18.6%
Poland	16.5%	8.6%	29.9%	22.9%	22.1%
Romania	18.9%	10.7%	34.9%	18.2%	17.3%
Average	19.3%	8.0%	29.8%	24.4%	18.4%
Relative contribution over early years of reform (to 2000 only)					
Bulgaria	13.8%	3.6%	36.3%	32.0%	14.3%
Hungary	26.5%	5.7%	9.7%	37.1%	21.1%
Poland	17.8%	9.4%	28.9%	24.9%	18.9%
Romania	10.9%	14.4%	37.5%	21.3%	16.0%
Average	15.3%	8.7%	31.7%	27.7%	16.7%

Conclusion

Broad and significant changes in country institutions and policies can, and do, happen. Despite knowing the clear importance of these changes for prosperity and well-being, there is a relatively sparse literature on this process other than several isolated pockets of research regarding specific issues such as the post-socialist transition economies or the growth of the U.S. government in the 20th century. There is little understanding of whether the process of institutional decline is similar to or different than the process of institutional improvement, the timing and duration of such changes, and the areas of policy that tend to move first. This chapter attempts to uncover empirical regularities in the major institutional changes that have occurred in countries between 1970 and 2013 using the data from the 2015 EFW index.

The data point to several conclusions that may help to advance future research in this area. First, there is clear evidence that institutional decline happens more rapidly and abruptly than institutional improvement. While significant improvements in institutional quality generally unfold over periods of roughly 25 years, significant deteriorations are mostly complete within 10-year periods. This suggests that the driving forces may be different. It is supportive of Higgs' (1987) "crisis," or "ratchet," type of theory of government growth in both size and scope (which implies a decline in economic freedom). The process of positive institutional reform, however, is a continuous process of smaller improvements over a longer period of time. Similar to the way in which small differences in economic growth rates can produce large differences in prosperity over longer time intervals, the key is sustained positive institutional reforms over time. Despite the apparent visibility of single transformative events, such as the fall of the Berlin Wall or of the Soviet Union, and the Arab Spring movement, true significant increases in institutional quality seem to be accomplished over longer time spans.

Second, there seems to be no evidence that the speed of the reform matters in terms of its durability. Despite the ongoing debate in the post-socialist transition literature on the relative merits of "shock" vs. "gradual" policy reforms, the data do not point to a clear conclusion when we examine all of the countries of the world that have experienced major institutional changes. Some countries that have improved rapidly have sustained that improvement, while others have not. Similarly, some that improved more slowly have sustained that improvement, while others have not. In a broader cross-section, there is no correlation between the durability of the change and the time length of the process. There is simply no conclusive evidence from a meta-analysis of the data that either approach is better.

Finally, government policies related to the freedom to trade internationally in capital and goods seems to be the clearest and most robust "first mover" in cases of significant institutional reform, both upward and downward. It is also the largest contributor to the magnitude of the overall ending reform. This is consistent with the arguments made by Coyne (2008), Leeson, Sobel, and Dean (2012), and Sobel and Leeson (2007) regarding the role of free trade in initiating and spreading positive institutional reform, as well as the correlation present between the Smoot-Hawley Tariff Act of 1930 and the New Deal programs in the United States during the early 20th century (as well as the more recent decline in the institutional ranking of the United States over the past two decades). Policies related to the legal structure and security of property rights and the size of government are the second most frequent early-moving areas, and thus early reforms in these areas (either upward or downward) need to be closely monitored as early indicators of transitions. On the opposite end of the spectrum, monetary policy and regulatory policy rarely move early in the process, tending to lag behind the other areas—especially in the case of larger institutional reforms. However, there is some evidence that, over the entire period of reform, monetary stability is one of the largest areas contributing to institutional change. One implication for current policy is that negotiating for more trade openness with Cuba (for example by easing restrictions on foreign investment and ownership, and travel restrictions) is indeed a worthwhile first step if the desire is to initiate a long-term process of positive institutional improvement in that country.

Notes

* "The Rise and Decline of Nations: The Dynamic Properties of Institutional Reform" was originally published in the *Journal of Institutional Economics*, volume 13, No. 3 (September 2017), pp. 549–574. It is reprinted here with the permission of the journal.

1 For good survey overviews of this literature, see De Haan, Lundstrom, and Sturm (2006), Hall and Lawson (2014), and Berggren (2003). For some of the most influential individual studies, see Gwartney, Lawson, and Holcombe (1999), Gwartney, Holcombe, and Lawson (2004, 2006), Dawson (1998, 2003), Heckelman (2000), Sobel (2008), Kreft and Sobel (2005), Sobel, Clark, and Lee (2007), Hall, Sobel, and Crowley (2010), Gehring (2013), Scully (2002), Grubel (1998), and Easton and Walker (1997). For recent evidence on the relationship with income inequality, see Holcombe and Boudreaux (2016), and Bologna, Lacombe, and Young (2016).

2 See, e.g., Glaeser and Shleifer (2002); La Porta, Lopez-de-Silanes, and Shleifer (2008); Acemoglu, Johnson, and Robinson (2001); and Robinson, Acemoglu, and Johnson (2005).

3 Examples include Easterly (2014), Glaeser and Shleifer (2002), La Porta, Lopez-de-Silanes, and Shleifer (2008), Acemoglu, Johnson, and Robinson (2001), Robinson, Acemoglu, and Johnson (2005), Glaeser, Laporta, Lopez-de-Silanes, and Shleifer (2004), Easterly and Levine (1997), Sachs and Warner (1999), and Collier (2010).

4 For examples, see Powell and Ryan (2006), and Heckelman and Knack (2009).

5 See Meltzer and Richard (1981), and Peltzman (1980).

6 See Pitlik and Wirth (2003), March, Lyford, and Powell (2015), and Young and Bologna (2016).

7 See, e.g., Husted and Kenny (1997), and Coyne (2008).

8 See Boettke (2001), Fischer and Gelb (1991), Heybey and Murrel (1999), Kolodko (2000), Murphy, Shleifer, and Vishny (1992), Murrell (1992), Roland (1994), Sachs (1996), and Shleifer and Treisman (2005).

9 Unless otherwise noted, all data that follow use the chain-linked values from 2015 Economic Freedom of the World report data. All analysis in this paper was conducted using the data in the file "2015 corrected dataset (Excel 3.3MB)," downloaded from http://www.freetheworld.com/release.html on September 10, 2015. Note that the data used throughout focus on properties of the first-differenced (change) series, which is justified (and stationary), unlike the levels of EFW: see Sobel and Coyne (2011), and Coyne and Sobel (2010).

10 Note that the EFW index is not a random sample of the world because countries without available data (such as Cuba and North Korea) are omitted. So the data is biased in that some of the countries with the worst institutions are not included in the sample. However, countries can and do move into the index as they reform, so the only countries omitted completely are those that have been poor since the start of recording of this data in 1970, such as Cuba and North Korea. These are countries that would have low EFW scores, but which scores would have changed relatively little since 1970, so which scores probably would not skew the distribution because any changes would likely be near zero. However, it would have been useful had the data reached back far enough to include data pre-dating the collapse of communism in Eastern Europe.

11 These use the full sample available and present every possible calculation of the time span indicated for all countries.

12 The question of early movers or an ordering of changes is also interesting in light of the work by Friedman (1962) and Lawson and Clark (2010), who examine whether changes in economic freedom precede changes in political freedom.

13 See Gwartney, Stroup, Sobel, and Macpherson (2015: 630).

14 Tariff policy was also a key factor contributing to early tensions between the southern and northern U.S. states prior to the Civil War to the extent that the newly formed Confederate government wrote its Constitution with an explicit prohibition of using tariffs to discriminatorily impact commerce (Holcombe 1992).

References

Acemoglu, D., S. Johnson and J. Robinson. 2001. The colonial origins of comparative development. *American Economic Review*, *91*(5): 1369–1401.

Anderson, T., and P. Hill. 1980. *The birth of a transfer society*. Stanford, CA: Hoover Institution Press.

Baumol, W. 1990. Entrepreneurship: Productive, unproductive and destructive. *Journal of Political Economy*, *98*(5): 893–921.

Berggren, N. 2003. The benefits of economic freedom: A survey. *The Independent Review*, *8*(2): 193–211.

Boettke, P. 2001. *Calculation and coordination: Essays on socialism and transitional political economy*. New York: Routledge.

Bologna, J., D. Lacombe and A. Young. 2016. A spatial analysis of incomes and institutional quality: Evidence from US metropolitan areas. *Journal of Institutional Economics*, *12*(1): 191–216.

Collier, P. 2010. The political economy of natural resources. *Social Research*, *77*(4): 1105–1132.

Coyne, C. 2008. *After war: The political economy of exporting democracy*. Stanford, CA: Stanford University Press.

Coyne, C., and R.S. Sobel. 2010. How are institutions related? In J. Gwartney and R. Lawson (eds.), *Economic freedom of the world: 2010 annual report* (pp. 163–174). Vancouver, BC: Fraser Institute.

Dawson, J. 1998. Institutions, investment, and growth: New cross-country and panel data evidence. *Economic Inquiry*, *36*(4): 603–619.

Dawson, J. 2003. Causality in the freedom–growth relationship. *European Journal of Political Economy*, *19*(3): 479–495.

De Haan, J., S. Lundstrom and J. Sturm. 2006. Market-oriented institutions and policies and economic growth: A critical survey. *Journal of Economic Surveys*, *20*(2): 157–191.

Easterly, W. 2001. *The elusive quest for growth*. Cambridge, MA: MIT Press.

Easterly, W. 2014. *Tyranny of experts*. New York: Basic Books.

Easterly, W., and R. Levine. 1997. Africa's growth tragedy: Policies and ethnic divisions. *Quarterly Journal of Economics*, *112*(4): 1203–1250.

Easton, S., and M. Walker. 1997. Income, growth, and economic freedom. *American Economic Review*, *87*(2): 328–332.

Fischer, S., and A. Gelb. 1991. The process of socialist economic transformation. *Journal of Economic Perspectives*, *5*(4): 91–105.

Friedman, M. 1962. *Capitalism and freedom*. Chicago, IL: University of Chicago Press.

Gehring, K. 2013. Who benefits from economic freedom? Unraveling the effect of economic freedom on subjective well-being. *World Development*, *50*(C): 74–90.

Glaeser, E., and A. Shleifer. 2002. Legal origins. *Quarterly Journal of Economics*, *117*(4): 1193–1229.

Glaeser, E., R. Laporta, F. Lopez-de-Silanes and A. Shleifer. 2004. Do institutions cause growth? *Journal of Economic Growth*, *9*(3): 271–303.

Grubel, H. 1998. Economic freedom and human welfare: Some empirical findings. *Cato Journal*, *18*(2): 287–304.

Gwartney, J., R. Holcombe and R. Lawson. 2004. Economic freedom, institutional quality, and cross-country differences in income and growth. *Cato Journal*, *24*(3): 205–233.

Gwartney, J., R. Holcombe and R. Lawson. 2006. Institutions and the impact of investment on growth. *Kyklos, 59*(2): 255–273.

Gwartney, J., R. Lawson and J. Hall. 2015. *Economic freedom of the world: 2015 annual report.* Vancouver, BC: Fraser Institute.

Gwartney, J., R. Lawson and R. Holcombe. 1999. Economic freedom and the environment for economic growth. *Journal of Institutional and Theoretical Economics, 155*(4): 643–663.

Gwartney, J., R. Stroup, R.S. Sobel and D. Macpherson. 2015. *Economics: Private and public choice.* 15th edn. Stamford, CT: South-Western Cengage Learning.

Hall, J., and R. Lawson. 2014. Economic freedom of the world: An accounting of the literature. *Contemporary Economic Policy, 32*(1): 1–19.

Hall, J., R.S. Sobel and G. Crowley. 2010. Institutions, capital, and growth. *Southern Economic Journal, 77*(2): 385–405.

Hayek, F.A. 1945. The use of knowledge in society. *American Economic Review, 35*(4): 519–530.

Hayek, F.A. 1994 [1944]. *The road to serfdom.* Chicago, IL: University of Chicago Press.

Heckelman, J. 2000. Economic freedom and economic growth: A short-run causal investigation. *Journal of Applied Economics, 3*(1): 71–91.

Heckelman, J., and S. Knack. 2009. Aid, economic freedom, and growth. *Contemporary Economic Policy, 27*(1): 46–53.

Heybey, B., and P. Murrel. 1999. The relationship between economic growth and the speed of liberalization during transition. *Journal of Policy Reform, 3*(2): 121–137.

Higgs, R. 1987. *Crisis and Leviathan critical episodes in the growth of American government.* Oxford: Oxford University Press.

Holcombe, R. 1992. The distributive model of government: Evidence from the confederate constitution. *Southern Economic Journal, 58*(3): 762–769.

Holcombe, R. 1999. Veterans interests and the transition to government growth, 1870–1915. *Public Choice, 99*(3/4): 311–326.

Holcombe, R. 2002. *From liberty to democracy: The transformation of American government.* Ann Arbor, MI: University of Michigan Press.

Holcombe, R., and C. Boudreaux. 2016. Market institutions and income inequality. *Journal of Institutional Economics, 12*(2): 263–276.

Husted, T., and L. Kenny. 1997. The effect of the expansion of the voting franchise on the size of government. *Journal of Political Economy, 105*(1): 54–82.

Kolodko, G. 2000. *From shock to therapy: Political economy of postsocialist transformation.* Oxford: Oxford University Press.

Kreft, S., and R.S. Sobel. 2005. Public policy, entrepreneurship, and economic freedom. *Cato Journal, 25*(3): 595–616.

La Porta, R., F. Lopez-de-Silanes and A. Shleifer. 2008. The economic consequences of legal origins. *Journal of Economic Literature, 46*(2): 285–332.

Lawson, R., and J. Clark. 2010. Examining the Hayek–Friedman hypothesis on economic and political freedom. *Journal of Economic Behavior and Organization, 74*(3): 230–239.

Leeson, P. 2007. Better off stateless: Somalia before and after government collapse. *Journal of Comparative Economics, 35*(4): 689–710.

Leeson, P., and C. Coyne. 2012. Sassywood. *Journal of Comparative Economics, 40*(4): 608–620.

Leeson, P., R.S. Sobel and A. Dean. 2012. Comparing the spread of capitalism and democracy. *Economics Letters*, *114*(1): 139–141.

March, R., C. Lyford and B. Powell. 2015. *Causes and barriers to increases in economic freedom*. Working paper.

Meltzer, A., and S. Richard. 1981. A rational theory of the size of government. *Journal of Political Economy*, *89*(5): 914–927.

Murphy, K., A. Shleifer and R. Vishny. 1992. The transition to a market economy: Pitfalls of partial reform. *Quarterly Journal of Economics*, *107*(3): 889–906.

Murrell, P. 1992. Evolutionary and radical approaches to economic reform. *Economics of Planning*, *25*(1): 79–95.

North, D. 1990. *Institutions, institutional change and economic performance*. New York: Cambridge University Press.

North, D. 1991. Institutions. *Journal of Economic Perspectives*, *5*(1): 97–112.

Olson, M. 1982. *The rise and decline of nations*. New Haven, CT: Yale University Press.

Peltzman, S. 1980. The growth of government. *Journal of Law and Economics*, *23*(2): 209–287.

Pitlik, H., and S. Wirth. 2003. Do crises promote the extent of economic liberalization: An empirical test. *European Journal of Political Economy*, *19*(3): 565–581.

Powell, B., and M. Ryan. 2006. Does development aid lead to economic freedom? *Journal of Private Enterprise*, *22*(1): 1–21.

Robinson, J., D. Acemoglu and S. Johnson. 2005. Institutions as a fundamental cause of long-run growth. *Handbook of Economic Growth*, *1A*: 386–472.

Roland, G. 1994. On the speed and sequencing of privatisation and restructuring. *Economic Journal*, *104*(426): 1158–1168.

Sachs, J. 1996. The transition at mid-decade. *American Economic Review*, *86*(2): 128–133.

Sachs, J., and A. Warner. 1999. The big rush, natural resource booms and growth. *Journal of Development Economics*, *59*(1): 43–76.

Scully, G. 2002. Economic freedom, government policy and the trade-off between equity and economic growth. *Public Choice*, *113*(1): 77–96.

Shleifer, A., and D. Treisman. 2005. A normal country: Russia after communism. *Journal of Economic Perspectives*, *19*(1): 151–174.

Smith, A. 1976 [1776]. *An inquiry into the nature and causes of the wealth of nations*. New York: Oxford University Press.

Sobel, R.S. 2008. Testing Baumol: Institutional quality and the productivity of entrepreneurship. *Journal of Business Venturing*, *23*(6): 641–655.

Sobel, R.S., and C. Coyne. 2011. Cointegrating institutions: The time-series properties of country institutional measures. *Journal of Law and Economics*, *54*(1): 111–134.

Sobel, R.S., and P. Leeson. 2007. The spread of global freedom. In J.D. Gwartney and R.A. Lawson (eds.), *Economic freedom of the world: 2007 annual report* (pp. 29–37). Vancouver, BC: Fraser Institute.

Sobel, R.S., J. Clark and D. Lee. 2007. Freedom, barriers to entry, entrepreneurship, and economic progress. *Review of Austrian Economics*, *20*(4): 221–236.

Young, A., and J. Bologna. 2016. Crises and government: Some empirical evidence. *Contemporary Economic Policy*, *34*(2): 234–249.

5 The persistence of historical influences on current economic freedom

Stephan F. Gohmann

Introduction

In *Fatal Conceit*, Hayek (1988, p. 9) says that "our values and institutions are determined not simply by preceding causes, but as part of a process of unconscious self-organization of a structure or pattern." This long and slow evolutionary process results in diverse institutions across countries. The diversity of and path dependency from these historic institutions play a role in the current institutions that influence economic freedom and economic growth. In his examination of the influence of institutions on historical development, North (1990, 1991, 1994) finds that the "rules of the game" that develop in a region change the incentives for investment in human capital, increased productivity, and rent-seeking. In other words, institutions change the cost and benefits for individuals to engage in productive, unproductive, or destructive entrepreneurship (Baumol 1990). Through these incentives, institutions influence economic growth.

Economists examining differences in economic growth between countries find that contemporary levels of human capital accumulation, technological innovation, and investment play a major role (Mankiw, Romer and Weil 1992). These relationships raise the question of why some countries have more capital and innovation than others. One explanation is that institutions influence incentives to innovate, invest, and produce (North 1990, 1991, 1994). If institutions are driving growth, then why do some countries have better (growth-enhancing) institutions than others? North indicates that institutions are historically based, slow to change, and influenced by path dependence. If this is the case, then events occurring in the past should have persistence in terms of their influence on current institutions and economic outcomes. Several studies have examined how historical variables influence the institutions. Gutmann and Voigt (2015) find a historical influence on the rule of law, and Chilton and Posner (2015) find a similar relationship on human rights.

This study examines how a country's geography (that is, location and climate) and biogeography (that is, locally available wild plants and animals in BC 11000 – Hibbs and Olsson 2004), history of state-level institutions (Bockstette, Chanda and Putterman 2002), history of technology adoption (Comin, Easterly and

Gong 2006), and geographic roots of immigrants (Putterman 2008; Putterman and Weil 2008) influence institutions as represented by economic freedom (Gwartney, Lawson and Hall 2015) – particularly measures of property rights and free trade. Economic freedom is important because countries with greater economic freedom tend to have better outcomes in economic growth (Dawson 1998, 2003; Berggren 2003; Williamson and Mathers 2011), entrepreneurship (Bjørnskov and Foss 2008; Nyström 2008; Gohmann 2012), income equality (Krieger and Meierrieks 2016), and other measures of well-being (Esposto and Zaleski 1999; Stroup 2007).[1]

In this chapter, we first briefly discuss the theory of institutional development and it relationship to the various areas (or sub-indices) in the Economic Freedom of the World (EFW) index. Next, we offer an overview of the use of historical data in economic growth studies and describe the data used in this study. We go on to discuss the empirical results. The final section concludes.

Institutional development and economic freedom

The idea of property has been around at least since the time of the Ten Commandments in Exodus 20:2–17, the eighth of which directs, "Thou shalt not steal." One must have property for it to be stolen. Property rights were written into law in the Reforms of Urukagina in BC 2550 (World History Project 2016). These reforms included rules against the seizure of property by rulers. Private individual property rights allow individuals to choose how to use their property and, in particular, whether to trade their property with others. Note that, here, property rights are individual rights. Some may argue that slave owners had property rights to their slaves. Property rights in this chapter refer to individual property rights – that is, each individual has a property in their own person, as well as in what they put their labor into (Locke 2014 [1690]).

Two aspects of economic freedom – respect for private property and the ability to engage in trade – make up the backbone of economic growth. The degree of respect for and protection of property rights by governments has varied over time, resulting in different growth rates across countries. Historical events and local customs allowed some countries to secure stronger property rights and freer trade more quickly. North (1990) discusses the cost–benefit analysis of why property rights develop. The institution of property rights develops as resource prices change in a way that makes it beneficial to incur the additional costs of providing property rights. Rules leading to inefficient property rights can be maintained if policymakers find such rules beneficial to themselves and their constituents. The consequence is that poor institutions may persist if policymakers benefit from them.

Institutions "define and limit the set of choices of individuals" (North 1991, p. 4). They change incrementally, and these incremental changes influence the choice set that individuals face and result in path dependency based on initial institutions and the direction of change in these institutions. For example, the types of institution set up in colonies of North and South

America differed. In South America, the Spanish extracted wealth, enslaved the natives, and set up institutions that were not supportive of property rights. In North America, colonists intent on staying for a long period increased the benefits of well-defined property rights. As a result, even if property rights were similar in North and South America prior to colonization, the differences in colonization changed how property rights were viewed, and property rights institutions were put on a slower growth path in South America than in North America. This difference persists today. The average EFW sub-index for legal structure and the security of property rights in 2000 (based on a scale of 0–10, with 10 being the greatest level of property right freedom) in South America was 4.80. In Central America, the value was 5.26. The average for Canada, the United States, and Mexico was 7.58. A slower start toward increased property rights because of poorer initial institutions results in path dependency and may persist for long periods. A consequence of this path dependency is that the level of economic freedoms that countries have today are dependent upon the types of institution that developed historically.

However, events in history may line up in a way that allows institutions to evolve or move to another path. Acemoglu and Robinson (2013) discuss critical junctures, such as the bubonic plague in 1346, which killed about half of the English population and had similar fatality rates throughout Europe. This reduced the supply of labor, and led to an increase in wages and demands by the peasants, aiming to be free of compulsory services to their kings and lords. In England, laborers obtained greater freedoms, but in Eastern Europe laborers were less well organized and lords took over larger tracts of land, gaining an edge over the laborers. As a consequence, these institutions became more extractive in Eastern Europe and less extractive in England. Such critical junctures can diminish the persistence of institutions as countries move to greater or lesser freedom.

The importance of institutions to economic outcomes has been known at least since Adam Smith's *Wealth of Nations*:

> The natural effort of every individual to better his own condition, when suffered to exert itself with freedom and security is so powerful a principle that it is alone, and without any assistance, not only capable of carrying on the society to wealth and prosperity, but of surmounting a hundred impertinent obstructions with which the folly of human laws too often incumbers [*sic*] its operations; though the effect of these obstructions is always more or less either to encroach upon its freedom, or to diminish its security.
>
> (Smith 1776, p. 277)

As much as economists discuss the importance of institutions, few widely available cross-country time-series measures of institutions existed until the development of the EFW index (Gwartney et al. 2015), which first appeared in 1996 (Gwartney, Lawson and Block 1996).[2] This index measures political institutions that support free choice, market-coordinated voluntary exchange, free entry and exit into markets, and property rights protection. The index is the average of economic freedom measured in five areas (or sub-indices): "Size of Government; Legal System and Security of Property Rights; Sound Money; Freedom to Trade Internationally; Regulation" (Gwartney et al. 2015, p. 3).

The overall index is made up of 24 components, many of which include subcomponents, resulting in 42 variables used in the overall measure. Each variable ranges from 0 to 10, with 10 reflecting the greatest level of freedom. We use the 2000 index in this study.[3] Any component that has subcomponents is the average value of its subcomponents. Likewise, the areas (or sub-indices) are the average of the components.

The two main sub-indices examined in this chapter are "Legal System and Security of Property Rights" and "Freedom to Trade Internationally." *Legal System and Security of Property Rights* is the average of eight components:

1) judicial independence;
2) impartial courts;
3) protection of property rights;
4) military inference in rule of law and politics;
5) integrity of the legal system;
6) legal enforcement of contracts;
7) regulatory costs of the sale of real property;
8) reliability of the police; and
9) business costs of crime.

For the (year) 2000 data used in this study, observations for 122 countries are available. However, for the various components, the number of observations ranges from 63 to 121.

The *Freedom to Trade Internationally* sub-index has four components. The first is tariffs, which includes three subcomponents: revenue from trade taxes as a percentage of the trade sector; mean tariff rate; and the standard deviation of tariff rates. The second component comprises regulatory trade barriers, made up of non-tariff trade barriers and the compliance costs of importing and exporting. The third component is black-market exchange rates. The final component, controls of the movement of capital and people, includes three subcomponents: foreign ownership/investment restrictions; capital controls; and freedom of foreigners to visit. The free trade sub-index includes observations for 114 countries.

We will also examine the overall index and the remaining three sub-indices, but the main focus will be on *property rights* and *free trade*.

The five sub-indices and the overall EFW index are all connected to historical political developments. Property rights are a prerequisite for the other sub-indices in the sense that, without property rights, the other freedoms are of minor significance since individuals will have little property to trade; changes in monetary policy will not influence individuals directly since they will have nothing to trade for; regulation will still influence other behaviors, but production and trade without property rights will be less influenced than when property rights exist; and governments may be a huge portion of a non-property economy.

Stronger individual property rights lead to greater private investment and economic growth (Svensson 1998). Free trade is an extension of property rights in that it allows individuals to trade *their* property with others regardless of political boundaries. This results in larger markets, more specialization, and greater growth. We expect that historical data will have the greatest explanatory power on property rights and a greater influence on the ability to trade internationally relative to the remaining three sub-indices (money, regulation, and government), because trade has been in existence since primitive societies first interacted peacefully.

Although governments have controlled money for many centuries, an understanding of monetary policy and the "scientistic" control of monetary policy, and its influence on the economy, is a recent and ongoing phenomenon. Regulations have existed since governments were formed. However, both regulations and the size of government have grown considerably since the Industrial Revolution, and even more so in the past 100 years. This greater growth in government allows for greater intervention in the marketplace. As a result, the influence of past historical events on these measures is likely to be smaller than on property rights and free trade.

Although some countries, such as the Soviet Union, moved away from recognizing property rights during communist rule, the fact that property rights may have been recognized in the past makes it more likely that property rights will be recognized after regime change occurs. In contrast, countries that were ruled by colonizers who extracted wealth may have less experience with property rights, and may be less likely to have strong and secure property rights today even with regime changes.

Historical data

Spolaore and Wacziarg (2013) give an overview of the major studies examining the historical antecedents of growth. We use data for three of these studies to examine the influence of historical variables on economic freedom.[4] This section briefly describes each study and the data. The next section will use these data in regressions on the EFW sub-indices.

All of the historical factors examined in this study show a relationship between the historical factors and economic growth, implying a long-term constraint on economic growth. About 60 percent of the variation among countries in income per capita and 40 percent of the variation in current technology are explained by this historical data. The historical influence leaves the remaining 40–60 percent of variation to be influenced by more contemporaneous variables (Spolaore and Wacziarg 2013). We find that similar results hold for the institutions of property rights and free trade examined in this study.

Bio and geographic conditions

Researchers have examined Jared Diamond's (1999) idea that people in ancient cultures who lived in areas with greater numbers of edible wild plants and domesticable animals were likely to move sooner from hunting/gathering to agriculture. This early start gave them the ability to feed more people and freed up time for some individuals to engage in other productive activities. This led to greater specialization and innovation in both production and governance structure. Hibbs and Olsson (2004) use measures of geography (location and climate) and biogeography (locally available wild plants and animals) in BC 11000 in a regression on log gross domestic product (GDP) in 1997, and they find that a move from the worst geographic and biogeographic area to the best is associated with a US$600–8,800 increase in 1997 GDP per capita.

Olsson and Hibbs (2005) argue that better initial biogeographic conditions bestow a head start on economic development. Their initial biological conditions include the number of annual and perennial wild grasses that have large edible kernels and the number of domesticable mammals weighing over 45 kg. Areas with a large initial endowment of these plants and animals were more likely to develop agriculture earlier. Since agricultural production increases the amount of food available, it allows for a class of artisans, chiefs, and thinkers to arise. As a result, output, knowledge, and population grow.

Olsson and Hibbs (2005) offer data for seven regions of the world and show that the Near East, Europe, and North Africa had a much greater number of edible-kernel-producing plants than elsewhere (33 compared to the next highest, 6 plants, in East Asia) and domesticable animals (9, compared to the next highest, 7, in East Asia, and then only 2 or fewer in all other regions). Olsson and Hibbs (2005) use two main variables in their analysis. The first, *geo conditions*, is the first principal component of climate, latitude, East–West orientation, and landmass size. The second, *bio conditions*, is the first principal component of the number of wild grasses with mean kernel weight greater than 10 mg and the number of domesticable animals with weight greater than 45 kg. They find that these two variables account for some 40–50 percent of the variation in log 1997 per capita income. From the perspective of this chapter, countries that developed agriculture earlier would also have institutions evolving earlier, allowing for more iterations in institutional development, which will lead to institutions better suited to greater economic freedom.

Statehood experience

Similar to the way in which better biological and geographic conditions give regions a head start on development, areas with a long experience of statehood will have had more time not only to develop their institutions, but also to better develop rent-seeking behaviors. Bockstette and colleagues (2002) find a strong relationship between countries with a long experience with governmental institutions and their current institutional quality and political stability. They argue that countries with longer statehood experience will have developed better institutions since they have been experiencing these institutions for a longer period of time. Individuals in these countries will have learned from past experience. Since institutions are slow to change, Bockstette and colleagues' (2002) data helps to describe how some countries with historical experiences of governmental institutions, such as China, can more easily develop industrially even after more recent experience with central planning than can Mozambique, for example, which has little statehood experience and little development of its human capital or industry.

To develop their index, Bockstette and colleagues (2002) divide the period spanning 1–1950 CE into nineteen 50-year periods. They then assign values between 0 and 1 for three areas based on the extent to which the government was above the tribal level, was locally based, and how much territory was ruled by this government. They combine the data for the 39 periods using a discount rate. For each period, they divide by the maximum value of the discounted series in each period to normalize their measure to fall between 0 and 1. We use their preferred 5 percent discount rate in this study.

One problem with the measure used by Bockstette and colleagues (2002) is that it is difficult to account for the economies of the New World. Recognizing that many of the colonists in the United States and other New World countries migrated from countries that had long statehood experiences, Putterman (2008) and Putterman and Weil (2008) use data that includes the 1500 AD ancestral roots of the current population of countries' immigrants to weight the historical variables. These ancestry-weighted values of statehood experience have been found to be better predictors of current per capita income. We hypothesize that countries with an earlier start and greater statehood experience will have had more time to experiment with institutions, and hence may be more likely to have developed property rights and free trade. These institutions will be better explained by the ancestry-weighted data.

Technology adoption

The historical antecedents of economic freedom include technological innovation. In *Guns, Germs and Steel*, Diamond (1999) claims that, in communities in which agriculture developed, some individuals had free time to engage in other activities. This additional free time lead to greater development of technologies and greater growth for these communities. Comin and colleagues (2006) test whether the adoption of technology in the past influences current per capita income and current technology adoption. They develop a data set of the technologies available in BC 1000, 0 AD, and 1500 AD for each country in the world today, and they find that this measure has strong predictive power for both current technology usage and for per capita income. Following Diamond's argument of individuals having time to develop other technologies, as economies adopt more technologies, they free up time for some individuals to develop better governmental institutions. In this case, technology adoption may be influencing per capita income through the institutions that it enabled societies to develop. Further, better institutions in the past are likely to lead to greater technology development in the past; thus technology may be a proxy for the quality of institutions in the past.

Comin and colleagues (2006) use a measure for technology adoption measure in 1500 AD that is based on 24 technologies in five sectors: communications, industry, transportation, agriculture, and military. In *communications*, they examine four areas: the use of the movable printing block; the use of woodblock printing; the use of books; and the use of paper. For the other four areas, they use different numbers of variables to determine the extent to which a country had technology. *Military* has the most variables, with eight, and *industry*, the fewest, with two. We use the 1500 AD technology measure in this study, and expect a positive relationship between technology development and economic freedom.

Empirical results

Our empirical strategy is to estimate regressions with the EFW index and each sub-index as dependent variables and to use the early development variables described above as independent variables. In particular, we will separately examine geographic and biologic variables (Olsson and Hibbs 2005), state history (Bockstette et al. 2002; Putterman and Weil 2008), and technological adoption in 1500 AD (Comin et al. 2006). For state history and technology, we also include the ancestry-adjusted values (Putterman and Weil 2008).

Table 5.1 shows the relationship between geography and the EFW sub-indices. The regressions include only those countries used in Olsson and Hibbs (2005). As they defined, these exclude the neo-European countries of Australia, Canada, New Zealand, and the United States. The data also exclude countries built on extractive wealth (that is, oil production based on foreign technology and labor). Columns 1 and 2 in Table 5.1 include geographic diversity and biological diversity separately, while column 3 includes both. The coefficients for both geographical and biological conditions are positive and significant for all of the EFW sub-indices, except for *size of government*, which has a negative coefficient. Geographical conditions explain 39 percent of the international variation in the *property rights* sub-index. *Free trade* has the next highest adjusted-R^2, at 0.24. Likewise, the biological conditions explain 40 percent of the variation in *property rights* freedom and 18 percent of *free trade*. The *regulation* and *money* sub-indices have little of their international variation explained by these variables. When both the geographical and biological conditions are included together in the regression, the international variation explained does not markedly increase and the significance of the coefficient for biological conditions diminishes or disappears. Including dummy variables for island/landlocked, percentage tropical/subtropical, and average latitude increases the variation explained and also

Table 5.1 Influence of bio conditions and geographic conditions on economic freedom

Variables	(1)	(2)	(3)	(4)
Property rights				
Geographical conditions	1.164[a]		0.557[c]	0.801[b]
	(0.00)		(0.08)	(0.02)
Biological conditions		1.248[a]	0.730[b]	0.0298
		(0.00)	(0.03)	(0.93)
Constant	5.730[a]	5.797[a]	5.760[a]	6.233[a]
	(0.00)	(0.00)	(0.00)	(0.00)
Observations	94	94	94	89
Adjusted R^2	0.382	0.393	0.407	0.530
Free trade				
Geographical conditions	0.739[a]		0.760[b]	0.954[a]
	(0.00)		(0.01)	(0.00)
Biological conditions		0.675[a]	−0.0261	−0.332
		(0.00)	(0.93)	(0.33)
Constant	7.039[a]	7.097[a]	7.038[a]	7.056[a]
	(0.00)	(0.00)	(0.00)	(0.00)
Observations	88	88	88	83
Adjusted R^2	0.235	0.173	0.226	0.278
Economic freedom				
Geographical conditions	0.405[a]	0.398[a]	0.327	0.562[a]
	(0.00)	(0.00)	(0.11)	(0.01)
Biological conditions			0.0935	−0.248
			(0.65)	(0.26)
Constant	6.595[a]	6.620[a]	6.598[a]	6.604[a]
	(0.00)	(0.00)	(0.00)	(0.00)
Observations	94	94	94	89
Adjusted R^2	0.158	0.135	0.150	0.300
Size of government				
Geographical conditions	−0.644[a]		−0.459[c]	−0.280
	(0.00)		(0.08)	(0.294)
Biological conditions		−0.650[a]	−0.222	−0.173
		(0.00)	(0.41)	(0.57)
Constant	6.331[a]	6.292[a]	6.323[a]	5.898[a]
	(0.00)	(0.00)	(0.00)	(0.00)
Observations	94	94	94	89
Adjusted R^2	0.222	0.201	0.219	0.270

(continued)

Table 5.1 (continued)

Regulation				
Geographical conditions	0.285[a]		0.373[c]	0.698[a]
	(0.00)		(0.06)	(0.00)
Biological conditions		0.242[b]	−0.105	−0.395[c]
		(0.02)	(0.61)	(0.06)
Constant	6.293[a]	6.313[a]	6.288[a]	6.097[a]
	(0.00)	(0.00)	(0.00)	(0.00)
Observations	94	94	94	89
Adjusted R^2	0.085	0.051	0.078	0.252
Money				
Geographical conditions	0.432[b]		0.403	0.588
	(0.01)		(0.27)	(0.16)
Biological conditions		0.410[b]	0.0352	−0.394
		(0.03)	(0.93)	(0.36)
Constant	7.644[a]	7.672[a]	7.645[a]	7.833[a]
	(0.00)	(0.00)	(0.00)	(0.00)
Observations	94	94	94	89
Adjusted R^2	0.055	0.042	0.045	0.109

Notes: Column (4) includes dummy variables for landlocked and island nations; *p*-values in parentheses
[a] $p < 0.01$
[b] $p < 0.05$
[c] $p < 0.1$

increases the significance of the geographical conditions for all dependent variables, except for the *size of government* sub-index.

In Table 5.1, column 1, moving from the worst geo conditions to the best increases *property rights* from 4.26 to 7.93 – an 86 percent increase. Likewise, for bio conditions, a move from worst to best increases *property rights* from 4.59 to 7.53 – a 64 percent increase. When both variables are included in the regression in column 3, movement from the worst of both conditions to the best result in *property rights* freedom increasing from 4.35 to 7.83 – that is, by 80 percent. All in all, geographical conditions tend to be associated with higher economic freedom – particularly property rights and free trade.

Bockstette and colleagues (2002) find that earlier state history is related to economic growth. Likewise, we expect that countries that have had more statehood experience will have developed better institutions since they have had more years of experimenting and developing their institutions. Further, the ancestry-adjusted measures of statehood experience should do a better job of explaining the variation among countries in their EFW sub-indices.[5]

Table 5.2 shows how statehood experience is related to the EFW sub-indices. When no other variables are included in the regressions, the state history variable has a positive and significant association with *property rights*, but a low adjusted R-squared of 0.069. However, the ancestry-adjusted state history has a positive and significant association with property rights, free trade, overall economic freedom, regulation, and money. The adjusted R-squareds are low, indicating that little of the variation among countries in these EFW sub-indices is explained by the ancestry-adjusted state history. The inclusion of the locational variables raises the adjusted R-squared and the ancestry-adjusted state history variables remain significant for all but the *size of government* and *regulation* sub-indices. Over 54 percent of the variation among countries in the *property rights* sub-index is explained when these variables are included.

When only adjusted state history is included in the regression, the beta is 0.443. This might be similar to moving from Russia with *property rights* freedom of 4.44 to Uruguay, with a value of 6.38, or from Uruguay to Japan (8.18). A move from the least state history experience to the most results in an increase in *property rights* freedom from 3.64 to 7.51 – a 106 percent increase.

Table 5.2 Years of state history influence on economic freedom

	Property rights	Free trade	Economic freedom	Size of government	Regulation	Money
State history	2.238[a]	0.809	0.567	−1.294[b]	0.123	0.770
	(0.00)	(0.23)	(0.19)	(0.02)	(0.77)	(0.28)
Adjusted R^2	0.069	0.005	0.007	0.045	−0.009	0.002
Observations	108	102	108	108	108	108
Ancestry-adjusted state history	4.220[a]	2.611[a]	2.101[a]	−0.553	1.224[b]	2.832[a]
	(0.00)	(0.00)	(0.00)	(0.39)	(0.01)	(0.00)
Adjusted R^2	0.189	0.095	0.154	−0.002	0.051	0.100
Observations	108	102	108	108	108	108

Including other independent variables (island/landlocked, average latitude, and percentage tropical and subtropical)

State history	−0.122	−0.085	−0.126	−0.292	−0.311	0.109
	(0.85)	(0.89)	(0.76)	(0.59)	(0.45)	(0.89)
Adjusted R^2	0.528	0.261	0.268	0.214	0.214	0.061
Observations	104	98	104	104	104	104
Ancestry-adjusted state history	1.664[b]	1.652[b]	1.323[a]	0.342	0.598	2.316[b]
	(0.03)	(0.02)	(0.01)	(0.60)	(0.22)	(0.01)
Adjusted R^2	0.541	0.302	0.311	0.214	0.206	0.112
Observations	103	97	104	104	104	104

Note: p-value in parentheses
[a] $p < 0.01$
[b] $p < 0.05$
[c] $p < 0$

Table 5.3 examines the association of technology in AD 1500 with current economic freedom. As with the previous results, the ancestry-adjusted technology variable explains much more of the variation in overall economic freedom

Table 5.3 Overall technology association with economic freedom

	Property rights	Property rights	Free trade	Free trade	Economic freedom	Economic freedom
Total technology	2.400[a]		1.355[b]		0.688[b]	
	(0.00)		(0.01)		(0.05)	
Ancestry-adjusted total technology		4.417[a]		3.782[a]		2.251[a]
		(0.00)		(0.00)		(0.00)
Observations	96	96	92	92	96	96
Adjusted R^2	0.144	0.297	0.055	0.285	0.030	0.246

Including other independent variables (island/landlocked, average latitude, and percentage tropical and subtropical)

	Property rights	Property rights	Free trade	Free trade	Economic freedom	Economic freedom
Total technology	−0.912		−0.544		−0.888[b]	
	(0.15)		(0.36)		(0.03)	
Ancestry-adjusted total technology		0.886		3.347[a]		1.579[a]
		(0.33)		(0.00)		(0.01)
Observations	90	90	86	86	90	90
Adjusted R^2	0.501	0.494	0.274	0.403	0.291	0.314

	Size of government	Size of government	Regulation	Regulation	Money	Money
Total technology	−1.409[a]		0.141		0.834	
	(0.00)		(0.68)		(0.14)	
Ancestry-adjusted total technology		−1.017[c]		1.292[a]		2.665[a]
		(0.06)		(0.00)		(0.00)
Observations	96	96	96	96	96	96
Adjusted R^2	0.111	0.027	−0.009	0.083	0.013	0.130

Including other independent variables (island/landlocked, average latitude, and percentage tropical and subtropical)

	Size of government	Size of government	Regulation	Regulation	Money	Money
Total technology	−1.070[b]		−1.227[a]		−0.704	
	(0.04)		(0.00)		(0.36)	
Ancestry-adjusted total technology		0.593		0.358		2.697[b]
		(0.44)		(0.55)		(0.01)
Observations	90	90	90	90	90	90
Adjusted R^2	0.182	0.146	0.243	0.158	0.081	0.138

Note: p-value in parentheses
[a] $p < 0.01$
[b] $p < 0.05$
[c] $p < 0$

than the unadjusted variable. When the ancestry-adjusted variable is the only independent variable included in the regression, between 28 and 30 percent of the variation in *property rights* freedom and *free trade* freedom is explained. The technology variable also explains over 24 percent of the variation in overall economic freedom, but has little explanatory power for *size of government, regulation,* and *money* sub-indices.[6]

The model including only adjusted technology has a beta of 0.55. A 1 standard deviation change in adjusted technology would be similar to going from Uganda, with technology of 0.26 and property rights of 5.35, to Mali, with technology of 0.50 and property rights of 5.35. Likewise, an increase from the worst technology to the best results in an increase in *property rights* from 3.76 to 7.57 – a 100 percent increase.

Tables 5.4a and 5.4b show the correlations between the main variables used in this study – geographical conditions, biological conditions, ancestry-adjusted state history, and ancestry-adjusted total technology in AD 1500. Table 5.4a is for the full sample and Table 5.4b shows the correlations for those countries where missing observations for any of the variables are excluded, which leads to a sample size of 70. All of the significant correlations are positive, except for those with the *size of government* sub-index. For the smaller sample size of 70, similar significance and signs remain.

The correlation between biological and geographical conditions is high, but recall that these variables are for seven regions of the world, so that the same value is assigned for the variable to any country in a region. The ancestry-adjusted total technology is strongly correlated to the geographical and biological conditions, as well as the ancestry-adjusted state history.

Table 5.5 shows a set of regressions including the main independent variables. Four different sets of regressions are estimated. The first two include all of the historical variables: geographical conditions, biological conditions, ancestry-adjusted state history, and ancestry-adjusted total technology. The first panel includes only these variables and the second panel includes additionally island/landlocked, average latitude, and the percentage tropical and subtropical. As with the other models, the greatest amount of variation is explained for *property rights* and then *free trade* at 51 percent and 39 percent in panel 1, and 65 percent and 41 percent in panel 2. The number of observations is limited to a maximum of 70. In panel 1, biological conditions and ancestry-adjusted total technology are both positive and significant for *property rights*. Ancestry-adjusted technology is positive and significant for all of the sub-indices other than *size of government*. Ancestry-adjusted state history has a positive and significant coefficient for *size of government*. However, the inclusion of the additional independent variables results in only ancestry-adjusted technology being positive and significant for *free trade* and overall economic freedom. Biological conditions are now negative and significant for *free trade*.

Because of the small sample size with biological and geographical conditions, we omit them from the regressions in panels 3 and 4. Panel 3 includes only

Table 5.4 (a) Correlations

	Geo cond.	1.	2.	3.	4.	5.	6.	7.	8.
1. Biological conditions	0.88 (0.00)* 112**								
2. Ancestry-adjusted state history	0.48 (0.00) 99	0.51 (0.00) 99							
3. Ancestry-adjusted total technology	0.73 (0.00) 87	0.73 (0.00) 87	0.69 (0.00) 109						
4. Economic freedom overall	0.41 (0.00) 94	0.38 (0.00) 94	0.40 (0.00) 108	0.50 (0.00) 96					
5. Property rights freedom	0.62 (0.00) 94	0.63 (0.00) 94	0.44 (0.00) 108	0.55 (0.00) 96	0.75 (0.00) 122				
6. Free trade freedom	0.49 (0.00) 88	0.43 (0.00) 88	0.32 (0.00) 102	0.54 (0.00) 92	0.84 (0.00) 114	0.59 (0.00) 114			
7. Government freedom	−.48 (0.00) 94	−0.46 (0.00) 94	−0.08 (0.39) 108	−0.19 (0.06) 96	0.14 (0.13) 122	−0.35 (0.00) 122	−0.08 (0.40) 114		
8. Regulation freedom	0.31 (0.00) 94	0.25 (0.02) 94	0.25 (0.01) 108	0.30 (0.00) 96	0.79 (0.00) 122	0.58 (0.00) 122	0.63 (0.00) 114	0.10 (0.27) 122	
9. Money freedom	0.26 (0.01) 94	0.23 (0.03) 94	0.33 (0.00) 108	0.37 (0.00) 96	0.83 (0.00) 122	0.53 (0.00) 122	0.63 (0.00) 1.14	0.04 (0.63) 122	0.53 (0.00) 122

Notes: * p-value; ** No. of observations

(b) Correlations including only observations available for all variables ($n = 70$)

	Geo cond.	1.	2.	3.	4.	5.	6.	7.	8.
1. Biological conditions	0.89 (0.00)*								
2. Ancestry-adjusted state history	0.53 (0.00)	0.50 (0.00)							
3. Ancestry-adjusted total technology	0.72 (0.00)	0.70 (0.00)	0.74 (0.00)						
4. Economic freedom overall	0.40 (0.00)	0.37 (0.00)	0.45 (0.00)	0.58 (0.00)					
5. Property rights freedom	0.67 (0.00)	0.70 (0.00)	0.44 (0.00)	0.63 (0.00)	0.74 (0.00)				
6. Free trade freedom	0.45 (0.00)	0.38 (0.00)	0.42 (0.00)	0.63 (0.00)	0.87 (0.00)	0.63 (0.00)			
7. Government freedom	-0.50 (0.00)	-0.50 (0.00)	-0.05 (0.71)	-0.25 (0.04)	0.06 (0.62)	-0.44 (0.00)	-0.10 (0.40)		
8. Regulation freedom	0.33 (0.01)	0.27 (0.03)	0.29 (0.01)	0.40 (0.00)	0.81 (0.00)	0.59 (0.00)	0.68 (0.00)	-0.01 (0.95)	
9. Money freedom	0.26 (0.03)	0.23 (0.06)	0.32 (0.01)	0.42 (0.00)	0.83 (0.00)	0.53 (0.00)	0.67 (0.00)	-0.06 (0.63)	0.57 (0.00)

Note: * p-value

Table 5.5 Influence of select historical variables on economic freedoms

	Property rights	Free trade	Economic freedom overall	Size of government	Regulation	Money
Sample including only historical variables						
Ancestry-adjusted state history	−0.228 (0.83)	−0.776 (0.43)	0.207 (0.76)	1.922[c] (0.06)	−0.075 (0.92)	0.174 (0.89)
Geographical conditions	0.155 (0.67)	0.346 (0.30)	0.074 (0.75)	−0.511 (0.13)	0.273 (0.28)	0.089 (0.83)
Biological conditions	0.877[b] (0.02)	−0.476 (0.16)	−0.117 (0.62)	−0.455 (0.19)	−0.228 (0.37)	−0.310 (0.47)
Ancestry-adjusted total technology	2.013[c] (0.09)	4.628[a] (0.00)	2.340[a] (0.00)	0.393 (0.71)	1.447[c] (0.07)	3.221[b] (0.02)
Intercept	4.607[a] (0.00)	4.770[a] (0.00)	5.122[a] (0.00)	5.084[a] (0.00)	5.418[a] (0.00)	5.762[a] (0.00)
Observations	72	70	72	72	72	72
Adjusted R^2	0.51	0.39	0.32	0.24	0.14	0.14
Including other independent variables (island/landlocked, average latitude, and percentage tropical and subtropical)						
Ancestry-adjusted state history	0.374 (0.70)	−0.490 (0.63)	0.410 (0.53)	1.342 (0.20)	0.098 (0.89)	0.681 (0.60)
Geographical conditions	−0.360 (0.38)	0.036 (0.93)	−0.138 (0.62)	−0.410 (0.35)	0.258 (0.38)	−0.228 (0.68)
Biological conditions	0.419 (0.25)	−0.638[c] (0.10)	−0.268 (0.27)	−0.170 (0.66)	−0.365 (0.16)	−0.614 (0.21)
Ancestry-adjusted total technology	0.662 (0.54)	3.925[a] (0.00)	1.578[b] (0.03)	0.534 (0.64)	0.384 (0.62)	2.507[c] (0.08)
Intercept	3.155[a] (0.00)	3.634[a] (0.00)	4.211[a] (0.00)	5.162[a] (0.00)	4.724[a] (0.00)	4.471[a] (0.00)
Observations	70	68	70	70	70	70
Adjusted R^2	0.65	0.41	0.40	0.23	0.24	0.18
Including only ancestry-adjusted variables						
Ancestry-adjusted state history	0.004 (1.00)	−1.124 (0.30)	0.385 (0.59)	1.622[c] (0.09)	0.068 (0.93)	1.349 (0.26)
Ancestry-adjusted total technology	4.804[a] (0.00)	4.335[a] (0.00)	2.013[a] (0.00)	−2.234[a] (0.01)	1.330[b] (0.04)	1.765[c] (0.09)
Intercept	2.838[a] (0.00)	4.994[a] (0.00)	5.136[a] (0.00)	6.678[a] (0.00)	5.385[a] (0.00)	5.846[a] (0.00)
Observations	90	87	90	90	90	90
Adjusted R^2	0.34	0.26	0.23	0.06	0.08	0.12

Including only ancestry-adjusted variables and other independent variables (island/landlocked, average latitude, and percentage tropical and subtropical)

Ancestry-adjusted state history	1.500 (0.16)	−0.290 (0.76)	0.840 (0.22)	0.726 (0.44)	0.540 (0.46)	1.685 (0.20)
Ancestry-adjusted total technology	0.455 (0.70)	3.328[a] (0.00)	1.009 (0.19)	−0.189 (0.86)	0.137 (0.87)	1.379 (0.35)
Intercept	2.991[a] (0.00)	3.990[a] (0.00)	4.579[a] (0.00)	6.058[a] (0.00)	4.555[a] (0.00)	5.378[a] (0.00)
Observations	87	84	87	87	87	87
Adjusted R^2	0.54	0.36	0.31	0.16	0.17	0.13

Note: *p*-value in parentheses
[a] $p < 0.01$
[b] $p < 0.05$
[c] $p < 0$

ancestry-adjusted state history and ancestry-adjusted total technology. The technology variable is positive and significant in all regressions except *size of government*, which is negative and significant. State history has a positive and marginally significant coefficient for *size of government*. Including the location independent variables tends to increase the adjusted *R*-squareds, but now only technology is positive and significant for *free trade*.

We examined the robustness of the results to the inclusion of combinations of regional dummy variables, dummies for landlocked/island and tropical countries, and dummy variables for colonial origin. The regional dummies are sub-Saharan Africa, Northern Africa, Southeast Asia, South Central Asia, Southern Asia, Mideast, Western Europe, Eastern Europe, Latin American and the Caribbean, and Oceania. North America was the omitted region. The colony dummy variables are for English, French, German and Scandinavian colonies.[7]

Table 5.6a shows these results for the *property rights* variable. We estimate regressions for the inclusion of each of the historical variables. The geographical conditions variables is consistently positive and is significant in all regressions except for that which includes only regional dummy variables. The biological conditions variable is not significant in any of the regressions. When these two variables are included together, the geographic conditions variables remains positive and significant in all of the regressions except for that including only the regional dummies. The ancestry-adjusted state history is positive and significant in all specifications, and ancestry-adjusted technology is positive and significant in two of the four specifications. One important takeaway is that, in the models that include regional, colonization, and the island/land locked and tropical dummy variables, all of the *R*-squared values are above 0.68. So these historical and location-related variables explain over 68 percent of the variation in the *property rights* sub-index.

Table 5.6b shows similar results for the *free trade* sub-index. The results for the *free trade* sub-index do not hold up as well as those for *property rights*. None of the coefficients on geographical or biological conditions are significant. The ancestry-adjusted state history is significant when regional and colonial dummies are included. The ancestry-adjusted technology variable is significant for all regressions except when all of the dummy variables are included for region, colonialism, and locational environment.

Table 5.6 (a) Robustness check for property rights

	Property rights	Property rights	Property rights	Property rights	Property rights
Only regional dummies					
Geographical conditions	0.481 (0.12)		0.471 (0.15)		
Biological conditions		0.298 (0.57)	0.049 (0.93)		
Ancestry-adjusted state history				2.706[a] (0.00)	
Ancestry-adjusted total technology					2.279[c] (0.05)
Adjusted R^2	0.500	0.487	0.494	0.548	0.479
Observations	94	94	94	108	96
Includes regional dummies, island/landlocked, tropical					
Geographical conditions	0.918[b] (0.05)		0.921[c] (0.05)		
Biological conditions		0.091 (0.86)	−0.023 (0.97)		
Ancestry-adjusted state history				2.042[b] (0.03)	
Ancestry-adjusted total technology					0.740 (0.54)
Adjusted R^2	0.580	0.557	0.574	0.630	0.572
Observations	89	89	89	103	90

Only regional dummies and colonial

Geographical conditions	0.489[c] (0.07)		0.478[c] (0.10)		
Biological conditions		0.353 (0.46)	0.052 (0.92)		
Ancestry-adjusted state history				3.165[a] (0.00)	
Ancestry-adjusted total technology					2.969[a] (0.00)
Adjusted R^2	0.651	0.638	0.646	0.688	0.650
Observations	94	94	94	108	96

Includes regional dummies and colonial, island/landlocked, tropical

Geographical conditions	0.647[c] (0.08)		0.662[c] (0.08)		
Biological conditions		−0.051 (0.91)	−0.150 (0.74)		
Ancestry-adjusted state history				2.059[b] (0.02)	
Ancestry-adjusted total technology					1.299 (0.23)
Adjusted R^2	0.736	0.725	0.733	0.729	0.685
Observations	89	89	89	103	90

Note: p-value in parentheses
[a] $p < 0.01$
[b] $p < 0.05$
[c] $p < 0$

We also examined whether the choice of year made a difference in the results. The EFW index is available for every five years from 1970 to 2000, and then annually from 2000 until 2014. We estimated the same regressions as in Tables 5.1–5.3 and found fairly consistent results. Table 5.7 shows these results for *property rights* and each of the historical variables.

Table 5.6 (b) Economic freedom robustness

	Economic freedom	Economic freedom	Economic freedom	Economic freedom	Economic freedom
Only regional dummies					
Geographical conditions	0.302 (0.21)		0.306 (0.23)		
Biological conditions		0.141 (0.73)	−0.020 (0.96)		
Ancestry-adjusted state history				1.339 (0.11)	
Ancestry-adjusted total technology					2.054c (0.06)
Adjusted R^2	0.541	0.532	0.535	0.448	0.445
Observations	88	88	88	102	92
Includes regional dummies, island/landlocked, tropical					
Geographical conditions	0.128 (0.73)		0.120 (0.75)		
Biological conditions		0.115 (0.78)	0.104 (0.80)		
Ancestry-adjusted state history				0.952 (0.19)	
Ancestry-adjusted total technology					1.528c (0.07)
Adjusted R^2	0.602	0.601	0.596	0.603	0.682
Observations	83	83	83	97	86

Only regional dummies and colonial

Geographical conditions	0.361 (0.14)		0.394 (0.13)		
Biological conditions		0.086 (0.84)	−0.162 (0.72)		
Ancestry-adjusted state history				1.439**c** (0.08)	
Ancestry-adjusted total technology					2.520**b** (0.01)
Adjusted R^2	0.557	0.544	0.552	0.572	0.565
Observations	88	88	88	102	92

Includes regional dummies and colonial, island/landlocked, tropical

Geographical conditions	0.081 (0.82)		0.094 (0.80)		
Biological conditions		−0.137 (0.75)	−0.148 (0.73)		
Ancestry-adjusted state history				0.414 (0.61)	
Ancestry-adjusted total technology					1.371 (0.11)
Adjusted R^2	0.619	0.620	0.614	0.625	0.692
Observations	83	83	83	97	86

Note: p–value in parentheses
[a] $p < 0.01$
[b] $p < 0.05$
[c] $p < 0$

Table 5.7 Results for property rights for each year of the EFW index

Year	Geographical conditions			Biological conditions			Ancestry-adjusted state history			Ancestry-adjusted total technology		
	Coef.	Obvs.	Adj. R²	Coef.	Obvs.	Adj. R²	Coef.	Obvs.	Adj. R²	Coef.	Obvs.	Adj. R²
1970	1.07[a] (0.00)	41	0.21	0.86[b] (0.02)	41	0.12	3.40[c] (0.07)	48	0.05	6.73[a] (0.00)	46	0.26
1975	0.58[b] (0.05)	41	0.07	0.56[c] (0.07)	41	0.06	1.97 (0.19)	48	0.02	3.76[b] (0.01)	46	0.12
1980	0.90[a] (0.00)	69	0.21	0.75[a] (0.00)	69	0.13	4.83[a] (0.00)	80	0.21	4.60[a] (0.00)	71	0.27
1985	1.03[a] (0.00)	82	0.34	0.95[a] (0.00)	82	0.26	3.14[a] (0.00)	93	0.11	3.65[a] (0.00)	81	0.21
1990	1.10[a] (0.00)	83	0.33	0.98[a] (0.00)	83	0.23	3.29[a] (0.00)	93	0.11	4.30[a] (0.00)	82	0.27
1995	1.04[a] (0.00)	87	0.35	1.13[a] (0.00)	87	0.36	4.16[a] (0.00)	102	0.21	4.18[a] (0.00)	90	0.29
2000	1.18[a] (0.00)	93	0.39	1.27[a] (0.00)	93	0.40	4.23[a] (0.00)	107	0.19	4.42[a] (0.00)	95	0.30
2001	1.07[a] (0.00)	93	0.32	1.15[a] (0.00)	93	0.32	4.01[a] (0.00)	107	0.17	3.93[a] (0.00)	95	0.23
2002	1.15[a] (0.00)	93	0.36	1.19[a] (0.00)	93	0.34	3.92[a] (0.00)	107	0.16	4.02[a] (0.00)	95	0.24
2003	1.09[a] (0.00)	93	0.30	1.13[a] (0.00)	93	0.29	3.62[a] (0.00)	107	0.13	3.84[a] (0.00)	95	0.21
2004	1.07[a] (0.00)	93	0.30	1.10[a] (0.00)	93	0.28	3.62[a] (0.00)	107	0.13	3.80[a] (0.00)	95	0.21

Year		N				N				N				N	
2005	1.09^a (0.00)	93	0.30	1.15^a (0.00)	93	0.30	3.71^a (0.00)	107	0.14	3.99^a (0.00)	95	0.23
2006	1.06^a (0.00)	93	0.32	1.09^a (0.00)	93	0.30	3.46^a (0.00)	107	0.13	3.77^a (0.00)	95	0.23
2007	1.02^a (0.00)	93	0.28	1.08^a (0.00)	93	0.28	3.37^a (0.00)	107	0.12	3.72^a (0.00)	95	0.21
2008	0.96^a (0.00)	93	0.26	1.01^a (0.00)	93	0.26	3.22^a (0.00)	107	0.11	3.54^a (0.00)	95	0.20
2009	0.92^a (0.00)	93	0.25	0.98^a (0.00)	93	0.25	3.01^a (0.00)	107	0.10	3.34^a (0.00)	95	0.18
2010	0.93^a (0.00)	93	0.25	0.98^a (0.00)	93	0.25	3.04^a (0.00)	107	0.10	3.33^a (0.00)	95	0.18
2011	0.91^a (0.00)	93	0.25	0.96^a (0.00)	93	0.24	2.93^a (0.00)	107	0.10	3.21^a (0.00)	95	0.17
2012	0.88^a (0.00)	93	0.24	0.92^a (0.00)	93	0.23	2.78^a (0.00)	107	0.09	3.14^a (0.00)	95	0.17
2013	0.88^a (0.00)	93	0.25	0.92^a (0.00)	93	0.24	2.74^a (0.00)	107	0.09	3.18^a (0.00)	95	0.18
2014	0.88^a (0.00)	93	0.24	0.92^a (0.00)	93	0.23	2.69^a (0.00)	107	0.08	2.99^a (0.00)	95	0.15

Note: p–value in parentheses
[a] $p < 0.01$
[b] $p < 0.05$
[c] $p < 0$

Finally, there may be concern that the relationship between the historical variables and current economic freedom might be influenced by other unobserved factors. We used genetic diversity and its square from Ashraf and Galor (2013) as an instrument for each of the full regressions in Tables 5.1–5.3 that also included the geographic and tropical variables. For most of the regressions, the Durbin and Wu-Hausman tests were not significant, indicating that the historical variable is exogenous. The main exception was for adjusted state history, where endogeneity was indicated for *free trade*, overall economic freedom, and *regulation*. For these regressions, the coefficient on adjusted state history became larger and more significant.

Discussion and conclusion

This exploratory study shows that much of the variation among countries in their institutions is explained by influences from over 500 years ago. In almost all cases, more of the variation in property rights – a bedrock of free trade – was explained than the variation in any of the other indices. Free trade has the second most variation explained. The fact that Table 5.5 resulted in 60 percent of the variation in property rights being explained by historical and geographical variables shows the persistence of institutions: they are slow to change and rooted in their starting points. The remaining 40 percent of the variation can be explained by other variables and these variables may be changed over time to bring countries to greater or lesser economic freedom.

As Spolaore and Wacziarg (2013) argue, these long-term constraints on change can be overcome since long-term history does not explain all of the variation, leaving much to be determined by other variables that may not be long-term. Second dynamics between populations mean that changes can be more readily adopted. Given immigration, current technology, and information transfers, interactions between populations are much greater today than in the past and should result in faster changes in institutions.

We examined the overall EFW index, as well as its sub-indices. The expectation that the *property rights* and *free trade* sub-indices would be better explained by the data was borne out. The overall EFW index was also the next best explained. The *money* and *regulation* indices were less well explained. Although monarchs and governments in the past used inflation to reduce debt payments, monetary policy, both good and bad, is a more recent phenomenon and would be expected to have less persistence from the perspective of long-term historical roots.

The negative coefficient that often appeared for the *size of government* sub-index may be reflective of the tendency of countries with greater economic growth to have larger governments (Ram 1986). This greater growth may come from a positive government externality or from greater economic freedom in the other categories. Barro (1996) finds that wealthier countries have more democracy, and greater democracy in these countries tends to dampen growth. As countries become wealthier, they may push for more government policies. This can lead to greater growth in government and less economic freedom in the *size of government* sub-index. Another explanation may be that these historical variables indicate a head start. As a result, rent-seeking institutions also had more time to develop. So the negative coefficient on the *size of government* sub-index may be an indicator of better organized rent-seeking behavior.

Our results for institutional variables are consistent with the results found by Gutmann and Voigt (2015) for the rule of law. Using data similar to that included in this chapter, they find that better geographic conditions matter for the rule of law. They also find similar positive associations of the rule of law with ancestry-adjusted state history.

The timing of regime changes that have severely restricted or enhanced property rights may play an important role. If a regime change is short-lived, spanning perhaps fewer than three generations, then the adverse effects of restricted property rights might dissipate more quickly than in situations in which restrictions on property rights lasted for many generations. People in a society with longer-standing restrictions will have less institutional knowledge passed down from generation to generation. As a result, they may be less likely to revert back to property rights. Also, the more recent the reduction in property rights, the more likely a society is to revert back to respect for property rights after regime change, since information flows more freely today than it did in the past. It is difficult to eliminate the human tendency to truck, barter, and trade. Sobel (2017) finds that countries can recover from recently instituted poor institutions, but the process is slower than their decline. Countries that do move to better institutions usually lead with improvements in free trade.

Future research might examine how these past historical events influence culture (Hofstede and Hofstede 2001) and through culture, and how this directly mediates economic freedom and economic growth. Further, the change in institutions over time after accounting for historical variables may shed light on what drives more recent changes in economic freedom. This study has shown that institutions are strongly influenced by past historical events. Institutions are slow to change. However, room exists for further changes toward economic freedom and, given the migration of people and the greater flow of information in today's world, these changes may occur more quickly now than they did in the past.

Notes

1 See Hall and Lawson (2014) for an overview of studies using the Economic Freedom of the World (EFW) index.
2 Kaufmann, Kraay, and Mastruzzi (2011) developed the Worldwide Governance Indicators, which also appeared in 1996. They measure: voice and accountability; political stability and absence of violence; government effectiveness; regulatory quality; rule of law; and control of corruption.
3 The number of components in each sub-index have changed over time. In 2000, the sub-index included legal security of private ownership rights, viability of contracts, and rule of law. By 2012, this sub-index included: judicial independence; impartial courts; protection of property rights; military interference in rule of law and politics; integrity of the legal system; legal enforcement of contracts; regulatory restrictions

on the sale of real property; reliability of police; and business costs of crime. Many of these are more oriented toward modern institutions. Similar changes were made to the other sub-indices. Later in the chapter, we examine the influence of the historical variables for each year that the EFW data is available. Our results tend to be consistent over the years.

4 These data are from Romain Wacziarg's website: http://www.anderson.ucla.edu/faculty_pages/romain.wacziarg/papersum.html

5 Putterman and Weil (2008) developed a measure for agricultural history, i.e. the time since agriculture first started in a country. We estimated equations using this variable and an ancestry-adjusted agriculture variable, but found no significant coefficients at the 5 percent level of significance.

6 A regression using only the ancestry-weighted technology in 0 AD had a coefficient of 5.34, a p-value of 0.001 and an adjusted R-square of 0.19. The coefficient on the BC 1000 ancestry-adjusted technology variable was 2.11, with a p-value of 0.026 and an adjusted R-squared of 0.05.

7 We also examined whether a reversal of fortune (Acemoglu, Johnson and Robinson 2001) occurred for European colonies and found support that countries with greater population densities in 1500, when institutions were more likely to be extractive, had fewer economic freedoms today.

References

Acemoglu, D., and J. A. Robinson. 2013. *Why nations fail: The origins of power, prosperity, and poverty.* New York: Crown Business.

Acemoglu, D., S. Johnson and J. A. Robinson. 2001. *Reversal of fortune: Geography and institutions in the making of the modern world income distribution.* Working paper.

Ashraf, Q., and O. Galor. 2013. The "Out of Africa" hypothesis, human genetic diversity, and comparative economic development. *American Economic Review,* 103(1): 1–46.

Barro, R. J. 1996. Democracy and growth. *Journal of Economic Growth,* 1(1): 1–27.

Baumol, W. J. 1990. Entrepreneurship: Productive, unproductive and destructive. *Journal of Political Economy,* 98(5): 893–921.

Berggren, N. 2003. The benefits of economic freedom: A survey. *The Independent Review,* 8(2): 193–211.

Bjørnskov, C., and N. Foss. 2008. Economic freedom and entrepreneurial activity: Some cross-country evidence. *Public Choice,* 134(3): 307–328.

Bockstette, V., A. Chanda and L. Putterman. 2002. States and markets: The advantage of an early start. *Journal of Economic Growth,* 7(4): 347–369.

Chilton, A. S., and E. A. Posner. 2015. *The influence of history on states' compliance with human rights obligations.* Working paper.

Comin, D., W. Easterly and E. Gong. 2006. *Was the wealth of nations determined in 1000 BC?* Working paper.

Dawson, J. W. 1998. Institutions, investment, and growth: New cross-country and panel data evidence. *Economic Inquiry,* 36(4): 603–619.

Dawson, J. W. 2003. Causality in the freedom–growth relationship. *European Journal of Political Economy,* 19(3): 479–495.

Diamond, J. 1999. *Guns, germs, and steel: The fates of human societies.* New York: W.W. Norton & Co.

Esposto, A. G., and P. A. Zaleski. 1999. Economic freedom and the quality of life: an empirical analysis. *Constitutional Political Economy,* 10(2): 185–197.

Gohmann, S. F. 2012. Institutions, latent entrepreneurship, and self-employment: An international comparison. *Entrepreneurship Theory and Practice, 36*(2): 295–321.

Gutmann, J., and S. Voigt. 2015. *The rule of law: Measurement and deep roots.* Working paper.

Gwartney, J. D., R. A. Lawson and W. Block. 1996. *Economic freedom of the world, 1975–1995.* Vancouver, BC: Fraser Institute.

Gwartney, J. D., R. A. Lawson and J. Hall. 2015. *Economic freedom of the world: 2015 annual report.* Vancouver, BC: Fraser Institute.

Hall, J. C., and R. A. Lawson. 2014. Economic freedom of the world: An accounting of the literature. *Contemporary Economic Policy, 32*(1): 1–19.

Hayek, F. A. 1988. *The fatal conceit: The errors of socialism.* Chicago, IL: University of Chicago Press.

Hibbs, D. A., and O. Olsson. 2004. Geography, biogeography, and why some countries are rich and others are poor. *Proceedings of the National Academy of Sciences of the United States of America, 101*(10): 3715–3720.

Hofstede, G. H., and G. Hofstede. 2001. *Culture's consequences: Comparing values, behaviors, institutions and organizations across nations.* Thousand Oaks, CA: Sage.

Kaufmann, D., A. Kraay and M. Mastruzzi. 2011. The worldwide governance indicators: Methodology and analytical issues. *Hague Journal on the Rule of Law, 3*(2): 220–246.

Krieger, T., and D. Meierrieks. 2016. Political capitalism: The interaction between income inequality, economic freedom and democracy. *European Journal of Political Economy, 45*(C): 115–132.

Locke, J. 2014 [1690]. *Second treatise of government: An essay concerning the true original, extent and end of civil government.* Hoboken, NJ: John Wiley & Sons.

Mankiw, N. G., D. Romer and D. N. Weil. 1992. A contribution to the empirics of economic growth. *Quarterly Journal of Economics, 107*(2): 407–437.

North, D. C. 1990. *Institutions, institutional change and economic performance.* Cambridge: Cambridge University Press.

North, D. C. 1991. Institutions. *Journal of Economic Perspectives, 5*(1): 97–112.

North, D. C. 1994. Economic performance through time. *American Economic Review, 84*(3): 359–368.

Nyström, K. 2008. The institutions of economic freedom and entrepreneurship: evidence from panel data. *Public Choice, 136*(3–4): 269–282.

Olsson, O., and D. A. Hibbs. 2005. Biogeography and long-run economic development. *European Economic Review, 49*(4): 909–938.

Putterman, L. 2008. Agriculture, diffusion and development: Ripple effects of the Neolithic revolution. *Economica, 75*(300): 729–748.

Putterman, L., and D. N. Weil. 2008. *Post-1500 population flows and the long-run determinants of economic growth and inequality.* Working paper

Ram, R. 1986. Government size and economic growth: A new framework and some evidence from cross-section and time-series data. *American Economic Review, 76*(1): 191–203.

Smith, A. 1776. *An inquiry into the nature and causes of the wealth of nations.* London: Adam Smith Institute.

Sobel, R. S. 2017. The rise and decline of nations: The dynamic properties of institutional reform, 1. *Journal of Institutional Economics, 13*(3): 549–574.

Spolaore, E., and R. Wacziarg. 2013. How deep are the roots of economic development? *Journal of Economic Literature, 51*(2): 325–369.

Stroup, M. D. 2007. Economic freedom, democracy, and the quality of life. *World Development*, *35*(1): 52–66.

Svensson, J. 1998. Investment, property rights and political instability: Theory and evidence. *European Economic Review*, *42*(7): 1317–1341.

Williamson, C. R., and R. L. Mathers. 2011. Economic freedom, culture, and growth. *Public Choice*, *148*(3–4): 313–335.

World History Project. 2016. *The reforms of Urukagina*. Available at http://history-world.org/reforms_of_urukagina.htm

6 Institutional convergence

Exit or voice?

Joshua C. Hall

Introduction*

While the study of the institutions of economic freedom has a long history in economics going back at least to Adam Smith, the creation of the Economic Freedom of the World (EFW) index by Gwartney, Lawson, and Block (1996) has led a large number of economists to study the effect of economic freedom on social, political, and economic outcomes.[1] Hall and Lawson (2014) provide an accounting of a subset of the literature using the EFW index. Focusing only on journals listed in the *Social Science Citation Index*, they find 402 articles citing the EFW index since 1996. Of those 402 articles, 198 are empirical papers using the EFW index as an explanatory variable. After reading and categorizing all of the articles, Hall and Lawson (2014) find that fewer than 4 percent of the articles surveyed found economic freedom to be associated with a normatively "bad" outcome such as income inequality or obesity.[2]

A large number of papers in the literature using the EFW index focus on the relationship between economic freedom and growth. This literature almost uniformly shows that an institutional environment more consistent with economic freedom is conducive to long-term growth. An early paper by Gwartney, Lawson, and Holcombe (1999) finds that a 1-unit change in the EFW index during the period 1975–85 was associated with a 0.8 percentage point increase in a country's long-term growth rate. Looking at the 1990s and controlling for the effect that economic freedom has on the productivity of investment, Gwartney, Holcombe, and Lawson (2006) find that a 1-unit change in the EFW index is associated with a 1.5 percentage point increase in growth. A critical survey of the literature by De Haan, Lundström, and Sturm (2006) finds strong evidence that increases in the EFW index stimulate growth. A 2011 meta-regression analysis by Efendic, Pugh, and Adnett (2011) finds similar results, albeit with some suggestions for improvement for scholars working in the area. Other important recent works include Williamson and Mathers (2011), Rode and Coll (2012), and Young and Sheehan (2014).

If the institutions of economic freedom are associated with economic growth, then the next logical question is: what causes countries to turn towards or away from market-oriented institutions? What exactly are the determinants of economic freedom? While many have been discussed in the literature, a prominent determinant in the literature has been political freedom, or democratic institutions. An early paper in this literature is that by Dawson (1998), who finds that the level of economic freedom in 1990 is related to political freedom in 1975. Wu and Davis (1999), however, find no effect of political freedom on economic freedom. More recent work by De Haan and Sturm (2003), Pitlik and Wirth (2003), Lundström (2005), and Rode and Coll (2012) finds that political freedom or democratic transitions lead to economic freedom. This finding is supported by papers by Dawson (2003), Vega-Gordillo and Alvarez-Arce (2003), and Aixalá and Fabro (2009), who present evidence that political freedom Granger-causes economic freedom. Sobel and Coyne (2011) find that political and economic institutions are cointegrated, and therefore move together through time within a country.[3] The case for political freedom has also been backed by within-country case studies, such as the work of Beaulier and Subrick (2006) on Botswana.

Other long-run determinants of the institutions of economic freedom include the historical origins of a country's laws (La Porta et al., 1999; La Porta, Lopez-de Silanes, and Shleifer 2008). Legal origin theory is based on the idea that the British common law created more effective constraints on the power of the executive than did French civil law or Scandinavian or socialist legal origins (Du, 2010).[4] Similarly, countries that are fractionalized in terms of ethnicity, religion, or language might have lower levels of economic freedom because it is harder for diverse individuals to agree on publicly provided goods (Alesina et al., 2003). In a paper looking at the long-run determinants of growth, Easterly, Ritzen, and Woolcock (2006) find that ethnolinguistic fractionalization affects institutional quality, which in turn influences growth.

An important addition to this literature is the work of Brown (2014), building on the work of Diamond (1997), who briefly notes that the shapes of Europe and China could have influenced their institutional development. Europe, unlike China, is geographically indented, and has more peninsulas and islands, which created natural barriers to population centralization and control. Brown (2014) links this literature to institutional competition, which requires the ability of citizens to "vote with their feet" (Tiebout, 1956). The closer an individual is in a country to a border, the closer they are to an alternative institutional environment. Brown (2014) creates a variable called "exitability" to capture this concept.[5] Defined as the sum of land borders and coastline divided by total geographic area, his measure of the "exitability" of a country is a long-run determinant of economic freedom in his empirical work.[6]

This chapter adds to the literature on the determinants of economic freedom by seeing how specific determinants contributed to institutional convergence from 1980 to 2010. This is an important question for four reasons. First, the question of income convergence across countries has interested economists since the seminal papers by Barro and Sala-i-Martin (1992) and Sala-i-Martin (1996). Second, Knack and Keefer (1995), Knack (1996), and Keefer and Knack (1997) show that convergence depends on the quality of institutions. By better understanding the process of convergence in economic freedom across countries, scholars can better understand the causes of continued income differences across countries. Third, while many studies have documented how various determinants such as political freedom have influenced economic freedom, no studies have quantified how these determinants contribute to the speed at which countries with poor institutional quality catch up to those with good institutional quality. Finally, this chapter contributes to the literature on exit versus voice in determining the quality of institutions (Hirschman, 1978).[7]

The chapter proceeds as follows. In the next section, the data and empirical approach is described. The third section presents the empirical results and the final section concludes.

Empirical approach and data

In the growth literature, there is a large body of work on the convergence of incomes across countries or regions (Barro and Sala-i-Martin, 1992; Mankiw, Romer, and Weil 1992). A large portion of this literature focuses on β-convergence. Beta-convergence occurs when the partial correlation between growth in income over some time period is negatively related to the initial level of income (Young, Higgins, and Levy, 2008). There exist a number of papers testing for β-convergence in incomes. There is a much smaller literature, however, on β-convergence in economic freedom or institutions. A search for papers on institutional convergence yielded only three. The first, by Savoia and Sen (2012), looks for β-convergence across a number of different institutional measures, including Area 2 of the EFW index. In addition to not using the entire EFW index, the focus of their paper is only on testing for convergence; they do not report coefficients for their conditional convergence regressions and they employ largely time-invariant data using a panel approach. The second paper, by Elert and Halvarsson (2012), does use the entire EFW index as its measure of institutions and finds evidence for convergence using a panel data approach. However, the authors do not control for any other determinants of the change in economic freedom other than the initial value of economic freedom and the change in economic freedom over the time period.[8] Finally, a very recent paper by Boudreaux and Holcombe (2015) looks at institutional convergence for an unbalanced panel of countries from 1970 to 2010.

Economic freedom is measured by the EFW index by Gwartney, Lawson, and Hall (2015). A widely used political economy indicator, the EFW index measures the economic freedom present in a country based on 42 variables in five areas: size of government; legal system and property rights; sound money; freedom to trade internationally; and the regulation of business, credit, and labor. Each component is placed onto a 0–10 scale and then aggregated to create a summary measure of economic freedom for a country as a whole. The index contains 157 countries in the most recent year at time of writing (2013) and a smaller number of countries going back to 1970.[9] The analysis begins in 1980 instead of 1970 because the number of countries rated in 1980 is considerably higher than in 1970 for the chain-linked version of the index, which tries to adjust for changes in the components of the index over time. Only the chain-link measure of economic freedom is employed in the analysis.

Convergence in institutional quality is tested using Equation 6.1:

$$InEFW_{2010} - InEFW_{1980} = \alpha + \beta\, EFW_{1980} + \gamma X_{1980} + \varepsilon \quad (6.1)$$

where X_{1980} is a matrix of variables that might explain long-run determinants of the change in the natural log of economic freedom from 1980 to 2010. A negative sign on the parameter β implies that there is convergence in economic freedom. Conversely, a positive sign on β would imply divergence in economic freedom from 1980 to 2010 among this sample of countries. Variables included in the X matrix are motivated by the literature on the determinants of economic freedom discussed in the introduction.

Gross domestic product (GDP) per capita in 1980 in constant 2005 U.S. dollars was obtained from the World Bank (2015). To capture the quality of human capital in 1980, the average years of secondary schooling for the total population aged 25 and over in 1980 from Barro and Lee (2013) is included. Descriptive statistics for all non-binary data used in the chapter is presented in Table 6.1.

To see how the initial level of political institutions contributed to the change in economic freedom from 1980 to 2010, the level of political democracy in 1980 from Marshall, Gurr, and Jaggers (2014) is included. Widely used as a measure of democracy in a number of studies (Glaeser et al., 2004; Leeson and Dean, 2009), the measure ranges from −10 ("total autocracy") to +10 ("total democracy"). This variable captures political openness, the competitiveness of the political process, and constraints on the chief executive (Leeson and Dean, 2009). Presumably, countries that are more democratic allow their citizens a greater voice in public affairs. As

Table 6.1 Summary statistics

Name	Observations	Mean	SD	Min.	Max.
EFW growth	102	0.01	0.01	−0.02	0.03
1980 EFW	102	5.31	1.26	2.76	9.03
1980 GDP (ln)	100	7.97	1.06	5.78	10.60
1980 Education	98	1.29	1.08	0.05	5.10
Democracy	90	0.21	8.08	−10.00	10.00
Checks and balances	100	3.13	1.14	1.00	5.73
Exitability	100	0.050	0.103	0.003	0.699
Ethnic fractionalization	102	0.438	0.268	0.002	0.930
Language fractionalization	100	0.391	0.297	0.002	0.923
Religious fractionalization	102	0.430	0.240	0.003	0.860

an additional political institution variable, *Checks* from Beck and colleagues (2001) is included. As created by Keefer and Stasavage (2003), *Checks* is an attempt to capture the number of veto players in government. This variable is based on whether the executive and legislative branches are controlled by different parties (in a presidential system) or the number of parties in the government coalition (in parliamentary systems). The measure is also adjusted for political rules that make coalitions more cohesive. Countries with a higher score on *Checks* are expected to have higher economic freedom because the scope for collective activity is limited.

To test whether the threat of exit plays an important role in explaining convergence in economic freedom over this period, *Exitability* from Brown (2014) is included. As discussed in the introduction, this variable is defined as the "sum of land borders and coastline divided by total geographic area" (Brown, 2014, p. 110). A country's *Exitability* score is higher when the ratio of the length of its border and coastline to its total area is greater. So countries with irregular borders, such as Denmark and Panama, have relatively high scores (0.17 and 0.039, respectively), while a country such as Chad, with a large land mass and smooth borders, has a low score of 0.004. This variable – at least historically – has been an attempt to capture how easy it is for a country's population to "exit" a country in response to bad or stagnating policy.

The inclusion of these two variables provides the ability to test how these structural characteristics contribute to conditional convergence in economic freedom from 1980 to 2010. Have countries that were similar in terms of democracy in 1980 converged faster than countries that were similar in terms of exit? The coefficient estimates on *Democracy* and *Exitability* should be able to shed some light on this question. In addition, legal origins (La Porta et al., 1999, 2008), and ethnic, religious, and linguistic fractionalization (Alesina et al., 2003), are included because conditional β-convergence might also depend on these determinants of institutional quality.

Empirical results

Column (1) of Table 6.2 presents the unconditional convergence estimates over the 1980–2010 period for the EFW index. The negative and statistically significant coefficient on *1980 EFW* demonstrates that economic freedom has been converging since 1980. To put these estimates in context, consider that Argentina had a score in the EFW index in 1980 of 3.96. According to the unconditional convergence estimates in column (1), the expected annual growth in economic freedom will be $0.0329 - 0.00450 \times 3.96 = 0.015$ percentage points. This implies that, over the 30-year period, economic freedom in Argentina would reach an EFW score of $3.96 \times e^{30 \times 0.015} = 6.21$ if it were converging at the average rate. In reality, Argentina had an EFW score of 5.86 in 2010.

Convergence not only means that countries that begin the period with low levels of economic freedom "catch up," but also that some countries that begin the period with a high level of economic freedom might stagnate institutionally or decline. Once you have eliminated conscription, for example, there is no way to get freer on that component of the EFW. Consider the United States, which began 1980 with an EFW score of 7.92. Again, using the estimates from column (1), the expected annualized growth rate in economic freedom for the United States will be $0.0329 - 0.00450 \times 7.92 = -0.0027$ percentage points. After 30 years, this would predict an EFW score of $7.92 \times e^{30 \times -0.0027} = 7.29$. In reality, the United States had a chain-link EFW score of 7.76 in 2010.

Clearly, it is necessary to look at institutional convergence conditional on other factors such as initial GDP levels and human capital levels. Columns (2) and (3) from Table 6.2 introduce both of these variables. The natural log of 1980 GDP per capita is positively related to the speed of economic freedom convergence in column (2), but its statistical significance disappears once *1980 Education* is introduced in column (3), with years of secondary education of those over the age of 25 (in 1980) being statistically significant at the 1 percent level. The coefficient on *1980 EFW* in column (3) suggests that a country with a low initial EFW will close the institutional gap with countries at the top of the EFW rankings, such as Hong Kong and Singapore at a rate of 0.5 percent annually, other things being equal.

What about *Democracy* and *Exitability*? Table 6.3 introduces *Democracy*, *Checks*, and *Exitability* one at a time. *Democracy*, as measured by the Polity IV data, is not statistically significant in any of the specifications. The same is also true of *Checks*.

Table 6.2 Convergence in economic freedom: baseline results

	(1)	*(2)*	*(3)*
1980 EFW	0.00450***	0.00532***	0.00559***
	(0.000408)	(0.000498)	(0.000518)
1980 GDP		0.00143**	0.000589
(ln)		(0.000448)	(0.000510)
1980			0.00157***
Education			(0.000380)
Constant	0.0329***	0.0260***	0.0321***
	(0.00227)	(0.00311)	(0.00407)
N	102	100	96
Adjusted R^2	0.593	0.651	0.663

Notes: Dependent variable is the change in the natural log of the EFW index from 1980 to 2010; robust standard errors in parentheses.
* $p < 0.05$
** $p < 0.01$
*** $p < 0.001$

Table 6.3 Convergence in economic freedom: politics and exit

	(1)	(2)	(3)
1980 EFW	0.00590***	0.00591***	0.00630***
	(0.000533)	(0.000529)	(0.000508)
1980 GDP (ln)	0.000637	0.000637	0.0000453
	(0.000702)	(0.000706)	(0.000720)
1980	0.00166**	0.00173***	0.00209***
Education	(0.000494)	(0.000476)	(0.000505)
Democracy	0.0000185	0.0000300	0.0000247
	(0.0000865)	(0.000102)	(0.0000993)
Checks		−0.000208	0.00000958
		(0.000515)	(0.000538)
Exitability			0.0303**
			(0.0108)
Constant	0.0331***	0.0337***	0.0382***
	(0.00577)	(0.00610)	(0.00607)
N	85	84	83
Adjusted R^2	0.0654	0.65	0.678

Notes: Dependent variable is the change in the natural log of the EFW index from 1980 to 2010; robust standard errors in parentheses.

* $p < 0.05$
** $p < 0.01$
*** $p < 0.001$

Exitability, however, is positively related to institutional convergence in column (3) of Table 6.3. This implies that countries with more uneven borders or longer borders relative to their total area converged more than other countries, conditional on initial levels of economic freedom. Other important things to note are that *1980 Education* retains its significance with the inclusion of these additional variables. Once more similar countries are taken into account in these conditional convergence specifications, it is not surprising that the estimated β becomes larger, since institutional convergence should be faster for countries that are similar in important structural ways, such as having the same degree of *Exitability*.

In Table 6.4, the robustness of the findings of Table 6.3 are tested by including measures of ethnic, language, and religious fractionalization. None of these variables contributea to the convergence of economic freedom over the 1980–2010 period in a statistically significant manner. Most importantly, however, *Exitability* retains its statistical significance across all three columns, as does *1980 Education*. The estimate of β in column (3) of Table 6.4 is −0.00648, suggesting that a country with a low EFW score in 1980 will erode the economic freedom gap at a rate of 0.648 percent a year.

Table 6.4 Convergence in economic freedom: including fractionalization

	(1)	(2)	(3)
1980 EFW	−0.00632***	−0.00651***	−0.00648***
	(0.000510)	(0.000675)	(0.000640)
1980 GDP (ln)	0.0000996	0.000509	0.000582
	(0.000717)	(0.000883)	(0.000879)
1980 Education	0.00212***	0.00202***	0.00182**
	(0.000527)	(0.000524)	(0.000554)
Democracy	0.0000242	0.0000332	0.0000252
	(0.0000996)	(0.0000963)	(0.0000961)
Checks	0.0000185	−0.0000258	0.0000355
	(0.000532)	(0.000495)	(0.000517)
Exitability	0.0307**	0.0290**	0.0279**
	(0.0108)	(0.0102)	(0.00924)
Ethnic fractionalization	0.000583	−0.000617	−0.00107
	(0.00174)	(0.00290)	(0.00307)
Language fractionalization		0.00204	0.00144
		(0.00308)	(0.00281)
Religious fractionalization			0.00262
			(0.00221)
Constant	0.0375***	0.0353***	0.0340***
	(0.00600)	(0.00632)	(0.00641)
N	83	82	82
Adjusted R^2	0.674	0.668	0.671

Notes: Dependent variable is the change in the natural log of the EFW index from 1980 to 2010; robust standard errors in parentheses.
* $p < 0.05$
** $p < 0.01$
*** $p < 0.001$

Countries fundamentally change their legal systems infrequently, usually as the result of colonization or initial settlement. Table 6.5 introduces legal origins. Column (1) introduces a dummy variable equal to 1 if the country follows the British common-law tradition. While the sign on this variable is positive, as expected, it is not statistically significant. Similarly, when the French legal origin binary variable is introduced in column (2), the sign is negative as expected, but statistically insignificant as well. Socialist legal origins are introduced in column (3). The variable not only is statistically insignificant, but also has the wrong sign (that is, it is positively related to the change in the natural log of economic freedom from 1980 to 2010).

In terms of the primary variables of interest, *Democracy* and *Exitability*, both retain the same conclusion once legal origins are introduced. While the

Table 6.5 Convergence in economic freedom: including legal origins

	(1)	*(2)*	*(3)*
1980 EFW	−0.00645***	−0.00645***	−0.00642***
	(0.000691)	(0.000687)	(0.000710)
1980 GDP (ln)	0.000860	0.00100	0.000996
	(0.000901)	(0.000921)	(0.000910)
1980 Education	0.00176**	0.00159**	0.00164**
	(0.000591)	(0.000577)	(0.000585)
Democracy	−0.00000803	−0.0000108	−0.00000551
	(0.0000990)	(0.0000992)	(0.000101)
Checks	0.0000444	0.0000479	0.0000614
	(0.000516)	(0.000513)	(0.000514)
Exitability	0.0247**	0.0237*	0.0241*
	(0.00931)	(0.00955)	(0.00949)
Ethnic	−0.00130	−0.000665	−0.000558
fractionalization	(0.00308)	(0.00309)	(0.00316)
Language	0.00111	0.00121	0.00136
fractionalization	(0.00281)	(0.00284)	(0.00282)
Religious	0.00139	0.000928	0.000676
fractionalization	(0.00222)	(0.00226)	(0.00237)
UK legal origins	0.00167	0.000522	0.000978
	(0.000986)	(0.00115)	(0.00117)
French legal origins		−0.00150	−0.00103
		(0.00110)	(0.00119)
Socialist legal			0.00209
origins			(0.00183)
Constant	0.0320***	0.0322***	0.0315***
	(0.00630)	(0.00616)	(0.00619)
N	81	81	81
Adjusted R^2	0.658	0.657	0.653

Notes: Dependent variable is the change in the natural log of the EFW index from 1980 to 2010; robust standard errors in parentheses.

* $p < 0.05$
** $p < 0.01$
*** $p < 0.001$

sign on *Democracy* is now negative, it is statistically indistinguishable from 0. *Exitability*, on the other hand, remains statistically significant even with the inclusion of a large number of covariates and the number of countries falling to 81. The same is also true of *1980 Education*, which retains its positive and significant relationship with the change in economic freedom.

Conclusion

There is a small, but growing, literature on the determinants of economic freedom. This chapter has contributed to this literature in two ways. First, it empirically shows that β-convergence in economic freedom occurred from 1980 to 2010. Countries that started 1980 with low levels of economic freedom are converging on those at the top of the EFW ranking, albeit at a slow rate. Second, the chapter documents the initial conditions that have contributed to this institutional convergence. For example, countries in which individuals aged 25 and over had more years of secondary schooling in 1980 saw stronger convergence, other things being equal.

Most interestingly, no evidence of stronger convergence among countries with similar levels of democracy is found. *Exitability*, a variable created by Brown (2014) to capture how easy it is for citizens to "vote with their feet," is related to the change in economic freedom from 1980 to 2010 in a statistically significant manner across all specifications. This provides some indirect evidence of the importance of "exit" versus "voice" with respect to the question of institutional reform. Countries from which it was easier to exit during this period converged, while countries with similar levels of democracy in 1980 did not.

The results here suggest several other avenues for future research. First, *Exitability* is likely to be stronger within a country, rather than across countries, given the importance of passport controls and immigration restrictions. This suggest that areas within a country with greater *Exitability* are likely to have higher levels of economic freedom, all other things being equal. This would be extremely easy to test with any of the sub-regional economic freedom indices, such as Stansel, Torra, and McMahon (2014). This would fit well with the literature on economic freedom and migration (Ashby, 2007; Cebula, Foley, and Hall, 2015). Second, across countries, there have been found many determinants of economic freedom that change considerably over a 30-year period, such as joining fiscal or monetary unions (Hall et al., 2011), financial crises (Rode and Coll, 2012), populism (Rode and Revuelta, 2015), or human rights violations (Carden and Lawson, 2010). The effect of these variables on the β-convergence of economic freedom could be analyzed in a panel data format. Finally, the β-convergence of economic freedom across U.S. states could be estimated to see if states were converging or diverging in terms of institutional quality since 1980.

Notes

[*] Reprinted by permission from Springer: *Journal of Economics and Finance*, "Institutional Convergence: Exit or Voice?" Joshua Hall. Volume 40, No. 4, pp. 829–840. Copyright 2015.

[1] Gwartney and Lawson (2003) provide a good overview of the theoretical foundations behind the construction of the EFW index.

[2] Apergis, Dincer and Payne (2014) actually find bidirectional causality between income inequality and economic freedom.

[3] Lawson and Clark (2010) find very few cases of countries with high levels of political freedom and economic freedom.

4 Nattinger and Hall (2012) find that the legal origins of U.S. states help to explain their current levels of economic freedom.

5 In many ways, this variable and the thesis behind it is related to the work of Scott (2009). For more on the relationship between Scott (2009) and competition in governance, see Powell and Nair (2012) and Stringham and Miles (2012).

6 In addition to this literature on the deep determinants, there are a number of papers on how economic freedom responds to more short-run changes, such as in preferences (Crampton, 2002), foreign aid (Powell and Ryan, 2006; Young and Sheehan, 2014), immigration (Clark et al., 2014), ideas (Leeson, Sobel and Dean, 2012), changes in nearby countries (Leeson et al., 2012), Internet access (Sheehan and Young, 2014), and joining a monetary and fiscal union (Hall, Lawson and Wogsland, 2011). While important, these are outside the scope of this chapter, which focuses on initial conditions and time-invariant determinants such as exitability.

7 When an organization or country is declining, or not improving as fast as its neighbors, individuals have two possible responses if they want to change things: leave for a better situation (exit), or exercise political action (voice). In this chapter, the level of democracy is a proxy for the degree of voice that citizens have to change policy.

8 Another similar recent paper is Heckelman (2015), who tests for σ-convergence in economic freedom.

9 The data is annual, back to 2000, and at five-year intervals from 1970 to 2000.

References

Aixalá, J., and Fabro, G. 2009. Economic freedom, civil liberties, political rights and growth: A causality analysis. *Spanish Economic Review, 11*(3): 165–178.

Alesina, A., Devleeschauwer, A., Easterly, W., Kurlat, S., and Wacziarg, R. 2003. Fractionalization. *Journal of Economic Growth, 8*(2): 155–194.

Apergis, N., Dincer, O., and Payne, J. E. 2014. Economic freedom and income inequality revisited: Evidence from a panel error correction model. *Contemporary Economic Policy, 32*(1): 67–75.

Ashby, N. J. 2007. Economic freedom and migration flows between U.S. states. *Southern Economic Journal, 73*(3): 677–697.

Barro, R. J., and Lee, J. W. 2013. A new data set of educational attainment in the world, 1950–2010. *Journal of Development Economics, 104*(C): 184–198.

Barro, R. J., and Sala-i-Martin, X. 1992. Convergence. *Journal of Political Economy, 100*(2): 223–251.

Beaulier, S. A., and Subrick, J. R. 2006. The political foundations of development: The case of Botswana. *Constitutional Political Economy, 17*(2): 103–115.

Beck, T., Clarke, G., Groff, A., Keefer, P., and Walsh, P. 2001. New tools in comparative political economy: The database of political institutions. *World Bank Economic Review, 15*(1): 165–176.

Boudreaux, C., and Holcombe, R. 2015. *Institutional convergence*. Working paper.

Brown, M. 2014. The geography of economic freedom. *The Annual Proceedings of the Wealth and Well-Being of Nations, 4*: 105–121.

Carden, A., and Lawson, R. A. 2010. Human rights and economic liberalization. *Business & Politics, 12*(2): 1–18.

Cebula, R. J., Foley, M., and Hall, J. C. 2015. Freedom and gross in-migration: An empirical study of the post-Great Recession experience. *Journal of Economics and Finance, 16*: 1–19.

Clark, J., Lawson, R., Nowrasteh, A., Powell, B., and Murphy, R. 2014. Does immigration impact institutions? *Public Choice, 163*(3–4): 321–335.

Crampton, E. 2002. You get what you vote for: Voter preferences and economic freedom. *Journal of Private Enterprise, 18*(Fall): 29–56.

Dawson, J. W. 1998. Institutions, investment, and growth: New cross-country and panel data evidence. *Economic Inquiry, 36*(4): 603–619.

Dawson, J. W. 2003. Causality in the freedom–growth relationship. *European Journal of Political Economy, 19*(3): 479–495.

De Haan, J., and Sturm, J.-E. 2003. Does more democracy lead to greater economic freedom? New evidence for developing countries. *European Journal of Political Economy, 19*(3): 547–563.

De Haan, J., Lundström, S., and Sturm, J.-E. 2006. Market-oriented institutions and policies and economic growth: A critical survey. *Journal of Economic Surveys, 20*(2): 157–191.

Diamond, J. 1997. *Guns, germs, and steel: The fates of human societies.* New York: W.W. Norton & Co.

Du, J. 2010. Institutional quality and economic crises: Legal origin theory versus colonial strategy theory. *Review of Economics and Statistics, 92*(1): 173–179.

Easterly, W., Ritzen, J., and Woolcock, M. 2006. Social cohesion, institutions, and growth. *Economics & Politics, 18*(2): 103–120.

Efendic, A., Pugh, G., and Adnett, N. 2011. Institutions and economic performance: A meta-regression analysis. *European Journal of Political Economy, 27*(3): 586–599.

Elert, N., and Halvarsson, D. 2012. *Economic freedom and institutional convergence.* Working paper.

Glaeser, E. L., La Porta, R., Lopez-de Silanes, F., and Shleifer, A. 2004. Do institutions cause growth? *Journal of Economic Growth, 9*(3): 271–303.

Gwartney, J. D., and Lawson, R. A. 2003. The concept and measurement of economic freedom. *European Journal of Political Economy, 19*(3): 405–430.

Gwartney, J. D., Holcombe, R. G., and Lawson, R. A. 2006. Institutions and the impact of investment on growth. *Kyklos, 59*(2): 255–273.

Gwartney, J. D., Lawson, R. A., and Block, W. 1996. Economic freedom of the world, 1975–1995. Vancouver, BC: Fraser Institute.

Gwartney, J. D., Lawson, R. A., and Hall, J. 2015. *Economic freedom of the world: 2015 annual report.* Vancouver, BC: Fraser Institute.

Gwartney, J. D., Lawson, R. A., and Holcombe, R. G. 1999. Economic freedom and the environment for economic growth. *Journal of Institutional and Theoretical Economics, 155*(4): 643–663.

Hall, J. C., and Lawson, R. A. 2014. Economic freedom of the world: An accounting of the literature. *Contemporary Economic Policy, 32*(1): 1–19.

Hall, J. C., Lawson, R. A., and Wogsland, R. 2011. The European Union and economic freedom. *Global Economy Journal, 11*(3): 1–14.

Heckelman, J. 2015. Economic freedom convergence clubs. In R. Cebula, J. Hall, F. Mixon, and J. Payne (eds.), *Economic behavior, economic freedom, and entrepreneurship.* Northampton, MA: Edward Elgar.

Hirschman, A. O. 1978. Exit, voice, and the state. *World Politics, 31*(1): 90–107.

Keefer, P., and Knack, S. 1997. Why don't poor countries catch up? A cross-national test of an institutional explanation. *Economic Inquiry, 35*(3): 590–602.

Keefer, P., and Stasavage, D. 2003. The limits of delegation: Veto players, central bank independence, and the credibility of monetary policy. *American Political Science Review, 97*(3): 407–423.

Knack, S. 1996. Institutions and the convergence hypothesis: The cross-national evidence. *Public Choice, 87*(3–4): 207–228.

Knack, S., and Keefer, P. 1995. Institutions and economic performance: Cross-country tests using alternative institutional measures. *Economics & Politics, 7*(3): 207–227.

La Porta, R., Lopez-de Silanes, F., and Shleifer, A. 2008. The economic consequences of legal origins. *Journal of Economic Literature, 46*(2): 285–332.

La Porta, R., Lopez-de Silanes, F., Shleifer, A., and Vishny, R. 1999. The quality of government. *Journal of Law, Economics, and Organization, 15*(1): 222–279.

Lawson, R. A., and Clark, J. R. 2010. Examining the Hayek–Friedman hypothesis on economic and political freedom. *Journal of Economic Behavior & Organization, 74*(3): 230–239.

Leeson, P. T., and Dean, A. M. 2009. The democratic domino theory: An empirical investigation. *American Journal of Political Science, 53*(3): 533–551.

Leeson, P. T., Sobel, R. S., and Dean, A. M. 2012. Comparing the spread of capitalism and democracy. *Economics Letters, 114*(1): 139–141.

Lundström, S. 2005. The effect of democracy on different categories of economic freedom. *European Journal of Political Economy, 21*(4): 967–980.

Mankiw, N. G., Romer, D., and Weil, D. 1992. A contribution to the empirics of economic growth. *Quarterly Journal of Economics, 107*(2): 407–437.

Marshall, M. G., Gurr, T. R., and Jaggers, K. 2014. *Polity IV Project: Political Regime Characteristics and Transitions, 1800–2013.* Dataset.

Nattinger, M. C., and Hall, J. C. 2012. Legal origins and state economic freedom. *Journal of Economics and Economic Education Research, 13*(1): 25–32.

Pitlik, H., and Wirth, S. 2003. Do crises promote the extent of economic liberalization? An empirical test. *European Journal of Political Economy, 19*(3): 565–581.

Powell, B., and Nair, M. 2012. On the governance of "not being governed." *Review of Austrian Economics, 25*(1): 9–16.

Powell, B., and Ryan, M. 2006. Does development aid lead to economic freedom? *Journal of Private Enterprise, 22*(1): 1–21.

Rode, M., and Coll, S. 2012. Economic freedom and growth: Which policies matter the most? *Constitutional Political Economy, 23*(2): 95–133.

Rode, M., and Revuelta, J. 2015. The wild bunch! An empirical note on populism and economic institutions. *Economics of Governance, 16*(1): 73–96.

Sala-i-Martin, X. X. 1996. The classical approach to convergence analysis. *Economic Journal, 106*(437): 1019–1036.

Savoia, A., and Sen, K. 2012. *Do we see convergence in institutions? A cross-country analysis.* Working paper.

Scott, J. C. 2009. *The art of not being governed: An anarchist history of upland Southeast Asia.* New Haven, CT: Yale University Press.

Sheehan, K. M., and Young, A. T. 2014. It's a small world after all: Internet access and institutional quality. *Contemporary Economic Policy, 33*(4): 649–667.

Sobel, R. S., and Coyne, C. J. 2011. Cointegrating institutions: the time-series properties of country institutional measures. *Journal of Law and Economics, 54*(1): 111–134.

Stansel, D., Torra, J., and McMahon, F. 2014. *Economic freedom of North America 2014.* Vancouver, BC: Fraser Institute.

Stringham, E. P., and Miles, C. J. 2012. Repelling states: Evidence from upland Southeast Asia. *Review of Austrian Economics, 25*(1): 17–33.

Tiebout, C. M. 1956. A pure theory of local expenditures. *Journal of Political Economy, 64*(5): 416–424.

Vega-Gordillo, M., and Alvarez-Arce, J. L. 2003. Economic growth and freedom: A causality study. *Cato Journal, 23*(2): 199–216.

Williamson, C. R., and Mathers, R. L. 2011. Economic freedom, culture, and growth. *Public Choice, 148*(3–4): 313–335.

World Bank. 2015. *World development indicators.* Washington, DC: World Bank.

Wu, W., and Davis, O. A. 1999. The two freedoms, economic growth and development: An empirical study. *Public Choice, 100*(1–2): 39–64.

Young, A. T., and Sheehan, K. M. 2014. Foreign aid, institutional quality, and growth. *European Journal of Political Economy, 36*(C): 195–208.

Young, A. T., Higgins, M. J., and Levy, D. 2008. Sigma convergence versus beta convergence: Evidence from US country-level data. *Journal of Money, Credit and Banking, 40*(5): 1083–1093.

7 Crises and government

Some empirical evidence

Jamie Bologna Pavlik and Andrew T. Young

Introduction*

In September 2008, the world seemed to fall apart. What seemed like economic slowdown in 2007 deteriorated into financial crisis, first in the United States, and then in Europe and elsewhere. Since then, it has been hard to scan the headlines without reading about an economic crisis of some sort, somewhere. From 2008 to 2010, worldwide, there were 21 sovereign debt crises, 28 currency crises, and a staggering 46 banking crises.[1]

Governments often intervene in markets and implement policies intended to halt or mitigate crises. Recent interventions include the UK's 2008 bank rescue package, the 2009 American Recovery and Reinvestment Act (ARRA), and the European Union's 2008 Stimulus Plan. These interventions were all associated with increases in government expenditures and the scope of government decision-making and control. Are they exceptional or the rule? If they are the rule, are the increases in government size and scope temporary expedients or are they permanent?

We address these questions using data for up to 70 countries on economic crises from the 1960s through to 2010. We estimate the relationship between crises and changes in the size and scope of government over both five-year and ten-year horizons. Unlike previous studies that consider banking crises, we also consider sovereign debt, currency, and inflation crises.

Rahm Emanuel, then chief of staff to U.S. President-Elect Barack Obama, was quoted as saying, "You never want a serious crisis to go to waste."[2] His point (at least as it was widely interpreted) was that a crisis "creates a sense of urgency[;] actions that once appeared optional suddenly seem essential" (Seib 2008). In other words, a crisis facilitates political actions that, from the policymaker's perspective, would have been desirable regardless. Presumably, then, these political actions are not temporary expedients.

Economists have also argued that temporary crises are likely to result in permanent expansions of government. Higgs (1987) argues that, during a crisis, individuals' confidence in the efficiency of markets is shaken. The demand for government intervention increases as a result. Increasing the scope for government, in particular, can require a relaxing of constitutional constraints that tend to persist beyond the crisis period. Furthermore, people become accustomed to the more extensive government. For these reasons, Higgs argues that while expansion of government may recede after the crisis, it is unlikely to return to pre-crisis levels. There is a ratchet effect and the expansion of government has a *permanent* component.

Alternatively, Pitlik and Wirth (2003, p. 565) argue that it is "commonly shared wisdom among economists and political scientists . . . that crises promote the adoption of market-oriented reforms."[3] Pitlik and Wirth cite a number of examples in support of this view, including the reforms of Latin American countries at the beginning of the 1980s and the reforms of transition economies in the wake of the Soviet Union's demise.[4] According to this view, crises represent "moments of clarity" for politicians—realizations that bad policies need to be abandoned to avoid economic collapse (Harberger 1993; Williamson and Haggard 1994). Crises will result in a decrease in the size and scope of government.

Relatedly, Alesina and Drazen (1991) and Drazen and Grilli (1993) argue that particular reforms impose costs on particular special interests and that conflicts over the distribution of such costs delay reforms generally. Economies become "sclerotic," to use Olson's (1982) term. However, during a crisis, the more widely spread costs (that is, those associated with the continuation of bad policies) increase. This increases the likelihood that reforms occur.

Furthermore, there is a third possibility: crises lead to political polarization and, as a result, gridlock. This hampers both reforms and expansions of government. Mian, Sufi, and Trebbi (2014) report cross-country evidence suggesting that financial crises do lead to polarization and fractionalization. However, based on the information contained in the International Monetary Fund (IMF) structural reforms database (Abiad, Detragiache, and Tressel 2008), Ostry, Prati, and Spilimbergo (2009) report that the link between increased polarization/fractionalization and the likelihood of financial reforms is unclear. While Mian and colleagues (2014) focus on financial reforms (such as the liberalization of interest-rate controls), their gridlock argument may also be applicable to the size and scope of government more generally.

The relationship between crises and government is ultimately an empirical question. Moreover, that relationship may be different over the short run versus the long run. This would be the case if, for example, crises were associated with the sort of ratchet effect described by Higgs (1987).[5] With a ratchet effect, we would expect to see government expansion over the short run and then a smaller cumulative expansion over the long run. In this chapter, we consider the potential effects of crises over five-year and ten-year horizons using panel data. We also consider overall 40-year cross-section effects.[6] In addition to different time horizons, we consider measures of both the size and scope of government. Higgs (1991) notes that expenditures are only one margin along which government can expand. Furthermore, government interventions can be substitutes for expenditures.[7]

We find that the estimated effects of crises on government are largely insignificant, both statistically and economically. The estimated effects also differ greatly across the type of crisis in question. Our most robust finding is that, over the entire 40-year period considered (1970–2010), countries that spend more years in any type of crisis are associated with weaker legal systems and property rights. However, even these effects are economically modest. Overall, the evidence does not support a "one size fits all" theory of crises and government.

We proceed as follows. In the next section, we provide an overview of existing empirical studies on the relationship between crises and government size/scope. In doing so, we discuss our contribution vis-à-vis these existing studies. We then describe our data and subsequently provide the results of our analysis. The final section then concludes the chapter with some discussion.

Previous work

There are only a few studies that address the relationship between crises and the size/scope of government. For a sample of Latin American countries, Lora and Olivera (2004) report a positive relationship between severe episodes of inflation and negative growth in gross domestic product (GDP) and an index of structural reform.[8] For a broader sample of countries, Bruno and Easterly (1996) find that countries having experienced high inflation episodes are more likely to subsequently achieve low and stable inflation than moderate-inflation countries. Drazen and Easterly (2001) report similar findings, not only for inflation crises, but also for large increases in black-market premiums. However, both of these papers infer the occurrence of reforms from improved performance; they do not speak directly to changes in the size/scope of government.

The cross-country panel studies of Pitlik and Wirth (2003), de Haan, Sturm, and Zandberg (2009), and Baier, Clance, and Dwyer (2012) are most closely related to our work. Pitlik and Wirth (2003) report that episodes of severe GDP contraction and inflation are associated with subsequent increases in the Fraser Institute's Economic Freedom of the World (EFW) index. The EFW index serves as an inverse measure of government size and scope. Based on EFW data, de Haan and colleagues (2009) find that banking crises are associated with increases in government in the short run (that is, one year) but decreases in the longer run (that is, five years).[9] Baier and colleagues (2012) find that banking crises are associated with lower economic freedom scores up to ten years later.[10]

Relative to these studies, we make a number of contributions. First, we consider not only banking crises, but also currency crises, inflation crises, and sovereign debt crises (both external and internal). Debt crises are of particular interest given their prevalence both during and subsequent to the Great Recession. These include the well-publicized episodes in Greece, Ireland, and Portugal. Furthermore, sovereign debt crises may be perceived as failures of the public, rather than the private, sector; as such, one may suspect that they increase the likelihood of market-oriented reforms. Unlike banking crises, for example, sovereign debt crises may not weaken beliefs in market efficacy as Higgs (1987) describes.

Second, while we control for initial government size/scope, output gaps, and foreign aid flows as do de Haan and colleagues (2009), we additionally control for internal conflicts, oil rents, and shocks to the terms of trade that a country faces.

These variables are suggested by the existing literature on institutional change and may be important omitted variables in those authors' analysis.[11]

Third, we report the estimated effects of crises over both five-year and ten-year horizons. By doing so, we allow for potentially different short- and long-run effects. This is in contrast with de Haan and colleagues (2009), who treat five years as the long run, and Pitlik and Wirth (2003), who consider five-year periods only. Government interventions often take months to be instituted and years to be fully enacted. For example, the U.S. ARRA stimulus was not passed until February 2009. As of April 2010, still only 65% of the legislated ARRA spending had been announced and only about 60% of that total had actually been paid out (Young and Sobel 2013, table 1).[12] Also, crises often last for multiple years. The average banking crisis in our sample lasts 3.75 years and 37 of them are at least 5 years long.[13] We believe that it makes sense to define the long run as longer than the typical crisis episode.

While our benchmarks are five-year (short-run) and ten-year (long-run) horizons, we recognize that any such distinctions are arbitrary. We also report estimations based on annual changes in the data. Then we consider cross-sectional specifications where overall changes in measures of government size/scope during 1970–2010 are related to total years spent in crisis during 1961–2000. Reporting results over 1-, 5-, 10-, and 40-year horizons, we provide a thorough characterization of what the data tell us about crises and government.

Data

We have two benchmark panels. Each consists of data from the 1960s through to 2010 for 70 countries. The first panel is divided into eight time observations, each corresponding to a five-year period during which a crisis may be observed and one, to a subsequent five-year period during which a change in the size and/or scope of government is observed. For example, a crisis observation during 1966–70 is related to a 1970–75 change in the size and/or scope of government. The second panel is divided into four time observations, each corresponding to analogous ten-year periods. For example, a crisis observation during 1961–70 is related to a 1970–80 change in the size and/or scope of government.[14]

We believe that, in this context, our consideration of five-year and ten-year horizons as, respectively, the short run and the long run is reasonable. That being said, in addition to these benchmarks, we also consider two other perspectives: one significantly shorter run and the other significantly longer run. First, we consider the relationship between crises in a given year and changes in the size and scope of government in the subsequent year. Second, we examine a long cross-section in which the total number of years spent in crisis from 1961 to 2000 is related to changes in the size and scope of government over the 1970–2010 period.

Our data can be broken into four categories: measures of the size and scope of government; economic crises; additional controls; and instrumental variables.

Size and scope of government

From the Penn World Tables (PWTs), version 7.1 (Heston, Summer, and Aten 2012), we utilize the government consumption share of GDP (*G/GDP*) as a measure of the size of government. By the *size* of government, then, we refer specifically to the share of final goods and services that are ultimately purchased and put to purpose by the government.

To measure the scope of government, we utilize the Fraser Institute's EFW index constituent area scores (Gwartney, Lawson, and Hall 2012).[15] The EFW index is designed to capture the extents of "personal choice; voluntary exchange coordinated by markets; freedom to compete in markets; and protection of persons and their property by others" (Gwartney et al. 2012, p. 1). The index has five constituent sub-indices and we focus on three of these: legal system and security of property rights (*PROPERTY*); freedom to trade internationally (*TRADE*); and regulation (*REGULATION*).[16] By utilizing these three EFW area sub-indices, we conceive of the *scope* of government as the range of transactions on which it exerts an influence and the extent of that influence.

- *PROPERTY* measures the extent to which government is constrained by the rule of law or, alternatively, is able to expropriate resources.
- *TRADE* gauges the extent to which firms and individuals can trade with other countries freely versus the government determining which goods and services are and are not exchanged.
- *REGULATION* measures the extent to which individuals and firms are free to execute consumption and production plans or, alternatively, government plays an active role in constraining and otherwise shaping those plans.

For our government size measure (*G/GDP*), a larger value clearly corresponds to a larger government. Alternatively, each of the government scope measures (*PROPERTY, TRADE*, and *REGULATION*) is an index scored on a 0–10 scale, with 10 indicating the most economically free. Thus larger values correspond to *less* extensive government.

We will use changes in *G/GDP, PROPERTY, TRADE*, and *REGULATION* as dependent variables in our regressions. For the five-year panel, the observations will be changes over the 1970–75, 1975–80, 1980–85, 1985–90, 1990–95, 1995–2000, 2000–05, and 2005–10 time periods. For the ten-year panel, the analogous time periods will be 1970–80, 1980–90, 1990–2000, and 2000–10. Furthermore, in every regression we will control for the initial level of government size/scope (for example, when the 1970–75 or 1970–80 change in *PROPERTY* is the dependent variable, one of the regressors will be the 1970 value of *PROPERTY*).

Crises

We use the crisis dates described in Reinhart and Rogoff (2009, 2011). The Reinhart and Rogoff (henceforth RR) data is yearly and goes back to 1800 (though EFW index availability constrains us to use RR data only from the

1960s onward). Reinhart and Rogoff provide dates for five specific types of economic crisis: banking crises (*BANK*); sovereign debt crises—both external and internal (*DEBT_EXT* and *DEBT_INT*, respectively); currency crises (*CURRENCY*); and inflation crises (*INFLATION*). Reinhart and Rogoff (2008, appendix) provide a comprehensive discussion of the details and issues surrounding their criteria for dating crises.[17]

For a given five-year or ten-year period, we introduce controls for both the occurrence of a crisis and the duration of that crisis. For each type of crisis, we define *CRISIS* = 1 if a crisis occurred in a given five-year (ten-year) period and 0 otherwise; *CRISIS_DUR* = the duration of an observed crisis episode beginning in a given five-year (ten-year) period, where *CRISIS* represents *BANK, DEBT_EXT, DEBT_INT, CURRENCY*, and *INFLATION*.[18]

In our empirical specifications, crises occurring during a given time period are determinants of the changes in government size/scope during the subsequent time period. For example, in the five-year panel we consider the relationship between *BANK* and *BANK_DUR* for 1966–70 and the 1970–75 change in *G/GDP*. The analog in the ten-year panel is an estimation of the 1970–80 change in *G/GDP* on *BANK* and *BANK_DUR* for 1961–70.

Other controls

All of our estimations include the initial size/scope of government as a control.[19] We also include several additional controls. Following de Haan and colleagues (2009), we include a dummy variable that takes a value of 1 if the observation on the dependent value occurs during a period of economic distress. For each country in the sample, we take the entire 1961–2010 real GDP series from the PWTs and calculate trend values using a Hodrick–Prescott filter.[20] We assign the dummy variable a value of 1 if the annual output gap (trend minus actual value) ever became larger than 4% of actual GDP during the relevant time period.

Following Djankov and colleagues (2008), Young and Sheehan (2014), and Sheehan and Young (2015), we also control for foreign aid flows, oil production as a share of GDP, and terms–of–trade shocks. Foreign aid flows and oil reserves can create rent-seeking games that can lead to the corruption of institutions.[21] Terms–of–trade shocks can lead to political instability and social unrest, which in turn can lead to changes in the size/scope of government.

Foreign aid is measured by official development assistance (ODA) flows, data on which comes from the Organisation for Economic Co-operation and Development (OECD). We include ODA as a share of real GDP. We obtain data on oil production and prices from the BP Statistical Review of World Energy, Historical Data. Oil production is then taken as a share of a country's real GDP.[22] As terms–of–trade shock measures, we separately take the average values of negative and positive growth rates of the terms of trade over the relevant time periods. Considering positive and negative shocks separately acknowledges that their effects on political stability may be asymmetric. The data are from the World Bank's Net Barter Terms of Trade Index.

In addition, we control for the number of intra-state conflicts. These conflicts may be either a source of institutional change or persistence. Acemoglu (2003) argues that "theories of social conflict" are most appropriate for analyzing institutional change. However, while institutional change may be the goal of conflicts, Roland (2004) argues that conflicts can make it difficult for agents to the overcome collective action problems that need to be solved for institutional change to occur. From either perspective, controlling for intra-state conflict is likely to be important.[23]

Each of these additional controls—labeled, respectively, *GAP, ODA, OIL, POS_SHOCKS, NEG_SHOCKS*, and *CONFLICT*—are recorded for the time period over which we observe a change in the size/scope of government. For example, if our dependent variable is the change in *G/GDP* during 1970–80, then *ODA* would be the average foreign aid share of GDP during those same years, 1970–80. We also include country-level and period fixed effects in our estimations.

In some specifications, we also include an interaction between the initial (for the five-year or ten-year period) (log) real GDP per capita level and the crisis dummy. When discussing the ratchet hypothesis, Higgs (1987) is mainly referring to crisis situations occurring in the United States. In a high-income country like the United States, the government may be better able to expand in response to crises. However, in middle- to low-income countries, such as many of those in Pitlik and Wirth's (2003) analysis, reforms taking place after a crisis may have a greater tendency towards liberalizing. Consequently, the effect a crisis has on institutional change may be dependent on the country's income level.

Descriptions, sources, and summary statistics for variables introduced above are reported in Table 7.1. The mean values for the crises dummies can be interpreted as the share of observations where a crisis is recorded. Currency crises are by far the most prevalent type of crisis in our sample and occur in about 38% of the five-year observations and nearly 60% of the ten-year observations. Internal sovereign debt crises are the least frequently occurring, observed in only about 4% of five-year observations and less than 7% of ten-year observations. External sovereign debt crisis are more than twice as common as those that are internal. We also note that for the *PROPERTY, TRADE*, and *REGULATION* indices, a decent rule of thumb is that they all have mean values around 6 and standard deviations around 2.[24]

Results

Our initial specifications relate changes in a size/scope of government variable (*G/GDP, PROPERTY, TRADE*, or *REGULATION*) over a five-year or ten-year period to the occurrence and duration of a crisis type during the previous five-year or ten-year period. The initial value of the size/scope of government variable is included as an additional control, as are *GAP, ODA, OIL, POS_SHOCKS, NEG_SHOCKS*, and *CONFLICT*, as well as period

Table 7.1 Descriptions, sources, and summary statistics for variables included in regression analysis

Variable	Description	Source	Five-year		Ten-year	
			Mean	σ	Mean	σ
G/GDP	Government consumption share of GDP	PWTs	8.902	5.677	8.857	5.533
PROPERTY	Legal system and security of property rights score	Gwartney et al.	5.809	2.048	5.881	2.068
TRADE	Freedom to trade internationally score	Gwartney et al.	6.176	2.369	6.184	2.355
REGULATION	Regulation score	Gwartney et al.	6.049	1.377	6.064	1.370
BANK	1 if banking crisis; 0 otherwise	Reinhart & Rogoff	0.190		0.320	
DEBT_EXT	1 if sovereign debt crisis (external); 0 otherwise	Reinhart & Rogoff	0.108		0.200	
DEBT_INT	1 if sovereign debt crisis (internal); 0 otherwise	Reinhart & Rogoff	0.040		0.066	
CURRENCY	1 if currency crisis; 0 otherwise	Reinhart & Rogoff	0.378		0.580	
INFLATION	1 if inflation crisis; 0 otherwise	Reinhart & Rogoff	0.189		0.289	
TOTAL	Sum of the number of crises in a given period	Reinhart & Rogoff	0.930		1.511	
BANK_DUR	Duration (in years) of banking crisis	Reinhart & Rogoff	3.750	2.661	4.027	2.690
DEBT_EXT_DUR	Duration (in years) of sovereign debt crisis (external)	Reinhart & Rogoff	6.662	7.007	6.743	6.909
DEBT_INT_DUR	Duration (in years) of sovereign debt crisis (internal)	Reinhart & Rogoff	4.080	5.923	4.435	6.215
CURRENCY_DUR	Duration (in years) of currency crisis	Reinhart & Rogoff	2.496	3.484	3.089	4.040
INFLATION_DUR	Duration (in years) of inflation crisis	Reinhart & Rogoff	4.378	5.426	5.406	5.979
TOTAL_DUR	Sum of the duration (in years) of all crises	Reinhart & Rogoff	6.435	8.535	9.614	11.479
BANK_CROSS	Total number of years spent in banking crisis	Reinhart & Rogoff				
DEBT_EXT_CROSS	Total number of years spent in sovereign debt crisis (external)	Reinhart & Rogoff				

Variable	Description	Source				
DEBT_INT_CROSS	Total number of years spent in sovereign debt crisis (internal)	Reinhart & Rogoff				
CURRENCY_CROSS	Total number of years spent in currency crisis	Reinhart & Rogoff				
INFLATION_CROSS	Total number of years spent in inflation	Reinhart & Rogoff				
TOTAL_CROSS	Total number of years spent in crisis	Reinhart & Rogoff PWTs				
GAP	1 if real GDP deviation from trend ever > 4% actual GDP; 0 otherwise					
ODA	Average ratio of real official development assistance to real GDP	OECD; IMF; PWTs	0.008	0.018	0.008	0.017
OIL	Average ratio of real oil production to real GDP	BP; IMF; PWTs	0.018	0.053	0.017	0.050
POS_SHOCKS	Average of positive annual terms of trade growth observations	UN; IMF	0.076	0.083	0.084	0.074
NEG_SHOCKS	Average of negative annual terms of trade growth observations	UN; IMF	0.071	0.072	0.069	0.055
CONFLICT	Average number of intra-state conflicts	Dept. of Peace and Conflict Research	0.270	0.752	0.258	0.739
GDP	PPP converted (log) GDP per capita, at 2005 constant prices	Penn World Tables	12,051	11,449	12,160	11,616
AGRICULTURE	Value added of agriculture as a share of GDP	World Development Indicators	13.360	11.761	13.396	11.855
LIFE_EXPECTANCY	Life expectancy at birth, total number of years	World Development Indicators	67.878	9.723	67.828	9.913
INFANT_MORT	Infant mortality rate, per 1,000 live births	World Development Indicators	38.510	36.567	39.027	37.572

Notes: Summary statistics for crisis duration variables are calculated only for non-0 observations. Means are included for basic crisis dummy variables because they can be interpreted as the share of observations.

and country fixed effects. Recall that we interpret an increase in *G/GDP* as an increase in the size of government and decreases in *PROPERTY, TRADE,* or *REGULATION* as an increase in the scope of government.

All regressions are estimated by ordinary least squares (OLS). The probability of crisis may be a function of government size and/or scope. However, we control for the initial value of the government variable in all regressions. Given that, it is unclear that the *change* in the size and scope of government affects the probability of crisis. Endogeneity may also arise from the simultaneity of government size/scope and other dimensions of institutional quality. For example, Dzhumashev (2014) models a two-way relationship between government spending and corruption levels. The inclusion of period and country fixed effects, as well as our additional control variables, mitigates the risk of omitted variable bias in our estimates.[25]

We begin by reporting results based on crisis dummy and duration variables taken one type at a time (*BANK, DEBT_EXT, DEBT_INT, CURRENCY,* or *INFLATION*). Given the collinearity of crisis types, this seems a reasonable approach to understanding how the variation in each type of crisis series is related to changes in the size/scope of government. However, we subsequently report estimations including all crisis types together.

Table 7.2 reports five-year horizon results. To conserve space, Table 7.2 and subsequent tables report only the coefficients on crisis variables and initial government size/scope levels.[26] Crisis variables are seldom statistically different from 0. When statistically significant results do occur, the point estimate on crisis duration has the opposite sign than that of the crisis dummy. Taken at face value, this suggests—perhaps surprisingly—that longer crises have smaller effects on the size/scope of government than shorter crises. Also, the results do not support speaking generally about *the effect of crises on government.* *CURRENCY* is positively and significantly related to changes in government size. Alternatively, in most statistically significant cases, crisis dummies are associated with decreases in government scope (*DEBT_INT* for Δ*PROPERTY* and Δ*TRADE; BANK* for Δ*TRADE*). Furthermore, while internal debt crises are positively and significantly related to Δ*PROPERTY,* external debt crises are negatively and significantly related to the same variable.

For ten-year horizon results (Table 7.3), significant results for crisis variables remain few and far between. Again, duration variables tend to enter with the opposite signs as crisis dummies. (This is true for both cases in which duration and dummy are statistically significant: *CURRENCY* for Δ*G/GDP* and *INFLATION* for Δ*REGULATION*.) Statistically significant crisis dummies in Table 7.3 correspond to significant dummies in Table 7.2 in only two cases (*CURRENCY* for Δ*G/GDP* and *DEBT_EXT* for Δ*PROPERTY*). Neither case is consistent with a ratchet effect per se, but they are consistent with long-term increases in government size and scope. Currency crises are associated with increases in the size of government over the five-year horizon, but a larger increase over the ten-year horizon (five-year crisis dummy point estimate = 0.568; ten-year point estimate = 1.581). The relationship between external debt crises and Δ*PROPERTY* is similar (five-year crisis dummy point estimate = −0.397; ten-year point estimate = −0.702).

Table 7.2 Effects of crises and crises duration on five-year changes in government size/scope, 1976–2010 (full set of controls included)

| | Δ *Government* | | | |
	G/GDP	PROPERTY	TRADE	REGULATION
BANK	0.675	0.166	0.414*	0.199
	(0.600)	(0.176)	(0.216)	(0.136)
BANK_DUR	−0.311*	0.019	−0.097**	0.006
	(0.166)	(0.039)	(0.047)	(0.028)
Government(−1)	−0.574***	−0.591***	−0.519***	−0.577***
	(0.097)	(0.066)	(0.062)	(0.071)
Observations	298	287	291	285
R^2	0.398	0.464	0.518	0.427
DEBT_EXT	−0.713	−0.397**	0.122	0.183
	(0.644)	(0.173)	(0.245)	(0.111)
DEBT_EXT_DUR	0.231**	0.022	−0.030	−0.012
	(0.115)	(0.018)	(0.024)	(0.013)
Government(−1)	−0.551***	−0.618***	−0.525***	−0.581***
	(0.083)	(0.066)	(0.062)	(0.072)
Observations	298	287	291	285
R^2	0.443	0.464	0.511	0.410
DEBT_INT	−0.450	0.457*	0.843**	0.199
	(0.410)	(0.236)	(0.397)	(0.156)
DEBT_INT_DUR	0.058	−0.105***	−0.121*	−0.127***
	(0.139)	(0.039)	(0.063)	(0.030)
Government(−1)	−0.611***	−0.594***	−0.501***	−0.595***
	(0.121)	(0.070)	(0.058)	(0.080)
Observations	298	287	291	285
R^2	0.367	0.462	0.521	0.434
CURRENCY	0.568*	−0.138	0.012	0.013
	(0.307)	(0.138)	(0.133)	(0.068)
CURRENCY_DUR	−0.154***	0.039	−0.003	−0.003
	(0.054)	(0.025)	(0.043)	(0.016)
Government(−1)	−0.624***	−0.612***	−0.519***	−0.581***
	(0.111)	(0.069)	(0.065)	(0.074)
Observations	298	287	291	285
R^2	0.383	0.460	0.507	0.405
INFLATION	−0.785	0.023	−0.114	0.069
	(0.563)	(0.221)	(0.227)	(0.108)
INFLATION_DUR	0.089	−0.015	−0.009	−0.006
	(0.092)	(0.032)	(0.040)	(0.018)
Government(−1)	−0.605***	−0.599***	−0.529***	−0.582***
	(0.113)	(0.068)	(0.064)	(0.072)
Observations	298	287	291	285
R^2	0.375	0.454	0.509	0.406

Notes: *, **, *** denote statistical significance at the 10, 5, and 1% levels, respectively. Clustered standard errors are in parentheses. Period and country-level fixed effects and a constant are included in all regressions. Full set of controls (see Table 7.1) included, although not reported.

Table 7.3 Effects of crises and crises duration on ten-year changes in government size/scope, 1971–2010 (full set of controls included)

	Δ Government			
	G/GDP	PROPERTY	TRADE	REGULATION
BANK	0.574	0.053	−0.104	−0.018
	(0.620)	(0.242)	(0.332)	(0.195)
BANK_DUR	0.018	0.011	0.035	0.010
	(0.091)	(0.061)	(0.070)	(0.031)
Government(−1)	−1.040***	−0.961***	−0.849***	−0.949***
	(0.123)	(0.126)	(0.135)	(0.119)
Observations	151	143	146	142
R^2	0.724	0.516	0.671	0.612
DEBT_EXT	0.653	−0.702*	−0.100	−0.254
	(0.608)	(0.363)	(0.412)	(0.210)
DEBT_EXT_DUR	0.069	0.032	0.006	0.026
	(0.078)	(0.025)	(0.035)	(0.021)
Government(−1)	−1.029***	−0.989***	−0.862***	−0.924***
	(0.140)	(0.114)	(0.128)	(0.117)
Observations	151	143	146	142
R^2	0.738	0.540	0.670	0.620
DEBT_INT	1.499	−0.410	0.163	0.350
	(0.966)	(0.305)	(0.409)	(0.244)
DEBT_INT_DUR	−0.148**	0.039	−0.061	−0.009
	(0.061)	(0.026)	(0.068)	(0.015)
Government(−1)	−1.062***	−0.966***	−0.864***	−0.903***
	(0.122)	(0.113)	(0.121)	(0.126)
Observations	151	143	146	142
R^2	0.728	0.522	0.676	0.621
CURRENCY	1.581***	0.036	0.379	0.487**
	(0.591)	(0.331)	(0.351)	(0.220)
CURRENCY_DUR	−0.129***	0.007	−0.001	−0.024
	(0.047)	(0.030)	(0.029)	(0.022)
Government(−1)	−1.064***	−0.966***	−0.820***	−0.930***
	(0.123)	(0.128)	(0.127)	(0.105)
Observations	151	143	146	142
R^2	0.738	0.516	0.677	0.646
INFLATION	0.341	0.157	0.202	0.543***
	(0.789)	(0.306)	(0.376)	(0.190)
INFLATION_DUR	−0.010	0.015	0.023	−0.056***
	(0.053)	(0.031)	(0.032)	(0.020)
Government(−1)	−1.062***	−0.963***	−0.796***	−0.964***
	(0.132)	(0.116)	(0.115)	(0.086)
Observations	151	143	146	142
R^2	0.720	0.527	0.681	0.683

Notes: *, **, *** denote statistical significance at the 10, 5, and 1% levels, respectively. Clustered standard errors are in parentheses. Period and country-level fixed effects and a constant are included in all regressions. Full set of controls (see Table 7.1) included, although not reported.

Next, we report results that are analogous to those of Table 7.2 and 7.3 except that, instead of the crisis duration variable, we include an interaction between the crisis dummy and the initial (log) level of GDP per capita. Once again, statistically significant crisis variables and interactions are in short supply. In all cases in which the results are statistically significant, the coefficient on the interaction term has the opposite sign to that of the crisis dummy by itself. There are four statistically significant coefficient pairs each from the five-year and ten-year results. Based on them, Tables 7.4 and 7.5 report the marginal conditional effects (along with *p*-values) of crisis dummies for minimum, mean, and maximum *GDP* sample values. In all cases, the turning point for the sign of the effect is at GDP per capita value less than the sample mean (at most US$6,002—comparable to that of Algeria and Guatemala in 2010). Over the five-year horizon, *BANK* is positively (negatively) related to $\Delta GDP/G$ for high (low) income countries. The converse is true considering scope-of-government effects associated with *DEBT_EXT* and *INFLATION*. Over the ten-year horizon, the four reported cases are all regarding scope of government and the signs vary. None of the cases reported in Table 7.4 correspond to those reported in Table 7.5. Therefore, these results further indicate that the effect of a crisis on government size/scope is idiosyncratic.

Our last set of estimation results for our benchmark five-year and ten-year horizons are reported in Tables 7.6 and 7.7. Those results are from estimations that include all of the different crisis variables together. If collinearity does not inflate the standard errors too much, the results of these estimations will be

Table 7.4 Select conditional marginal effect of crises on five-year changes in government size/scope at specified levels of initial GDP per capita, 1976–2010 (full set of controls included)

Type of crisis		Initial level of GDP per capita			GDP value at sign turning point
		Min.	Mean	Max.	
		318	6,995	55,882	
Banking	d($\Delta G/GDP$)/dBANK	−3.728	0.334	3.067	5,431
	p-value	0.004	0.212	0.008	
External	d($\Delta PROP\_$ RIGHTS)/d(DEBT_EXT)	−1.314	0.080	1.018	6,002
	p-value	0.002	0.660	0.051	
External	d($\Delta TRADE$)/d(DEBT_EXT)	−1.669	0.404	1.799	4,023
	p-value	0.000	0.100	0.002	
Inflation	d($\Delta TRADE$)/d(INFLATION)	−1.341	0.197	1.232	4,712
	p-value	0.006	0.529	0.081	

Notes: Period and country-level fixed effects and a constant are included in all regressions. Full set of controls (see Table 7.1) included, although not reported.

Table 7.5 Select conditional marginal effect of crises on ten-year changes in government size/scope at specified levels of initial GDP per capita, 1971–2010 (full set of controls included)

Type of crisis		Initial level of GDP per capita			GDP value at sign turning point
		Min.	Mean	Max.	
		346	6,374	45,342	
Banking	d($\Delta TRADE$)/d($BANK$)	1.269	−0.234	−1.247	4,044
	p-value	0.103	0.355	0.096	
External	d($\Delta REGULATION$)/d($DEBT\_EXT$)	−0.883	0.260	1.030	3,287
	p-value	0.007	0.285	0.073	
Internal	d($\Delta PROP\_RIGHTS$)/d($DEBT\_INT$)	2.200	−0.646	−2.429	3,130
	p-value	0.094	0.073	0.060	
Inflation	d($\Delta PROP\_RIGHTS$)/d($INFLATION$)	−1.034	0.685	1.843	1,998
	p-value	0.095	0.004	0.007	

Notes: Period and country-level fixed effects and a constant are included in all regressions. Full set of controls (see Table 7.1) included, although not reported.

more reliable than those based on including one crisis type at a time.[27] Tables 7.6 and 7.7 contain a number of statistically significant results. We emphasize the fact that they contain all of the results, as described above in Tables 7.2 and 7.3.[28] Again, for the five-year horizon, the duration point estimates imply no negative effects on government scope for crises lasting about four years or longer. Over the ten-year horizon, currency and inflation crises are associated with decreases in government regulation.

In Table 7.8, we report the OLS results of regressions of the 1970–2010 changes in government size/scope variables on the total number of years spent in a given type of economic crisis from 1961 to 2000. Notably, every type of crisis variable is significantly and negatively related to a country's score of legal structure and property rights.[29] However, most of them are small. For example, the standard deviation of banking crises in our sample is about 2.7 years. Based on the point estimate, an additional 2.7 years spent in a banking crisis during 1961–2000 is associated with nearly a 0.5 point decrease in *PROPERTY*. The only case in which a sample standard deviation increase is associated with more than a 1-point decrease in *PROPERTY* is years spent in internal debt crisis. The point estimate (−0.621) implies that a sample standard deviation increase (of about 6 years) is associated with about a 3.7-point decrease in *PROPERTY*. There are also statistically significant and negative effects on *REGULATION* associated with *DEBT_EXT_CROSS, CURRENCY_CROSS*, and *INFLATION_CROSS* that are all very small.

Table 7.6 Effects of crises and crises duration on five-year changes in government size/scope, 1976–2010 (full set of controls included)

	Δ Government			
	G/GDP	PROPERTY	TRADE	REGULATION
BANK	0.601	0.275*	0.416*	0.184
	(0.691)	(0.153)	(0.210)	(0.132)
BANK_DUR	−0.246	−0.002	−0.111**	0.005
	(0.185)	(0.037)	(0.048)	(0.029)
DEBT_EXT	−0.726	−0.489**	0.013	0.194
	(0.811)	(0.198)	(0.264)	(0.116)
DEBT_EXT_DUR	0.223*	0.028	−0.027	−0.013
	(0.119)	(0.018)	(0.025)	(0.015)
DEBT_INT	−0.446	0.461**	0.917**	0.071
	(0.525)	(0.199)	(0.432)	(0.134)
DEBT_INT_DUR	0.227**	−0.099**	−0.143**	−0.120***
	(0.108)	(0.040)	(0.062)	(0.031)
CURRENCY	0.838**	−0.163	−0.024	−0.066
	(0.349)	(0.134)	(0.153)	(0.065)
CURRENCY_DUR	−0.224***	0.068***	0.010	0.003
	(0.062)	(0.024)	(0.045)	(0.018)
INFLATION	−1.035**	0.111	−0.013	0.061
	(0.500)	(0.221)	(0.278)	(0.116)
INFLATION_DUR	0.141*	−0.033	−0.004	−0.007
	(0.073)	(0.023)	(0.042)	(0.019)
Government(−1)	−0.541***	−0.605***	−0.508***	−0.611***
	(0.065)	(0.071)	(0.064)	(0.078)
Observations	298	287	291	285
R^2	0.501	0.502	0.538	0.461

Notes: *, **, *** denote statistical significance at the 10, 5, and 1% levels, respectively. Clustered standard errors are in parentheses. Period and country-level fixed effects and a constant are included in all regressions. Full set of controls (see Table 7.1) included, although not reported.

Conclusions

Responses to the Great Recession have been associated with increases in government expenditures and interventions. Are these responses typical? Do crises tend to increases in government size and scope? And are these effects temporary or do they have a permanent component?

Economists offer two contradictory perspectives on these questions. Higgs (1987) argues that crises weaken beliefs in the efficacy of markets, opening the opportunity for government to increase its expenditures and expand its interventions. Constitutional constraints relax, and people become accustomed to the greater size and scope of government. As a result, government "ratchets"

Table 7.7 Effects of crises and crises duration on ten-year changes in government size/scope, 1971–2010 (full set of controls included)

| | Δ *Government* | | | |
	G/GDP	PROPERTY	TRADE	REGULATION
BANK	0.949	0.197	−0.042	−0.088
	(0.683)	(0.265)	(0.337)	(0.175)
BANK_DUR	−0.012	0.020	0.042	0.011
	(0.096)	(0.068)	(0.072)	(0.028)
DEBT_EXT	−0.665	−1.169**	−0.796	−0.352*
	(0.746)	(0.454)	(0.536)	(0.184)
DEBT_EXT_DUR	0.125*	0.031	0.020	0.024**
	(0.070)	(0.027)	(0.037)	(0.012)
DEBT_INT	1.906	0.487	1.086**	0.512**
	(1.319)	(0.419)	(0.468)	(0.215)
DEBT_INT_DUR	−0.165	−0.018	−0.107*	−0.029*
	(0.101)	(0.030)	(0.055)	(0.016)
CURRENCY	1.904***	0.377	0.787**	0.464**
	(0.608)	(0.342)	(0.371)	(0.211)
CURRENCY_DUR	−0.215**	−0.054	−0.076	0.015
	(0.085)	(0.036)	(0.058)	(0.018)
INFLATION	−0.026	0.160	0.225	0.554***
	(0.834)	(0.320)	(0.430)	(0.148)
INFLATION_DUR	0.098	0.066*	0.074	−0.069***
	(0.083)	(0.037)	(0.054)	(0.015)
Government(−1)	−0.984***	−0.929***	−0.733***	−0.869***
	(0.117)	(0.127)	(0.127)	(0.092)
Observations	151	143	146	142
R^2	0.776	0.589	0.713	0.754

Notes: *, **, *** denote statistical significance at the 10, 5, and 1% levels, respectively. Clustered standard errors are in parentheses. Period and country-level fixed effects and a constant are included in all regressions. Full set of controls (see Table 7.1) included, although not reported.

up and never recedes to its pre-crisis size and scope. Alternatively, Pitlik and Wirth (2003) argue that deteriorating economic conditions encourage the adoption of market-oriented policies. This leads to a smaller government that exerts less influence over the economy.

Both perspectives are plausible and, ultimately, these are empirical questions. We attempt to estimate the effects of crises on government size/scope. We employ the Reinhart and Rogoff (2009) data on the five different types of crisis (banking, currency, inflation, internal debt, and external debt) and consider both five-year and ten-year periods, as well as a long cross-section from 1970 to 2010.

We report few robust results. In general, the estimated effects of crises on government size/scope are statistically insignificant. We find little to no

Table 7.8 Effects of total numbers of years spent in crisis from 1961 to 2000 on the change in government size/scope, 1970–2010 (full set of controls included)

	Δ *Government*			
	G/GDP	*PROPERTY*	*TRADE*	*REGULATION*
BANK_CROSS	−0.132	−0.169***	−0.017	0.009
	(0.145)	(0.053)	(0.034)	(0.036)
Government(−1)	−0.576***	−0.586***	−0.982***	−0.520***
	(0.131)	(0.170)	(0.063)	(0.116)
Observations	66	44	53	35
R^2	0.419	0.516	0.925	0.529
DEBT_EXT_CROSS	0.043	−0.107*	0.019	−0.096*
	(0.091)	(0.061)	(0.022)	(0.051)
Government(−1)	−0.582***	−0.695***	−0.978***	−0.619***
	(0.137)	(0.211)	(0.066)	(0.108)
Observations	66	44	53	35
R^2	0.410	0.474	0.926	0.620
DEBT_INT_CROSS	0.060	−0.621***	−0.008	−0.338
	(0.069)	(0.209)	(0.015)	(0.239)
Government(−1)	−0.576***	−0.628***	−0.986***	−0.580***
	(0.133)	(0.160)	(0.064)	(0.114)
Observations	66	44	53	35
R^2	0.410	0.542	0.925	0.590
CURRENCY_CROSS	0.006	−0.104***	0.001	−0.055**
	(0.043)	(0.029)	(0.013)	(0.021)
Government(−1)	−0.572***	−0.814***	−0.984***	−0.610***
	(0.131)	(0.179)	(0.066)	(0.108)
Observations	66	44	53	35
R^2	0.407	0.551	0.925	0.625
INFLATION_CROSS	0.009	−0.093***	0.003	−0.049*
	(0.043)	(0.030)	(0.013)	(0.026)
Government(−1)	−0.570***	−0.805***	−0.981***	−0.601***
	(0.130)	(0.189)	(0.066)	(0.120)
Observations	66	44	53	35
R^2	0.407	0.533	0.925	0.601

Notes: *·**, *** denote statistical significance at the 10, 5, and 1% levels, respectively. Heteroscedastic robust standard errors are in parentheses. Full set of controls (see Table 7.1) included, although not reported.

evidence of an increase in government size/scope resulting from a "ratchet up" effect or a decrease in government size/scope resulting from the adoption of market-oriented policies. A "punchline" of this chapter is that the effects of crisis episodes are, in large part, idiosyncratic. Whether a crisis results in increases or decreases in the size and scope of government is conditional on the particulars of time and country. Mian and colleagues' (2014) contention that crises lead to political polarization and gridlock is also not inconsistent with many of our findings. The estimated effects that we report are, for the most part, absent and/or contradictory across types of crisis and government measures. As best we can tell, a satisfactory "one size fits all" theory of government and crises does not exist.

Our long cross-section results give more uniform results across crisis types. We find that the cumulative years spent in crisis *of any type* are associated with statistically significant *decreases* in a country's quality of legal system and property rights. Over a significant period of time, a country that spends a larger number of years in crisis will, all else equal, end up having a government less constrained by the rule of law and more able to expropriate resources—as well as one that may regulate more. However, even in this case, the estimated effects are modest.

Notes

* "Crises and Government: Some Empirical Evidence," was originally published in *Contemporary Economic Policy* volume 34, no. 2, pp. 234–249, (2016). It is reprinted here with permission of the journal.
1 These numbers are based on dates of crises in Reinhart and Rogoff (2011).
2 Rahm Emanuel made the statement in November 2008. It was a rephrasing of economist Paul Romer's 2004 statement, "A crisis is a terrible thing to waste" (Rosenthal, 2009).
3 See also the literature review by Rodrick (1996).
4 New Zealand in the middle of the 1980s and the experience of the UK during Thatcher's administration are also cited.
5 Higgs (1987) points toward the U.S. experience during and following the Great Depression and World War II (WWII). Federal government spending increased from less than 3% of gross domestic product (GDP) to over 31% in 1945. Spending subsequently fell, but never below 14% of GDP (or 5.5 times the pre-crisis level). Higgs argues that both the short-run and long-run effects of the crises were positive, but that the long-run effect was less than the short-run effect. However, Holcombe (1993) argues that, after taking into account a positive trend in government growth during the twentieth century, the Great Depression/WWII crisis is not a statistically significant event in the data. In a related study, Sobel and Crowley (2012) find statistically significant ratchet effects for U.S. state and local government budgets in response to federal grants during the period 1995–2008.
6 We also report estimates of effects based on annual data. These are available in an appendix from the authors upon request.
7 For example, if a crisis creates unemployment, government may respond by increasing unemployment benefits (expenditures). However, it may alternatively raise minimum wage rates, institute policies that make it more difficult to fire workers, or nationalize firms. All of these alternatives represent increases in the scope of government. Given substitution possibilities, certain types of crisis may tend to affect government size, while others will tend to affect its scope.
8 Their index includes trade policy, tax policy, financial policy, privatization, and labor legislation components.

9 This is based on estimated effects on the Area 1 sub-index (size of government) and the Area 2 sub-index (legal structure and security of property rights).

10 Unlike de Haan et al. (2009) and Pitlik and Wirth (2003), Baier at al. (2012) use the level of, rather than the change in, the EFW index as their dependent variable. Using the change seems more natural given the underlying theories: starting from some level of government size/scope, a crisis induces either an increase or decrease in government size/scope. Baier et al. (2012) also do not control for the initial level of the EFW in their estimations, or for output gaps and foreign aid flows as do de Haan et al. (2009).

11 Djankov, Montalvo, and Reynal-Querol (2008) argue that both can create political instability that directly affects institutional quality (including government institutions). Several studies have reported that oil wealth is negatively correlated with the quality of political institutions (e.g. Ross 2001; Collier and Hoeffler 2009; Ramsey 2011; Tsui 2011), but Brückner, Ciccone, and Tesei (2012) find that, for countries with high oil wealth generally, positive oil price shocks lead to long-run increases in democratic institutions. Catão and Kapur (2006) find that terms-of-trade shocks are associated with increased risk of government default; hence they are expected to be a determinant of debt crises. Rodrick (1998) reports that the well-documented positive correlation between openness and government size is strongest when the terms of trade are most volatile; openness is also a function of the government. Dawson (2010) finds that terms-of-trade shocks are an important omitted variable in regressions of macroeconomic volatility on an index of economic freedom; macroeconomic volatility is presumably a determinant of the probability of a crisis.

12 Fannie Mae and Freddie Mac, the government-sponsored mortgage entities, were taken into conservatorship on September 7, 2008. The investment bank Lehman Brothers collapsed on September 15, 2008.

13 The median duration is three years.

14 Modeling crises in a given (five- or ten-year) period as affecting outcomes in a subsequent period is, to some extent, arbitrary. However, the construction of tractable balanced panels dictates a specification of timing, and we believe that the one assumed is reasonable. Furthermore, in an appendix available from the authors upon request, we also report results for our benchmark horizons weighting crises in the given period according to whether their occurrence is relative close to or far away from the subsequent period. Most of these results are statistically insignificant.

15 The EFW index has been positively linked to "good" economic outcomes such as income levels and growth rates, life expectancy, and subjective reporting of happiness. See Hall and Lawson (2014) for a comprehensive survey of empirical studies employing the EFW index as an independent variable.

16 The other two constituent areas are *size of government* and *sound money*. We focus on the government expenditure share as a measure of size of government, so we do not focus on the former area of the EFW. The *sound money* area is largely based on indicators of "the consistency of monetary policy (or institutions) with long-term price stability" (Gwartney et al. 2012, p. 6). Monetary policy is often perceived as fundamentally different than other government functions, and monetary policy agencies are often, by design, granted considerable institutional independence. Therefore we also do not focus on this latter area.

17 *BANK* is characterized by (i) bank runs that result in the public sector closing, merging, or taking over financial institutions, and/or (ii) the large-scale public sector closing, merging, or taking over of an important (or a group of important) financial institution(s). *DEBT_EXT* is characterized by a government's repudiation of, restructuring of, or outright default on external debt obligations (i.e. liabilities

to non-residents). *DEBT_INT* is characterized by a government's repudiation of, restructuring of, or outright default on internal debt obligations; in identification of internal crises, the freezing or forcible conversion (from dollars to local currency) of bank deposits are considered failures to meet internal debt obligations. *CURRENCY* is characterized by an annual depreciation relative to the U.S. dollar (or a relevant anchor currency) exceeding 15%. Finally, *INFLATION* is characterized by an annual inflation rate exceeding 20%.

18 De Haan et al. (2009) simply employ a dummy variable (1 if crisis; 0 otherwise). Pitlik and Wirth (2003) weight crisis observations by years and severity. The values of our duration variables are independent of the panel's time dimension. For example, in the RR data, the Central African Republic is coded as experiencing a banking crisis during all years from 1988 to 1999 inclusive. Because of this, 12 years is the recorded banking crisis duration for both our 1986–90 (five-year panel) and 1981–90 (ten-year panel) observations of the Central African Republic.

19 Ordinary least squares (OLS) estimates of dynamic panel models may suffer from Nickell (1981) bias. Therefore, in addition to OLS, we employ the system generalized method of moments (GMM) estimation procedure suggested by Arellano and Bover (1995), and Blundell and Bond (1998), using lags of (log) GDP per capita (*GDP*), agriculture share of GDP (*AGRICULTURE*), life expectancy at birth (*LIFE_EXPECTANCY*), and the infant mortality rate (*INFANT_MORT*) as exogenous instruments, as suggested by the literature (e.g. Djankov et al. 2008; Heckelman and Knack 2008; Young and Sheehan 2014). Hansen–Sargan statistics do not reject the exogeneity null. However, these tests are unreliable in the presence of heteroskedasticity and a large number of instruments; therefore we emphasize the results that are reported based on OLS estimates and show that they do not change in any meaningful way when employing GMM. These GMM robustness results are available in an appendix available from the authors upon request.

20 The smoothing parameter for the HP filter is assigned a value of 6.25—typical for applications using annual data.

21 Svensson (2000) reports that aid flows are associated with greater corruption; Rajan and Subramanian (2007) find that aid is associated with decreased governance quality. Particularly relevant to this study, Heckelman and Knack (2008) and Young and Sheehan (2014) report negative relationships between aid and EFW index scores. (Alternatively, Heckelman and Knack 2009 report that aid does not affect overall EFW scores.) Isham et al. (2005) find that point natural resources are associated with deteriorations in policies and institutional quality.

22 Official development assistance flows are converted into 2005 U.S. dollars using the World Import Unit Value index from the International Monetary Fund (IMF). Oil production is reported in barrels and oil prices are given in 2009 U.S. dollars that we subsequently convert into 2005 U.S. dollars, also using the World Import Unit Value index.

23 Relatedly, O'Reilly and Powell (2015) focus on the occurrence of wars in a cross-country panel covering the period 1965–2010. They find that wars are associated with an increase in the scope of government regulation (measured by EFW area). These increases outlast the war episodes. Since Higgs (1987) notes WWII as an important source of a ratchet effect in U.S. government, O'Reilly and Powell's work evaluates the Higgs hypothesis from a different (and perhaps more supportive) perspective than the present chapter.

24 Note, however, that *REGULATION* has a bit less variation than the other two indices; its sample standard deviation is about 1.375. Despite this, mean of 6; standard deviation of 2 is easy to keep in mind and will not lead one too far astray quantitatively.

25 In the previous draft of this chapter, we also report results based on the GMM estimation procedure suggested by Arellano and Bover (1995) and Blundell and Bond (1998). As additional instruments, we employ four variables common in the institutional change literature (e.g. Djankov et al. 2008; Heckelman and Knack 2008; Young and Sheehan 2014). These are the lags of (log) GPD per capita (*GDP*), the agricultural share of GDP (*AGRICULTURE*), life expectancy at birth (*LIFE_EXPECTANCY*), and the infant mortality rate (*INFANT_MORT*). In the sense that the estimated effects of crises on government are largely insignificant, the GMM results are consistent with those produced by OLS. The GMM results are included in an appendix available from the authors upon request.

26 Full results are contained in an appendix available from the authors upon request.

27 Unfortunately, system GMM estimations-based instrumenting for levels and first-differences of all of the crisis variables together are not possible.

28 As with the OLS result from Table 7.3, *CURRENCY_DUR* does not enter statistically significantly.

29 The long cross-section has the virtue of not relying as heavily on arbitrary imposition of structure on the timing of effects. Focusing on the long cross-sectional variation, we run the risk of emphasizing (non-causal) correlations between institutional quality and the frequency with which a country has experienced crises, rather than the within-country effect of crises on institutional quality described in the previous estimations. That said, these correlations are interesting in and of themselves.

References

Abiad, A., Detragiache, E., and Tressel, T. 2008. *A New Database of Financial Reforms.* International Monetary Fund (IMF) Working Paper 08/266.

Acemoglu, D. 2003. Why not a political Coase theorem? Social conflict, commitment, and politics. *Journal of Comparative Economics, 31*(4), 620–652.

Alesina, A., and Drazen, A. 1991. Why are stabilizations delayed? *American Economic Review, 81*(5), 1170–1188.

Arellano, M., and Bover, O. 1995. Another look at the instrumental variable estimation of error-component models. *Journal of Econometrics, 68*(1), 29–51.

Baier, S. L., Clance, M., and Dwyer, G. P. 2012. Banking crises and economic freedom. In J. Gwartney, R. Lawson, and J. C. Hall (eds.), *Economic Freedom of the World: 2012 Annual Report.* Vancouver, BC: Fraser Institute.

Blundell, R., and Bond, S. 1998. Initial conditions and moment restrictions in dynamic panel data models. *Journal of Econometrics, 87*(1), 115–143.

Brückner, M., Ciccone, A., and Tesei, A. 2012. Oil price shocks, income, and democracy. *Review of Economics and Statistics, 94*(2), 389–399.

Bruno, M., and Easterly, W. 1996. Inflation's children: tales of crises that beget reforms. *American Economic Review, 86*(2), 213–217.

Catão, L., and Kapur, S. 2006. Volatility and the debt-intolerance paradox. *IMF Staff Papers, 53*(2), 195–218.

Collier, P., and Hoeffler A. 2009. Testing the neocon agenda: democracy in resource-rich societies. *European Economic Review, 53*(3), 293–308.

Dawson, J. W. 2010. Macroeconomic volatility and economic freedom: a preliminary analysis. In J. Gwartney, R. Lawson, and J. C. Hall (eds.) *Economic Freedom of the World: 2010 Annual Report.* Vancouver, BC: Fraser Institute.

De Haan, J., Sturm, J.-E., and Zandberg, E. 2009. The impact of financial and economic crises on economic freedom. In J. Gwartney and R. Lawson (eds.) *Economic Freedom of the World: 2009 Annual Report*. Vancouver, BC: Fraser Institute.

Djankov, S., Montalvo, J. G., and Reynal-Querol, M. 2008. The curse of aid. *Journal of Economic Growth*, *13*(3), 169–194.

Drazen, A., and Easterly, W. 2001. Do crises induce reform? Simple empirical tests of conventional wisdom. *Economics and Politics*, *13*(2), 129–157.

Drazen, A., and Grilli, V. 1993. The benefit of crises for economic reforms. *American Economic Review*, *83*(3), 598–607.

Dzhumashev, R. 2014. The two-way relationship between government spending and corruption and its effects on growth. *Contemporary Economic Policy*, *32*(2), 403–419.

Gwartney, J., Lawson, R., and Hall, J. C. 2012. *Economic Freedom of the World: 2012 Annual Report*. Vancouver, BC: Fraser Institute.

Hall, J. C., and Lawson, R. A. 2014. Economic Freedom of the World: an accounting of the literature. *Contemporary Economic Policy*, *32*(1), 1–19.

Harberger, A. 1993. The search for relevance in economics. *American Economic Review*, *83*(2), 1–17.

Heckelman, J. C., and Knack, S. 2008. Foreign aid and market-liberalizing reform. *Economica*, *75*(299), 524–548.

Heckelman, J. C., and Knack, S. 2009. Aid, economic freedom, and growth. *Contemporary Economic Policy*, *27*(1), 46–53.

Heston, A., Summer, R., and Aten, B. 2012. *Penn World Table Version 7.1*. Center for International Comparisons for Production, Income, and Prices at the University of Pennsylvania.

Higgs, R. 1987. *Crisis and Leviathan: Critical Episodes in the Growth of American Government*. New York: Oxford University Press.

Higgs, R. 1991. Eighteen problematic propositions in the analysis of the growth of government. *Review of Austrian Economics*, *5*(1), 3–40.

Holcombe, R. G. 1993. Are there ratchets in the growth of federal government spending? *Public Finance Review*, *21*(1), 33–47.

Isham, J., Woodcock, M., Pritchett, L., and Busby, G. 2005. The varieties of resource experience: natural resource export structures and the political economy of economic growth. *World Bank Economic Review*, *19*(2), 141–174.

Lora, E., and Olivera, M. 2004. What makes reforms likely: political economy determinants of reforms in Latin America. *Journal of Applied Economics*, *7*(1), 99–135.

Mian, A., Sufi, A., and Trebbi, F. 2014. Resolving debt overhang: political constraints in the aftermath of financial crises. *American Economic Journal: Macroeconomics*, *6*(2), 1–28.

Nickell, S. J. 1981. Biases in dynamic models with fixed effects. *Econometrica*, *49*(6), 1417–1426.

O'Reilly, C., and Powell, B. 2015. *War and the Growth of Government*. SSRN Working Paper.

Olson, M. 1982. *The Rise and Decline of Nations*. New Haven, CT: Yale University Press.

Ostry, J., Prati, A., and Spilimbergo, A. 2009. *Structural Reforms and Economic Performance in Advanced and Developing Economies*. International Monetary Fund (IMF) Occasional Paper 268.

Pitlik, H., and Wirth, S. 2003. Do crises promote the extent of liberalization? An empirical test. *European Journal of Political Economy*, *19*(3), 565–581.

Rajan, R., and Subramanian, A. 2007. Does aid affect governance? *American Economic Review*, 97(2), 322–327.

Ramsey, K. W. 2011. Revisiting the resource curse: natural disasters, the price of oil, and democracy. *International Organization*, 65(3), 507–529.

Reinhart, C. M., and Rogoff, K. S. 2008. *This Time Is Different: A Panoramic View of Eight Centuries of Financial Crises*. NBER Working Paper 13882.

Reinhart, C. M., and Rogoff, K. S. 2009. *This Time It Is Different: Eight Centuries of Financial Folly*. Princeton, NJ: Princeton University Press.

Reinhart, C. M., and Rogoff, K. S. 2011. From financial crash to debt crisis. *American Economic Review*, 101(5), 1676–1706.

Rodrick, D. 1996. Understanding economic policy reform. *Journal of Economic Literature*, 34(1), 9–41.

Rodrick, D. 1998. Why do more open economies have larger governments? *Journal of Political Economy*, 106(5), 997–1032.

Roland, G. 2004. Understanding institutional change: fast-moving and slow-moving institutions. *Studies in Comparative International Development*, 38(4), 109–131.

Rosenthal, J. 2009. A terrible thing to waste. *New York Times Magazine*, July 31.

Ross, M. 2001. Does oil hinder democracy? *World Politics*, 53(3), 325–361.

Seib, G. F. 2008. In crisis, opportunity for Obama. *Wall Street Journal*, November 21.

Sheehan, K. M., and Young, A. T. 2015. It's a small world after all: Internet access and institutional quality. *Contemporary Economic Policy*, 33(4), 649–667.

Sobel, R. S., and Crowley, G. R. 2012. Do intergovernmental grants create ratchets in state and local taxes? *Public Choice*, 158(1–2), 167–187.

Svensson, J. 2000. Foreign aid and rent-seeking. *Journal of International Economics*, 51(2), 437–461.

Tsui, K. K. 2011. More oil, less democracy: evidence from worldwide crude oil discoveries. *Economic Journal*, 121(551), 89–115.

Williamson, J., and Haggard, S. 1994. The political conditions for economic reform. In J. Williamson (ed.), *The Political Economy of Policy Reform*. Washington, DC: Institute for International Economics.

Young, A. T., and Sheehan, K. M. 2014. Foreign aid, institutional quality, and growth. *European Journal of Political Economy*, 36(C), 195–208.

Young, A. T., and Sobel, R. S. 2013. Recovery and reinvestment act spending at the state level: Keynesian stimulus or distributive politics? *Public Choice*, 155(3–4), 449–468.

8 Does immigration impact institutions?

*J. R. Clark, Robert Lawson, Alex Nowrasteh,
Benjamin Powell and Ryan Murphy*

Introduction*

The idea that international trade in goods and services increases efficiency and the long-run wealth of a nation is one of the most established principles of economics. However, the basic analytical framework driving the theory, comparative advantage, applies equally to international trade in labor as it does in goods and services (Freeman, 2006). But international trade in labor, immigration or emigration, differs in one important way from tradable goods and services trade: goods and services that move across borders cannot vote, protest, riot, or otherwise impact the public policies of the countries they move to, but immigrants can.

Institutions are an important fundamental cause of economic development (Rodrik, Subramanian, and Trebbi, 2004). As Adam Smith reportedly wrote:

> Little else is requisite to carry a state to the highest degree of opulence from the lowest barbarism, but peace, easy taxes, and a tolerable administration of justice: all the rest being brought about by the natural course of things.
> (Canaan, 1904: n.p.)

Borjas challenges the literature that claims there are trillions of dollars of gains available to the world economy (Clemens, 2011) from open borders because of the negative impact immigration could have on institutions. He asks, "What would happen to the institutions and social norms that govern economic exchanges in specific countries after the entry/exit of perhaps hundreds of millions of people" (Borjas, 2015: 3)? In a recent book, Borjas (2014: 169) succinctly states the problem and the state of our knowledge about it:

> As the important work of Acemoglu and Robinson (2012) suggests, "nations fail" mainly because of differences in political and economic institutions. For immigration to generate substantial global gains, it must be the case that billions of immigrants can move to the industrialized economies without importing the "bad" institutions that led to poor economic conditions in the source countries in the first place. It seems inconceivable that the North's infrastructure would remain unchanged after the admission of billions of

new workers. Unfortunately, remarkably little is known about the political and cultural impact of immigration on the receiving countries, and about how institutions in these receiving countries would adjust to the influx.

Borjas provides a number of simulations showing how varying degrees of importation of bad institutions impact the projected global gain from unrestricted immigration. He shows that these "general equilibrium effects can easily turn a receiving country's expected (static) windfall from unrestricted migration into an economic debacle" (Borjas, 2015: 21). As valuable as Borjas's simulations might be in highlighting the potential problem of immigrants importing inefficient institutions to richer countries, he offers no empirical evidence that this negative externality does in fact exist.

Collier (2013) shares Borjas's fears. He worries that immigrants might import both the institutions and cultural characteristics that are responsible for their former poverty at home: "Migrants are essentially escaping from countries with dysfunctional social models . . . The cultures—or norms and narratives—of poor societies, along with their institutions and organizations, stand suspected of being the primary cause of their poverty" (Collier, 2013: 34). Collier offers anecdotes of these impacts in Great Britain, but offers no systematic examination of whether the hypothesized negative effects actually materialize. This chapter is the first attempt to examine empirically whether immigrants import poor institutions from their countries of origin to recipient countries.

Borjas and Collier are both somewhat vague about exactly which institutions immigration could undermine. But their concern is clearly that, once undermined, the production function in destination countries will be damaged. A large literature has shown that institutions of economic freedom are important for economic growth. For example, Barro (1996) finds that the rule of law and free markets contribute to economic growth, but finds that democratic institutions have a "weakly negative" impact on growth. Barseghyan (2008) finds that entry barriers have large negative effects on total factor productivity. Many papers find that measures of economic freedom correlate positively with cross-country measures of economic growth (e.g. de Haan and Sturm 2000; Gwartney, Holcombe, and Lawson 2006). Dawson (2003) and Justesen (2008) essentially find that economic freedom Granger-causes economic growth. For surveys of this growing empirical literature, see de Haan, Lundstrom, and Sturm (2006), and Hall and Lawson (2013).[1]

We examine how migration impacts countries' economic institutions using the Economic Freedom of the World (EFW) index (Gwartney, Lawson, and Hall 2013). That index does not include any direct measure of the restrictiveness of immigration policies themselves. Although migration restrictions are not explicitly measured in the index, it is worth noting that immigration restrictions are, in and of themselves, restrictions on economic freedom. Migration restrictions reduce the freedom to trade internationally because they impede international trade in services (Area 4). Although Area 4 of the EFW index is the most likely place for immigration restrictions to appear, they could be reflected in other areas as well. Migration restrictions are a form of labor market regulation because they prohibit employers from contracting with prospective foreign-born employees whom they may prefer to hire (Area 5). Finally, as Meissner and colleagues (2013) have shown, the U.S. federal government spends more on border enforcement than on all other federal law enforcement combined, so migration restrictions may directly impact the amount of money the federal government spends (Area 1).

There is an enormous literature investigating the impact of immigration on the welfare of a native-born population. Leeson and Gochenour's (2015) and Kerr and Kerr's (2011) recent surveys, like prior surveys (e.g. Friedberg and Hunt 1995), acknowledge conflicting empirical results in the literature, but find the general consensus to be that current levels of immigration bring small, but positive, increases in the overall income of native-born citizens in recipient countries.[2] Some evidence exists of a negative impact on the least-skilled native-born workers, who are direct substitutes for low-skilled immigrants, but even in these cases the empirical magnitude is small (Kerr and Kerr 2011). Regardless, the economic gains to the world economy, and the immigrants themselves, can be quite large (Clemens 2011). Despite the size of the immigration literature, however, very little research has focused on how immigration can impact the institutional environment of recipient countries.

What research has been conducted on the impact of immigration—or on racial/ethnic heterogeneity more generally—has usually focused on immigrants' impact on the welfare state or provision of public goods. In each case, competing theoretical hypotheses and/or interpretations of the empirical studies are possible concerning how immigration would impact economic freedom on these margins.

Welfare and other public assistance programs typically are more generous in recipient nations than those in immigrants' homelands. Borjas (1999) and others have argued that these welfare benefits can be magnets that attract immigrants. The obvious question is how immigrants might impact levels of taxation and the welfare and social spending programs of the recipient nations.[3] Immigrants tend to have incomes below that of the median resident of developed countries. One hypothesis is that redistributionist policies in recipient nations will expand because immigrants will constitute a voting bloc (or social pressure group, if not allowed to vote) that agitates for higher taxes and greater redistribution. An alternative hypothesis is that welfare states will shrink because the native-born population will be less willing to have a large welfare state once many of the benefits are going to immigrants rather than to the native-born population.

Alesina and Glaeser (2004) argue that fractionalization and ethnic heterogeneity are the main reasons why the United States has a smaller welfare state than most Western European countries. The clear implication for this research is that if immigration leads to greater heterogeneity, it should shrink welfare states. Razin, Sadka, and Swagel (2002) propose a median voter model that relies on relative income positions, rather than ethnic fractionalization, to predict that native-born taxpayers will shift their preferences away from high-tax, high-benefits welfare policy more than immigrants, who join the pro-tax, pro-benefits coalition at the bottom of the income distribution. They study 11 European countries from

1974 to 1992, and find that a larger share of low-education immigrants in the population leads to smaller social transfers and lower rates of taxation on labor.

However, other scholarship disputes whether immigration reduces the size of the welfare state. Banting and Kymlicka (2006) point out that most of the evidence on fractionalization comes from sub-Saharan Africa and the United States. In the United States, much of the fractionalization comes from African Americans, whose ancestors were brought to the country as slaves rather than came as voluntary immigrants. They argue that it is a mistake to extrapolate too much from studies about immigration and welfare states.

A greater demand for public education is another way in which immigration might increase the size of government. Greer (1972), Everheart (1977), Butts (1978), Meyer and colleagues (1979), Ralph and Rubinson (1980), and Bowles and Gintis (2011) all argue that immigration to the United States increased the demand for public education—particularly from native-born Protestants, who wanted public schools to assimilate immigrant groups that came from Catholic backgrounds.

A literature in sociology finds that immigration heightens people's perceptions of greater risk of unemployment (despite the consensus of the economics literature that there is no such effect) and that people favor a more generous social safety net as a result (Svallfors 1997; Kunovich 2004; Finseraas 2008; Burgoon, Koster, and van Egmond 2012; Ervasti and Hjerm 2012).[4] Brady and Finnigan (2013) offer the most comprehensive and recent of these studies. They look at the effect of both the stock and the flow of immigrants on six measures of the population's views of the welfare state from 1996 to 2006. Their evidence fails to support the view that immigrants make the native-born more hostile to the welfare state and provides some evidence in support of the view that immigration makes the native-born desire the government to provide a more generous social safety net.

Ethnic fragmentation may impact governance institutions other than welfare state spending. Easterly and Levine (1997) find a negative relationship across countries between ethnic diversity and the shares of government-provided goods, such as schooling, electricity, roads, and telephones. Similarly, Alesina, Baqir, and Easterly (1999) find a negative correlation in U.S. cities, metropolitan areas, and counties between ethnic fragmentation and shares of spending on government-provided goods such as trash pick-up, roads, sewers, and education. These findings could be interpreted as support for the view that government will be smaller (and economic freedom higher) when there is greater fractionalization, but they could also be interpreted as indicating that the public goods of the rule of law and security of property rights will be weaker (and thus economic freedom lower) when fragmentation is greater.[5]

Potentially the largest impact that immigrants could have on the well-being of the native-born populations of recipient countries runs through their impact on countries' institutional environments. This chapter is the first to examine empirically the impact of immigration on institutions using a broad measure of economic freedom that has been shown to be associated with improved economic outcomes. The next section describes our data and methodology. We then outline our results and the final section concludes.

Data and methodology

Our institutional measure is taken from the Economic Freedom of the World annual report by Gwartney and colleagues (2013). The EFW index measures the consistency of a nation's policies and institutions with economic freedom. The report incorporates 43 variables across five broad areas:

1 Size of Government;
2 Legal Structure and Property Rights;
3 Access to Sound Money;
4 Freedom to Trade Internationally; and
5 Regulation of Credit, Labor, and Business.

At its most basic level, the EFW index measures the extent to which individuals and private groups are free to buy, sell, trade, invest, and take risks without interference by the state. To score high on the EFW index, a nation must keep taxes and public spending low, protect private property rights, maintain stable money, keep its borders open to trade and investment, and exercise regulatory restraint in the marketplace. Area 1 of the EFW index, "Size of Government," is of particular interest since it relates directly to the literature debating the impact of immigrants on the welfare state.

Our data on immigrant stocks come from the United Nation's International Migrant Stock by Destination and Origin data series (World Bank 2013). The stock of immigrants, expressed as a share of the population, is the main variable of interest. The percentage of immigrants in the population varied from a low of 0.03% in China to a high of 76.96% in Kuwait. The stock of immigrants from Organisation for Economic Co-operation and Development (OECD) and non-OECD countries was also entered to see whether immigrants from poorer countries impact economic freedom differently than immigrants from richer countries. Finally, we used the net inflow of immigrants during the period as an additional way of measuring the scale of immigration.

Our objective is to determine how immigration, measured either as the share of the immigrant population at the beginning of the period or as net inflows over the period, impacts the level of economic freedom at the end of the period. The data cover the 1990–2011 time frame. In the baseline regressions, we include a country's initial level of economic freedom in 1990 to control for various long-run historical, cultural, economic, and other factors that influence the level of freedom. Additional controls for political liberalism (measured using Polity IV) and per capita income, both at the beginning and the end of the period, are included as well. In our baseline regressions, entering both the beginning stock of immigrants and the flow of immigrants over time should alleviate concerns about endogeneity. Although increases in freedom may attract more immigrants, this would impact only their flow. It is less plausible that the beginning stock of immigrants, which was accumulated over decades of migration, came in expectation of future increases in economic freedom that would occur decades later.

Table 8.1 Descriptive statistics of primary data set

Variable	Obs.	Mean	SD	Min.	Max.
Economic freedom, 1990	110	5.698	1.354	2.690	8.730
Economic freedom, 2011	110	6.866	0.923	3.930	8.970
Immigrant percentage	110	0.074	0.123	0.000	0.770
OECD immigrant percentage	110	0.014	0.031	0.000	0.220
Non-OECD immigrant percentage	110	0.060	0.117	0.000	0.754
Immigrant net inflow, 1990–2010	110	0.078	0.336	−0.100	3.327
Polity, 1990	103	2.631	7.280	−10.000	10.000
Polity, 2011	102	5.500	5.310	−8.000	10.000
Log GDP (PPP) per capita, 1990	106	3.859	0.529	2.733	5.063
Log GDP (PPP) per capita, 2011	108	4.019	0.551	2.817	4.949
Area 1: Size of Govt., 2011	109	6.514	1.280	3.640	9.023
Area 1: Size of Govt., 1990	108	5.551	1.520	1.999	9.312
Area 2: Legal System, 2011	109	5.596	1.706	2.154	8.907
Area 2: Legal System, 1990	105	5.311	1.923	1.953	8.347
Area 3: Sound Money, 2011	109	8.122	1.3940	3.222	9.775
Area 3: Sound Money, 1990	109	6.430	2.411	0.000	9.794
Area 4: Int'l Trade, 2011	109	7.061	1.1809	1.782	9.356
Area 4: Int'l Trade, 1990	107	5.436	2.358	0.000	9.970
Area 5: Regulation, 2011	109	7.008	1.032	4.345	9.278
Area 5: Regulation, 1990	109	5.691	1.473	1.578	9.430

In addition, we run a set of difference-in-difference regressions that are even less subject to endogeneity concerns. The difference-in-difference regressions help to alleviate simultanity concerns about underlying unmeasured factors that may cause interventions into both migration freedom, as well as other economic freedoms. Table 8.1 contains descriptive statistics.

Results

Table 8.2a reports our core results for a cross-section of 110 countries. As expected, the level of economic freedom in 1990 is associated with greater economic freedom in 2011. Our main finding is that a larger percentage of immigrants in the population in 1990 is associated with a higher level of economic freedom in 2011. Specifically, in Regression 1, we find that a 1 standard deviation (*SD*) higher immigrant stock in 1990 is associated with a small, but positive, 0.14-unit higher score for economic freedom in 2011, or about 0.15*SD*. The impact of OECD and non-OECD immigrant shares was positive, although the coefficient is significant only for non-OECD immigrants (Regression 2). Finally, the net inflow of immigrants during the period, as opposed to the stock at the beginning of the period, was included, but is insignificant in the baseline regressions in Table 8.2a.

Table 8.2 (a) Economic freedom and immigration

Regression	1	2	3	4	5
LHS	*EFW, 2011*	*EFW, 2011*	*EFW, 2011*	*EFW, 2011*	*EFW, 2011*
Economic freedom, 1990	0.371*** (0.055)	0.357*** (0.062)	0.389*** (0.054)	0.371*** (0.056)	0.354*** (0.059)
Immigrant stock, 1990	1.130* (0.607)			1.073 (0.775)	0.980 (0.783)
OECD immigrant stock, 1990		2.484 (2.684)			
Non-OECD immigrant stock, 1990		1.067* (0.621)			
Immigrant net inflow, 1990–2010			0.270 (0.218)	0.033 (0.277)	0.993 (1.104)
Flow–stock interaction					−1.367 (1.522)
Constant	4.667*** (0.311)	4.732*** (0.337)	4.628*** (0.314)	4.670*** (0.314)	4.744*** (0.325)
Adjusted R^2	0.362	0.357	0.350	0.356	0.354
n	110	110	110	110	110
Years	1990–2011	1990–2011	1990–2011	1990–2011	1990–2011

*** Statistically significant at $p = 0.01$
** Statistically significant at $p = 0.05$
* Statistically significant at $p = 0.10$

(b) Economic freedom and immigration (cont'd)

Regression	6	7	8	9	10
LHS	*EFW, 2011*	*EFW, 2011*	*EFW, 2011*	*EFW, 2011*	*EFW, 2011*
Economic freedom, 1990	0.163** (0.064)	0.164** (0.066)	0.184*** (0.064)	0.168** (0.065)	0.167** (0.066)
Immigrant stock, 1990	1.471** (0.686)			1.184 (0.970)	1.179 (1.003)
OECD immigrant stock, 1990		1.449 (2.380)			
Non-OECD immigrant stock, 1990		1.472** (0.698)			
Immigrant net inflow, 1990–2010			0.362* (0.201)	0.119 (0.283)	0.142 (1.022)
Flow–stock interaction					−0.033 (1.352)

Log GDP (PPP) per capita, 1990	−1.401***	−1.401***	−1.391***	−1.441***	−1.441***
	(0.465)	(0.468)	(0.476)	(0.477)	(0.480)
Log GDP (PPP) per capita, 2011	2.034***	2.034***	2.042***	2.068***	2.067***
	(0.427)	(0.429)	(0.436)	(0.436)	(−0.439)
Constant	3.095***	3.093***	2.977***	3.104***	3.107***
	(0.491)	(0.528)	(0.484)	(0.493)	(0.514)
Adjusted R^2	0.506	0.501	0.500	0.502	0.497
n	106	106	106	106	106
Years	1990–2011	1990–2011	1990–2011	1990–2011	1990–2011

*** Statistically significant at $p = 0.01$
** Statistically significant at $p = 0.05$
* Statistically significant at $p = 0.10$

(c) Economic freedom and immigration (cont'd)

Regression	11	12	13	14	15
LHS	EFW, 2011	EFW, 2011	EFW, 2011	EFW, 2011	EFW, 2011
Economic freedom, 1990	0.123*	0.140**	0.143**	0.129**	0.100
	(0.063)	(0.065)	(0.062)	(0.063)	(0.063)
Immigrant stock, 1990	2.767***			1.498	1.010
	(0.813)			(1.056)	(1.062)
OECD immigrant stock, 1990		0.338			
		(2.298)			
Non-OECD immigrant stock, 1990		3.100***			
		(0.863)			
Immigrant net inflow, 1990–2010			0.812***	0.541*	2.855**
			(0.224)	(0.293)	(1.131)
Flow–stock interaction					−3.026**
					(1.431)
Polity, 1990	−0.008	−0.006	−0.010	−0.006	0.002
	(0.016)	(0.016)	(0.016)	(0.016)	(0.016)
Polity, 2011	0.061***	0.065***	0.065***	0.066***	0.073***
	(0.018)	(0.018)	(0.018)	(0.018)	(0.018)
Log GDP (PPP) per capita, 1990	−1.626***	−1.646***	−1.669***	−1.780***	−1.781***
	(0.468)	(0.467)	(0.465)	(0.469)	(0.460)
Log GDP (PPP) per capita, 2011	2.085***	2.105***	2.156***	2.190***	2.035***
	(0.434)	(0.434)	(0.434)	(0.432)	(0.431)
Constant	3.575***	3.461***	3.432***	3.711***	4.390***
	(0.690)	(0.696)	(0.660)	(0.685)	(0.745)
Adjusted R^2	0.550	0.551	0.556	0.561	0.577
n	99	99	99	99	99
Years	1990–2011	1990–2011	1990–2011	1990–2011	1990–2011

*** Statistically significant at $p = 0.01$
** Statistically significant at $p = 0.05$
* Statistically significant at $p = 0.10$

Tables 8.2b and 8.2c add additional controls for gross domestic product (GDP) per capita and Polity IV. In Table 8.2b, controlling for GDP per capita only, we find somewhat stronger results. In Regression 6, the coefficient indicates that a $1SD$ higher immigration share correlates with a 0.18 higher EFW index score in 2011, or about $0.20SD$. In Table 8.2c, controlling for both GDP per capita and Polity IV, the results are even stronger, with a $1SD$ larger flow of immigration yielding a 0.34 higher EFW index rating $(0.37SD)$. Also, in contrast to Tables 8.2a and 8.2b, the flow of immigrants is statistically related to the EFW index in Table 8.2c. In Regression 13, for example, the results indicate that a $1SD$ higher flow of immigrants between 1990 and 2010 corresponds to a 0.27 higher EFW index score in 2011.

The final regression in each version of Table 8.2 includes the immigrant share, immigrant flow, and an interaction term between them. The reasoning behind this specification is straightforward. Perhaps the impact of additional immigrants is especially pronounced when a nation already has attracted a large number of immigrants—that is, perhaps the impact of the flow variable is contingent on the level of the share variable (and vice versa). The only instance in which this interaction term was significant occurs in Table 8.2c (Regression 15). The negative sign on the interaction term indicates that, for any given level of immigration share (flow), a larger flow (stock) would generate less economic freedom. However, the net effect of immigration share (flow) nevertheless is positive for any reasonable value of immigration flow (stock). In short, the interaction term, although statistically significant, is not large enough to reverse the impact of the main coefficients on immigration stock and flow.

Table 8.3 reports the estimations found in Regression 4 of Table 8.2, but at the EFW area level. Whether measured as a stock or a flow, in no case do we find higher immigration to be a statistically significant threat to any area of economic freedom. For Areas 2 ("Legal Structure and Property Rights") and 5 ("Regulation of Credit, Labor, and Business"), the stock of immigrants at the beginning of the period is associated with higher area ratings—that is, countries with more immigrants in 1990 experienced stronger private property rights and less regulation over the ensuing two decades. We are not aware of any prior literature predicting either an increase or a decrease in property rights or regulation in response to immigration. However, the evidence does dissuade us of two potential fears of immigration: immigrants do not appear to bring a desire with them for the corrupt, highly regulated environment from which they often emigrate nor do the native-born respond to greater immigration by implementing a more stringent regulatory environment to preclude immigrants from participating in the economy.

The inflow of immigrants was found to be statistically related to higher ratings in Area 1 ("Size of Government"), meaning that more in-migration correlates with less government spending. This finding suggests that even if generous welfare benefits are "magnets" (Borjas 1999), the impact of attracting immigrants may end up weakening the magnet's force. This finding is consistent with the view that the native-born population desires a smaller welfare state when larger number of immigrants participate in the economy (Razin et al. 2002; Alesina and Glaeser 2004) and also with the fragmentation literature that finds

Table 8.3 Economic freedom area ratings and immigration

Regression	16	17	18	19	20
LHS	Area 1, 2011	Area 2, 2011	Area 3, 2011	Area 4, 2011	Area 5, 2011
Economic freedom, 1990	−0.044 (0.124)	0.363*** (0.107)	−0.056 (0.112)	0.104 (0.074)	0.265*** (0.088)
Immigrant stock, 1990	0.545 (2.098)	3.671** (1.804)	−0.595 (1.890)	1.407 (1.243)	2.674* (1.483)
Immigrant net inflow, 1990–2010	1.524** (0.576)	−0.271 (0.496)	0.700 (0.519)	0.556 (0.341)	0.179 (0.407)
Polity, 1990	0.038 (0.031)	−0.035 (0.027)	−0.034 (0.028)	−0.006 (0.018)	0.006 (0.022)
Polity, 2011	0.030 (0.035)	0.062** (0.030)	0.132*** (0.032)	0.084*** (0.021)	0.022 (0.025)
Log GDP (PPP) per capita, 1990	−2.786*** (0.927)	−2.002** (0.797)	−1.007 (0.835)	−1.922*** (0.549)	−1.259* (0.655)
Log GDP (PPP) per capita, 2011	1.271 (0.853)	3.508*** (0.733)	2.359*** (0.768)	2.599*** (0.505)	1.279** (0.603)
Constant	11.907*** (1.354)	−3.296*** (1.164)	2.265* (1.220)	2.909*** (0.802)	4.862*** (0.957)
Adjusted R^2	0.179	0.646	0.439	0.594	0.321
n	98	98	98	98	98
Years	1990–2011	1990–2011	1990–2011	1990–2011	1990–2011

*** Statistically significant at $p = 0.01$
** Statistically significant at $p = 0.05$
* Statistically significant at $p = 0.10$

governments spend a smaller amount on public goods when ethnic fragmentation is greater (Easterly and Levine 1997; Alesina et al. 1999).

Tables 8.4a, 8.4b, and 8.4c report the results of a set of difference-in-difference panel regressions using two ten-year time periods: 1990–2000 and 2001–2011. The four regressions reported there experiment with including and excluding time and country fixed effects. The dependent variable is the change in the EFW index. The main explanatory variable of interest is the change in the immigrant stock from 1990 to 2011—that is, the net inflow over the period. Table 8.4a shows the baseline model only; Table 8.4b adds differenced GDP per capita as a control; Table 8.4c adds both differenced GDP per capita and differenced Polity IV. Regardless of which controls are entered, only in the final regression in each table, which includes both year and country fixed effects, do we find a relationship between the immigration flow and the economic freedom variable, and once again the relationship is positive. In Regression 32, for instance, the results suggest that a 1 *SD* larger immigration flow is related to a 0.26 higher level of EFW index score in 2011 than in 1990, or about 0.24 *SD*.

Regardless of the immigration measure used or the precise regression specification, we have not found a single instance in which immigration is associated with less economic freedom. It does not appear that immigrants are bringing the poor economic freedom records of their home countries abroad with them.

Table 8.4 (a) Economic freedom and immigration, difference-in-difference results

Regression	21	22	23	24
LHS	Differenced EFW	Differenced EFW	Differenced EFW	Differenced EFW
Immigrant net inflow, 1990–2010	−0.330 (0.437)	−0.134 (0.408)	0.525 (1.104)	1.656* (0.975)
Constant	0.624*** (0.624)	0.926*** (0.074)	1.308** (0.637)	1.630*** (0.555)
Year fixed effects	N	Y	N	Y
Country fixed effects	N	N	Y	Y
Adjusted R^2	−0.002	0.139	−0.175	0.117
n	220	220	220	220
Years	1990–2011	1990–2011	1990–2011	1990–2011

*** Statistically significant at $p = 0.01$
** Statistically significant at $p = 0.05$
* Statistically significant at $p = 0.10$

(b) Economic freedom and immigration, difference-in-difference results (cont'd)

Regression	21	22	23	24
LHS	Differenced EFW	Differenced EFW	Differenced EFW	Differenced EFW
Immigrant net inflow, 1990–2010	−0.330 (0.437)	−0.134 (0.408)	0.525 (1.104)	1.656* (0.975)
Constant	0.624*** (0.624)	0.926*** (0.074)	1.308** (0.637)	1.630*** (0.555)
Year fixed effects	N	Y	N	Y
Country fixed effects	N	N	Y	Y
Adjusted R^2	−0.002	0.139	−0.175	0.117
n	220	220	220	220
Years	1990–2011	1990–2011	1990–2011	1990–2011

*** Statistically significant at $p = 0.01$
** Statistically significant at $p = 0.05$
* Statistically significant at $p = 0.10$

(c) Economic freedom and immigration, difference-in-difference results (cont'd)

Regression	29	30	31	32
LHS	Differenced EFW	Differenced EFW	Differenced EFW	Differenced EFW
Immigrant net inflow, 1990–2010	−0.058 (0.448)	0.151 (0.419)	0.870 (1.146)	2.098** (1.024)
Differenced polity	0.019 (0.015)	−0.006 (0.015)	0.026 (0.026)	−0.028 (0.024)
Differenced log GDP per capita	0.769 (0.663)	1.135* (0.621)	−0.548 (1.229)	0.208 (1.080)
Constant	0.532*** (0.086)	0.837*** (0.098)	1.396** (0.646)	1.622*** (0.564)
Year fixed effects	N	Y	N	Y
Country fixed effects	N	N	Y	Y
Adjusted R^2	−0.002	0.130	−0.152	0.124
n	193	193	193	193
Years	1990–2011	1990–2011	1990–2011	1990–2011

*** Statistically significant at $p = 0.01$
** Statistically significant at $p = 0.05$
* Statistically significant at $p = 0.10$

Conclusion

It is reasonably well established that immigrants bring small, but modest, economic benefits to the countries to which they migrate, but the literature has established little about the impact of migrants on recipient countries' institutions. In the case of open migration, as Borjas (2015, p. 12, emphasis original) put it, "Unfortunately we know little (read: *nothing*) about how host societies would adapt to the entry of perhaps billions of new persons."

This chapter is a step in learning *something* about the impact of immigrants on recipient countries' institutions. Our results indicate that immigration may improve a country's institutions marginally in a manner consistent with more economic freedom. Using our estimate that a 1 SD larger immigration stock increases economic freedom by 0.34 points and an estimate for the impact of economic freedom on growth (Gwartney et al. 2006), our results suggest that an increase in the immigrant share of this magnitude will generate a 0.45 percentage point higher long-run annual growth rate. This strikes us as a meaningful impact on economic growth.

Borjas (2015) simulates negative institutional impacts of immigrants to claim that the standard economic estimates of trillions of dollars of gains to the world economy (Clemens 2011) from open immigration are grossly overstated and may, in fact, be negative. Our results indicate that the opposite may be true. The static gains in traditional estimates underestimate the global gains by ignoring the positive general equilibrium impact on institutions. Of course, reasons exist why our results might not be applicable to a world of open borders. Perhaps the social capital of current immigrants is not representative of the social capital of the population that would migrate under alternative policy regimes. But, at a minimum, when starting from a baseline of knowing "nothing," our study, which shows that current levels of immigration either improve or fail to impact institutions, should make one skeptical of Borjas's unsubstantiated assumption that immigrants can only negatively impact recipient country institutions.

The usual caveats apply to this study. Although the use of economic freedom at the beginning of the period effectively controls for numerous omitted fixed effects, it is conceivable that relevant variables that vary over the time period have been omitted. Also, it is not obvious what the appropriate time horizon is to investigate the impact of immigration on the receiving countries' institutions. Most of the time, immigrants are not immediately eligible to vote, although they may still influence the political process by other means. Finally, we cannot tell with the data at hand whether any changes in institutional quality are a function of the preferences of immigrants themselves or of the reactions of the native-born to the immigrants. Furthermore, other factors that immigration may impact have been shown to be important for growth, such as culture and informal institutions (Williamson 2009), and these should be examined in future research.

Overall, we find some evidence that larger immigrant population shares (or inflows) yield positive impacts on institutional quality. At a minimum, our results indicate that no negative impact on economic freedom is associated with more immigration.

Notes

* Reprinted by permission of Springer. *Public Choice*. "Does Immigration Impact Institutions?" J. R. Clark, Robert Lawson, Alex Nowrasteh, Benjamin Powell and Ryan Murphy. Vol. 163, No. 3–4, pp. 321–336. Copyright 2015. We thank the participants at the Association of Private Enterprise Education's 2014 annual conference, the participants at Texas Tech's Free Market Institute's Research Workshop, and an anonymous referee for helpful comments on prior drafts. Support from the John Templeton Foundation is gratefully acknowledged.
1 Comparatively little work has been done on the causes of economic freedom. There is some evidence that economic freedom is enhanced by fiscal decentralization (Cassette and Paty 2010), more educated politicians (Dreher et al. 2009), and by the competitiveness of the political environment (Leonida, Patti and Navarra 2007). Djankov et al. (2003a, 2003b), and Bjornskov (2010) examined the determinants of legal institutions consistent with economic freedom. Finally, La Porta et al. (1999) looked at the determinants of various other aspects of economic freedom, such as marginal tax rates and government fiscal size and scope.
2 Despite the small net gain, Powell (2012) shows that, with substantial transfers, the rent-seeking costs to policy changes could be much larger than the standard Harberger triangles.
3 A separate and distinct question, on which there is a larger amount of research, is what the fiscal impact is of immigration, given current tax and spending policies. On this point, there is less consensus than on the impact of immigrants on the employment

opportunities and wages of natives. The fiscal impact of immigration varies considerably depending on the country studied, the characteristics of the immigrants, and the model estimated. In general, though, if a consensus has been reached, it is that the net fiscal impact is small: see Kerr and Kerr (2011) for a survey.

4 This is consistent with Rodrik (1998), who finds that the more open a country is to international trade, the larger government expenditures are as a percentage of GDP so as to mitigate the population's risk from fluctuations in the international market.

5 Dimant, Krieger and Redlin (2013) found that immigrants increase corruption in recipient countries when they come from corruption-ridden countries. Our measure of property rights and law is broader than only corruption, but contains some components related to corruption.

References

Acemoglu, D., and Robinson, J. A. 2012. *Why nations fail: The origins of power, prosperity, and poverty*. New York: Crown.

Alesina, A. F., and Glaeser, E. L. 2004. *Fighting poverty in the US and Europe*. New York: Oxford University Press.

Alesina, A. F., Baqir, R., and Easterly, W. 1999. Public goods and ethnic divisions. *Quarterly Journal of Economics, 114*(4): 1243–1284.

Banting, K., and Kymlicka, W. 2006. Introduction: Multiculturalism and the welfare state—Setting the context. In K. Banting and W. Kymlicka (eds.), *Multiculturalism and the welfare state*. New York: Oxford University Press, pp. 1–45.

Barro, R. J. 1996. Democracy and growth. *Journal of Economic Growth, 1*(1): 1–27.

Barseghyan, L. 2008. Entry costs and cross-country differences in productivity and output. *Journal of Economic Growth, 13*(2): 145–167.

Bjornskov, C. 2010. How does social trust lead to better governance? An attempt to separate electoral and bureaucratic mechanisms. *Public Choice, 144*(1–2): 323–346.

Borjas, G. J. 1999. Immigration and welfare magnets. *Journal of Labor Economics, 17*(4): 607–637.

Borjas, G. J. 2014. *Immigration economics*. Cambridge, MA: Harvard University Press.

Borjas, G. J. 2015. Immigration and globalization: A review essay. *Journal of Economic Literature, 53*(4): 961–974.

Bowles, A., and Gintis, H. 2011. *Schooling in capitalist America: Educational reforms and the contradictions of economic life*. Chicago, IL: Haymarket Books.

Brady, D., and Finnigan, R. 2013. Does immigration undermine public support for social policy? *American Sociological Review, 79*(1): 17–42.

Burgoon, B., Koster, F., and van Egmond, M. 2012. Support for redistribution and the paradox of immigration. *Journal of European Social Policy, 22*(3): 288–304.

Butts, F. R. 1978. *Public education in the United States: From revolution to reform*. New York: Holt, Rinehart & Winston.

Canaan, E. (ed.). 1904. Introduction. In A. Smith [1776], *An inquiry in the nature and causes of the wealth of nations*. London: Methuen & Co.

Cassette, A., and Paty, S. 2010. Fiscal decentralization and the size of government: A European country empirical analysis. *Public Choice, 143*(1–2): 173–189.

Clemens, M. A. 2011. Economics and emigration: Trillion-dollar bills on the sidewalk? *Journal of Economics Perspectives, 25*(3): 83–106.

Collier, P. 2013. *Exodus: How migration is changing our world*. Oxford: Oxford University Press.

Dawson, J. 2003. Causality in the freedom–growth relationship. *European Journal of Political Economy*, 19(3): 479–495.

De Haan, J., and Sturm, J. E. 2000. On the relationship between economic freedom and economic growth. *European Journal of Political Economy*, 16(2): 215–241.

De Haan, J., Lundstrom, S., and Sturm, J. E. 2006. Market-oriented institutions and policies and economic growth: A critical survey. *Journal of Economic Surveys*, 20(2): 157–191.

Dimant, E., Krieger, T., and Redlin, M. 2013. *A crook is a crook . . . but is he still a crook abroad? On the effect of immigration on destination-country corruption*. Discussion paper.

Djankov, A., McLiesh, C., Nenova, T., and Andrei Shleifer. 2003a. Who owns the media? *Journal of Law & Economics*, 46(2): 341–381.

Djankov, S., La Porta, R., Lopez-de-Silanes, F., and Shleifer, A. 2003b. Courts. *Quarterly Journal of Economics*, 118(2): 453–517.

Dreher, A., Lamla, M. J., Lein, S. M., and Somogyi, F. 2009. The impact of political leaders' profession and education on reforms. *Journal of Comparative Economics*, 37(1): 169–193.

Easterly, W., and Levine, R. 1997. Africa's growth tragedy: Policies and ethnic divisions. *Quarterly Journal of Economics*, 112(4): 1203–1250.

Ervasti, H., and Hjerm, M. 2012. Immigration, trust and support for the welfare state. In H. Ervasti, J. G. Andersen, T. Fridberg, and K. Ringdal (eds.), *The future of the welfare state*. Cheltenham: Edward Elgar, pp. 153–171.

Everheart, R. B. 1977. From universalism to usurpation: An essay on the antecedents to compulsory school attendance legislation. *Review of Education Research*, 47(3): 499–530.

Finseraas, H. 2008. Immigration and preferences for redistribution: An empirical analysis of European social survey data. *Comparative European Politics*, 6(4): 407–431.

Freeman, R. 2006. People flows in globalization. *Journal of Economic Perspectives*, 20(2): 145–170.

Friedberg, R. M., and Hunt, J. 1995. The effects of immigrants on host country wages, employment and growth. *Journal of Economic Perspectives*, 9(2): 23–44.

Greer, C. 1972. *The great school legend: A revisionist interpretation of American public education*. New York: Basic Books.

Gwartney, J., Holcombe, R., and Lawson, R. 2006. Institutions and the impact of investment on growth. *Kyklos*, 59(2): 255–273.

Gwartney, J., Lawson, R., and Hall, J. 2013. *Economic freedom of the world: 2013 Annual report*. Vancouver, BC: Fraser Institute.

Hall, J., and Lawson, R. 2013. Economic freedom of the world: An accounting of the literature. *Contemporary Economic Policy*, 32(1): 1–19.

Justesen, M. K. 2008. The effect of economic freedom on growth revisited: New evidence on causality from a panel of countries 1970–1999. *European Journal of Political Economy*, 24(3): 642–660.

Kerr, S. P., and Kerr, W. R. 2011. *Economic impacts of immigration: A survey*. Working paper.

Kunovich, R. M. 2004. Social structural position and prejudice: An exploration of cross-national differences in regression slopes. *Social Science Research*, 33(1): 20–44.

La Porta, R., Lopez-de-Silanes, F., Shleifer, A., and Vishny, R. 1999. The quality of government. *Journal of Law, Economics and Organization*, 15(1): 222–279.

Leeson, P., and Gochenour, Z. 2015. The economic effects of international labor mobility. In B. Powell (ed.), *The economics of immigration: Market-based approaches, social science, and public policy*. Oxford: Oxford University Press, pp. 11–37.

Leonida, L., Patti, D. M. A., and Navarra, P. 2007. Towards an equilibrium level of market reform: How politics affects the dynamics of policy change. *Applied Economics*, *39*(13): 1627–1634.

Meissner, D., Kerwin, D. M., Chishti, M., and Bergeron, C. 2013. *Immigration enforcement in the United States: The rise of a formidable machinery*. Washington, DC: Migration Policy Institute.

Meyer, J., Tyack, D., Nagel, J., and Gordon, A. 1979. Public education as nation-building in America. *American Journal of Sociology*, *85*(3): 591–613.

Powell, B. 2012. Coyote ugly: The deadweight cost of rent seeking for immigration policy. *Public Choice*, *150*(1–2): 195–208.

Ralph, J. H., and Rubinson, R. 1980. Immigration and the expansion of schooling in the United States, 1890–1970. *American Sociological Review*, *45*(Dec): 943–954.

Razin, A., Sadka, E., and Swagel, P. 2002. Tax burden and migration: A political economy theory and evidence. *Journal of Public Economics*, *85*(2): 167–190.

Rodrik, D. 1998. Why do more open economics have bigger governments? *Journal of Political Economy*, *106*(5): 997–1032.

Rodrik, D., Subramanian, A., and Trebbi, F. 2004. Institutions rule: The primacy of institutions over geography and integration in economic development. *Journal of Economic Growth*, *9*(2): 131–165.

Svallfors, S. 1997. Worlds of welfare and attitudes to redistribution: A comparison of eight Western nations. *European Sociological Review*, *13*(3): 283–304.

Williamson, C. 2009. Informal institutions rule: Institutional arrangements and economic performance. *Public Choice*, *139*(3): 371–387.

World Bank. 2013. *World Development Indicators*. Washington, DC: World Bank.

9 The genesis and evolution of China's economic liberalization

James A. Dorn[*]

Introduction

China has made much progress since it first opened to the outside world in 1978 under the guidance of paramount leader Deng Xiaoping. The devastation caused by Mao Zedong during the Great Leap Forward (1958–60), the Great Famine (1959–61), and the Cultural Revolution (1966–76) led Deng to rethink Marxist ideology and central planning. Rather than adhering to Chairman Mao's "Little Red Book" and engaging in class struggle, Deng elevated economic development to be the primary goal of socialism. His vision of "market socialism with Chinese characteristics"—and his mantra, "Seek truth from facts"—paved the way for the emergence of the non-state sector and the return of private entrepreneurs. The success of that vision is evident from the fact that China is now the world's largest trading nation and the second largest economy.

This chapter tells the story of how China's market economy with socialist characteristics rose from the ashes of Mao Zedong's failed experiments with central planning and control, and how it developed despite many bumps in the road. What is striking is that many of the reforms began at the local level and were motivated by the desire for greater economic freedom. Entrenched interests opposed departing from state-led development under the plan, but courageous individuals were willing to experiment with market alternatives to increase their freedom and prosperity.

This bottom-up reform movement, which might be called "spontaneous marketization," eventually led to the creation of a vibrant market economy sanctioned by the state. Indeed, the reform process could not have occurred without the support of local and higher-level officials. Thus one should think of the evolution of China's economic liberalization as both bottom-up and top-down. It was initiated by disgruntled farmers and others who suffered under state planning, and it was supported by leaders who understood that China's future depended on expanding markets and trade. Although China has moved toward a freer economic system, it would be misleading to think that the "People's Republic" has established a genuine free-market system. Such a change would require limited government, widespread private property rights enforced by an independent judiciary, and the safeguarding of basic human rights.

There is still no free market for ideas, and state planning is far from dead. The Chinese Communist Party (CCP) continues to hold a monopoly on political power and to thwart criticism. President Xi Jinping made it clear in his remarks at the Party's 95th anniversary (July 1, 2016) that Marxism, not liberalism, is the bedrock of China's political regime: "Turning our backs or abandoning Marxism means that our party would lose its soul and direction" (Wong 2016).

Initially, the goal of China's reform movement was to improve the performance of state-owned enterprises (SOEs). However, the non-state sector, including private enterprises, became the engine for creating new wealth and employment as constraints on entrepreneurship and trade were gradually relaxed. But, even before they were relaxed, brave individuals were willing to violate the law by engaging in private enterprise.

This chapter begins with the state of China's economic and social life under Mao, then proceeds to examine the genesis of economic reform that took place between Mao's death in September 1976 and the Third Plenum of the 11th Central Committee of the CCP in December 1978, which is considered to be the official start of Deng's economic liberalization. We then investigate the unfolding of reforms from 1978 to the present, what motivated those reforms, and the prospect for future reform. The focal point will be the quest for economic freedom and the relationship between the state and the market in the process of development.

Economic and social life under Mao

The system of state control of both economic and social life under Mao deprived the Chinese people of life, liberty, and happiness. The CCP repressed the free flow of information and tailored data to fit Mao's ambitions to make China self-sufficient in grain and steel, only to result in mass starvation and a huge misallocation of resources. The internal passport system (*hukou*) restricted peasants from leaving the countryside and made it difficult to exchange information, as well as goods and services. Families were destroyed by the large-scale communes that took the place of smaller collectives. The Great Proletarian Cultural Revolution turned everyday life upside down as children turned on their parents and trust was lost.

Jasper Becker (1998) gives a penetrating account of life under Mao's repressive regime.

- With the implementation of the internal passport in 1956, "the peasant could no longer travel without permission to attend fairs, or to seek work outside the village in slack seasons. News from the outside world was no longer brought by pedlars, strolling beggars, wandering musicians and mendicant priests" (Becker 1998: 52).
- In the same year, collectives were formed with the aim of increasing grain production at any cost. That obsession, along with the *hukou*, "discouraged handicrafts like embroidery or woodcarving that had been a part of peasant culture. All the small-scale private enterprises . . . withered and

died, leaving the peasants dependent on what the state could supply from its factories" (Becker, 1998: 52).

- The collectivization of agriculture, including livestock, eroded incentives to practice responsible farming and breeding methods: "Animals that survived collectivization were now publicly owned, no one felt responsible for them. Peasants worked the animals to death" (Becker, 1998: 53).
- In 1958, collectives were combined into large-scale communes as Mao launched his Great Leap Forward campaign. The CCP "set out to achieve the abolition of all private property" and to "destroy the family as an institution" (Becker, 1998: 105).

The purging of private entrepreneurs, the suppression of family life, and the fear of repression for any deviation from Party orthodoxy uprooted civil society and crushed individualism. Thus one reads in the *China Youth Journal* (September 27, 1958):

> The framework of the individual family, which has existed for thousands of years, has been shattered for all time. . . . We must regard the People's Commune as our family. . . . [T]he dearest people in the world are our parents, yet they cannot be compared with Chairman Mao and the Communist Party.
>
> (Becker, 1998: 105–6)

That mentality reached epic proportions during the Cultural Revolution as millions of youth were sent to the countryside for "re-education."

The massive starvation during the Great Famine and the devastation caused by the Cultural Revolution left a lasting impression on Deng Xiaoping, who was purged from his CCP posts and experienced the imprisonment, torture, and crippling of his eldest son, Deng Pufang, by the Red Guards.

Deng would also not forget the absurdities engineered by Mao that made it difficult for peasants to recover from the famine:

- "The Party outlawed all carpentry and handicrafts which were not undertaken by state-run units. Peasants in poor agricultural areas, who in the past had supplemented their income by carpentry, basket weaving and dozens of other trades, now had only farming on which to rely" (Becker, 1998: 258).
- "In the name of egalitarianism, no one was allowed to be seen to prosper from activities such as raising poultry or selling vegetables, even if they were permitted, without attracting censure and punishments as 'rich peasants.' . . . Anyone caught slaughtering a pig without permission would be sentenced to one or even three years in prison" (Becker, 1998: 258).
- "Peasant militia also patrolled the villages to stop the villagers from indulging in the most harmless pursuits if they smacked of bourgeois individualism. The small pleasures of life, even playing cards, became crimes against the state" (Becker, 1998: 258).

These are but a few examples of the suppression of economic freedom and civil society under Mao.[1] The illusion of success and the mania for power prevented Mao from changing course. With no market for ideas and no free press, the truth was largely hidden. As Becker (1998: 79) notes, "Even when the famine was over, Mao's faith in his agricultural methods does not appear to have been shaken in the slightest by their evident failure."

The death of Mao in September 1976 opened the door for positive change. That change had already begun earlier in the shadow economy. Mao and his cronies may have banned private entrepreneurship and placed the CCP above the family, but people naturally rebel against coercion and want to make themselves better off. Those incentives led to black markets, not the abolition of markets, and to a hidden social fabric, not the end of culture. With Mao's death, the time was ripe to bring what Frank Dikötter (2016) called "the silent revolution" to the forefront and let markets gain ground.[2]

Early reforms and the re-emergence of the private sector, 1976–78

By the time Deng Xiaoping took effective control of the CCP at the Third Plenum of the 11th Central Committee in December 1978, progress had already been made in moving from central planning to a market system. After Mao's death, Premier Hua Guofeng and others turned toward economic development as the primary focus of the CCP. That shift in attention led to the "Four Modernizations" and "Leap Forward" policies in 1976–77. More importantly, Hu Yaobang, as head of the Central Party School and editor of *Theoretical Trends*, fostered new thinking and debate. An article he helped publish in his journal, "Practice Is the Only Criterion for Testing Truth," gained CCP support for experimentation as an acceptable approach in moving from plan to market (Coase and Wang, 2012: 41–42).

The most significant change during the 1976–78 period was the re-emergence of the Household Responsibility System (*baochan daohu*). Earlier attempts by farmers to escape the vice grip of collectivization and gain autonomy were made in 1956–57, 1961–62, and 1967, but all failed as Mao and his cadres sought to maintain and strengthen their power (Zhou, 1996: ch. 3). Finally, with Mao's passing in 1976, the stage was set for "spontaneous privatization"—that is, grassroots, not centrally planned, privatization.

The Household Responsibility System was not officially adopted by the CCP until late 1981. However, after the death of Mao, areas devastated by the Great Leap Forward, the Great Famine, and the Cultural Revolution independently moved toward contracting out collectively owned land to individual households, who, after satisfying the agreed-upon quota, could sell their surplus produce on private markets.[3]

The first case in post-Maoist China of allowing households to engage in private farming occurred in September 1976, in Nine Dragon Hill, a village in Pengxi County, Sichuan, which was part of the Qunli Commune. That experiment, which was initiated by Deng Tianyuan, Party secretary of the commune, began by giving lower-quality land to two production teams. When crop yields on marginal private plots turned out to be three times higher than on more fertile collective plots, the experiment spread to the entire commune. However, since spontaneous privatization was illegal, it was kept secret until 1979 (Coase and Wang, 2012: 46–47).

In November 1977, Wan Li, the first Party secretary of Anhui Province, supported adopting the "Provincial Party Committee Six-Point Proposal" to address the dire plight of agriculture and continued starvation under the commune system. Point six of that program would assign land to production team members for their own use and allow them to sell surplus crops in local markets. Although such activities were illegal at the national level, Deng Xiaoping (then vice chairman of the Central Committee) and other officials understood the practicality of the Six-Point Proposal. The proposal was implemented and was successful in increasing production (Vogel, 2011: 437–38). Leftists, of course, were highly critical. Chen Yonggui, vice premier in charge of agriculture, strongly opposed Wan's experiment with contracting down to the household level. The official press criticized Wan for turning toward capitalism and for rejecting the Dazhai Model that glorified state planning.[4] In defending his experiment, Wan Li told Chen in November 1978: "You say you are speaking from the Dazhai experience; I say Dazhai is an ultra-leftist model. . . . You go your way and I'll go mine. . . . As for who is right and who is wrong, let's see which way works best" (Vogel, 2011: 438).

In early February 1978, Deng visited Sichuan and informed Zhao Ziyang (then first Party secretary) of Wan's success under the Six-Point Proposal. Deng urged Zhao to follow suit, which he did by implementing a Twelve-Point Program designed to stimulate crop production by devolving control rights and responsibility to small groups, but not to households (Vogel, 2011: 438).[5]

The most frequently cited case of spontaneous privatization occurred in November 1978, when peasants from 18 households in Xiaogang Village (in Fengyang County, Anhui) secretly got together and agreed to engage in private production. They would still meet state and collective quotas, but use the land at their disposal for private gain. In their contract, they promised to take care of the children of local cadres in the event that they were disciplined for failing to prohibit decollectivization (Zhou, 1996: 55–56). When farmers in Xiaogang were highly successful in increasing their yields and prospering from leaving the production teams to cultivate their own plots, nearby villagers had a strong incentive to join the movement (Coase and Wang, 2012: 47).

Although Deng was not in a position to openly support the silent revolution taking place in rural areas in 1976–78, once he became paramount leader after the Third Plenum of the 11th Central Committee of the CCP in December 1978, he gradually sanctioned reforms that had begun at the local level.

The evolution of reforms under Deng Xiaoping, 1978–89

Following the Cultural Revolution in 1977, Deng helped to launch the "Beijing Spring" movement in November 1978, which put a spotlight on Mao's failed policies and allowed intellectuals the freedom to debate a new path for China. Although that freedom soon ended, it was clear that the disastrous effects of forced collectivization and central planning made economic reform essential.

After the Third Plenum, Deng was in a position to act on the tenet, "Seek truth from facts." One fact was evident: the relationship between state and market had tilted too far toward comprehensive planning and away from competitive markets. By allowing markets to have more space in the state-directed economy, there was hope for greater freedom and prosperity. What Deng and his allies did not foresee was the spontaneous privatization and the growth of the non-state sector that would occur in the decade following the Third Plenum.

Four bottom-up reforms that occurred at the margins of the planned economy stand out: the rise of the Household Responsibility System (HRS); the creation of township and village enterprises (TVEs); the emergence of private businesses in urban areas; and the development of special economic zones (SEZs).[6]

The Household Responsibility System

The spontaneous spread of the HRS motivated Beijing to relax the ban on private farming in 1980; in October 1981, the National Work Conference helped to establish the legitimacy of that arrangement by declaring it to be consistent with China's socialist economy. In November 1981, the CCP Secretariat formally recognized the HRS (Tian, 2009: 1070); in January 1982, the Central Committee of the CCP issued a "No. 1 policy document," which officially recognized the right of peasants to directly market their products, thus ending the state monopoly of the rural supply cooperatives (Huang, 2008: 89–90; Coase and Wang, 2012: 49). That policy change revealed the need for competition and private entrepreneurship in rural areas, and thus the failure of collectivization to create prosperity.

The relaxation of constraints on decollectivization led to a rapid transition to the HRS. By the end of 1982, 80 percent of production teams were experimenting with various forms of contracting. The success of decentralization led the Central Committee to give further support to the HRS in January 1983, with the publication of its new Document No. 1. By the end of 1984, nearly 100 percent of rural households had joined the market-based contractual system (Tian, 2009: 1070).

The ultimate success of the HRS can be attributed to the lessons that farmers had learned from earlier failures and the fact that "they made deals with individual cadres while seizing every opportunity to pursue their goals. . . . They literally bribed their way out from under [the repressive state system]" (Zhou, 1996: 70). When local experiments were positive, they spread and eventually gained official recognition: "The most important and long-lasting effect of decollectivization was regained economic freedom" (Coase and Wang, 2012: 76). That benefit can also be seen in the rise of TVEs.

Township and village enterprises

During the Cultural Revolution, the mantra was, "Strike hard against the slightest sign of private ownership" (Becker, 2000: 157). However, as farmers gained autonomy in the post-Mao era, they began creating small-scale enterprises at the village and township level—first in the coastal areas, and then in more remote areas. It is not surprising that the entrepreneurial revolution began in the countryside. Weiying Zhang, a pioneer of China's reform movement, explains why: "As the household-contract responsibility system was implemented and as rural markets were gradually liberalized, peasants obtained some freedom to do business" (Zhang, 2015a: 176). Entrepreneurial farmers, who had little education, but a drive to improve their lives and their families' futures, took advantage of the cracks opening in the top-down system of planning to start TVEs, which officially were collectively owned, and rural *private* businesses.[7]

The number of TVEs exploded sevenfold between 1978 and 1985, reaching 18.5 million by 1990 and employing more than 92 million rural workers. The rural entrepreneurs/enterprises operated outside the state sector and "were the major driving force for economic growth in China during the 1980s" (Zhang, 2015a: 177).[8] The rise of TVEs reached a pinnacle in 1994 and declined thereafter as rural private enterprises took the high ground.

Unlike the commune and brigade enterprises that were set up by cadres during the Mao era, "the emergence of TVEs was not designed or guided by the state"; instead:

> The peasants took advantage of cheap land and labor, semi-formal or informal fund-pooling, the authority of the existing rural hierarchy or kinship, of local market and low transaction costs, of central government ignorance, and eroding control over income disparity since the adoption of the household responsibility system, and gradually shifted their resources into rural industry.
>
> (Wei, 2003: 4)

Deng (1987: 189) recognized the spontaneous nature of the rise and mushrooming of TVEs in the 1980s: "Our greatest success—and it is one we had by no means anticipated—has been the emergence of a large number of enterprises run by villages and townships. They were like a new force that just came into being spontaneously." But he also understood that the leadership had played a supporting role: "If the Central Committee made any contribution . . . it was only by laying down the correct policy of invigorating the domestic economy" (Deng, 1987: 189).

The general secretary of the CCP's Central Committee at the time was Zhao Ziyang, who held that office from November 1, 1987, to June 23, 1989, and was premier from September 10, 1982, to November 24, 1987. Zhao was instrumental in changing the intellectual climate and allowing more freedom to debate and discuss ideas on how best to spur development. He even met with Milton Friedman in Beijing following the Cato's Institute's September 1988 conference in Shanghai. During their dialogue, Zhao revealed a firm grasp of the importance of clearly defined property rights, open markets, and what Joseph Schumpeter (1942) called "creative destruction" for making people better off. The general secretary told Friedman:

- "Property rights should not be left ambiguous; they should be made clear" (Friedman, 1990: 131);
- "We must reform the price system. . . . Price reform does not involve simply a readjustment of prices, but more importantly the formation of a mechanism under which prices are determined by the market" (Friedman, 1990: 128); and
- "I am all for the idea that bankruptcy is a good thing. It allows the new to supersede the old" (Friedman, 1990: 129).

Earlier, in his speech at the 13th National Congress of the CCP, Zhao called for:

- "[giving] play to market forces and free competition" (Zhao, 1987: 25);
- "[creating] new types of institutions for commodity circulation, foreign trade and banking as well as networks of agencies to provide technology, information and service, all of which have full authority for management and full responsibility for their profits and losses" (Zhao, 1987: 36); and
- "strengthening the socialist legal system" to provide "a fundamental guarantee against a recurrence of the 'cultural revolution' and for lasting political stability" (Zhao, 1987: 59).

Both Deng and Zhao sought to build "socialism with Chinese characteristics," not the "free private markets" that Friedman called for on his first visit to China in 1980 (Friedman, 1989: 569). Yet Friedman recognized the political constraints facing those who sought to expand markets and limit the power of the state. Deng and Zhao get high marks for helping to navigate the economic reform movement through the political landmines set by special interests favoring the status quo.

The focus on economic development, rather than ideological correctness—as captured by Deng's famous dictum, "It doesn't matter whether the cat is black or white, as long as it catches mice"—meant that local officials could gain ground and move up the CCP ladder by increasing economic growth. The chief way of doing so was to allow experimentation with new ownership forms such as the TVEs. Deng and Zhao implicitly sanctioned those experiments, and their support helped to weaken resistance among hardliners. Moreover, openness to new ideas about how to improve productivity and the "modification of the rules of the game" lowered "the costs of inducing the privileged groups to accept a change" in thinking about the role of markets (Cheung, 1986 [1982]: 56–59). At the local level, farmers individually made deals with cadres to gain access to collective land for private use.[9]

The legal recognition of private enterprises in 1988 and Deng Xiaoping's political support during his post-Tiananmen Southern Tour in 1992 gave a boost to the non-state sector. New ownership arrangements appeared, and most TVEs were transformed into private enterprises. As Zhang (2015a: 178–79) notes, "Many local governments began to privatize their rural enterprises in various forms, such as by taking off 'red caps,' joint-stock corporatizations, or by simply selling out." By 2000, TVEs were such a minor aspect of the rural economy that they were not even listed in the China Statistical Yearbook (Zhang, 2015a: 179).

Urban private enterprises

Spontaneous privatization also was occurring in cities. Young workers coming back from "re-education" in the countryside during the Cultural Revolution could not find jobs in SOEs and began to "jump into the sea of private enterprise." The CCP also helped to fuel the private sector by allowing "self-employment," with the proviso that firms could not hire more than seven workers; anything beyond that limit was deemed "exploitation" and was illegal. However, risk-taking entrepreneurs were willing to bribe local officials to look the other way (Zhang, 2015b: 16). Corruption became an institutionalized part of China's market socialism—that is, it became a mechanism for overcoming the contradiction between using the market to spur economic development and adhering to Marxist ideology.

In one well-known case, Nian Guangjiu, a small-business owner in Wuhu City, Anhui, expanded his workforce far beyond the legal limit. His success made local police hesitant to arrest him for "exploitation." The case was taken to Deng Xiaoping, who said, "Don't arrest him. One person like Nian cannot shake socialism." The word spread that Deng did not consider the private sector a threat and thus fostered entrepreneurial activity (Zhang, 2015b: 17). The idea that private markets could work alongside state planning to promote development made its way into the Constitution of the People's Republic of China (PRC) in April 1988, when article 11 was amended to read:

> The State permits the private sector of the economy to exist and develop within the limits prescribed by law. The private sector of the economy is a complement to the socialist public economy. The State protects the lawful rights and interests of the private sector of the economy, and exercises guidance, supervision and control over the private sector of the economy.[10]

There were still major constraints on the private sector, but, compared to Mao's ban on private enterprise, the new era of private marketization was revolutionary. In 1978, the number of self-employed household businesses and sole proprietorships reached 140,000, and by 1981 it had grown to 2.6 million (Coase and Wang, 2012: 68). The private sector's success reflected the failure of SOEs to supply consumer goods that were in high demand, as well as essential services.[11] Black markets had operated, as in the Soviet Union under central planning, but the gradual removal of legal barriers and ideological straitjackets allowed the re-emergence of the private sector.

New thinking about marketization and urban enterprises was reflected in the Central Committee's "Decision on Reform and Economic Structure," which was adopted during the Third Plenary Session of the 12th Central Committee of the CCP in October 1984. That document cast aside Maoist rhetoric in favor of stating that the main goal of the CCP should be economic development—not class struggle—and that the market and price system should play a key role: "The full development of a commodity [i.e. market] economy is . . . a necessary requirement for the realization of the economic modernization of China"—and "price system reform is the key to the success of the reform of the whole economic system" (Wu, 2005: 75–76).

Special economic zones

One way of helping to rationalize the price system is to open the domestic economy to the forces of international competition. China took a small step in that direction in May 1980 when it decided to allow Guangdong and Fujian provinces to establish SEZs to attract foreign investors and integrate China into the global trading system. The first four SEZs were opened in the coastal cities of Shenzhen, Zhuhai, Shantou, and Xiamen. Fourteen additional SEZs were established in May 1984, including Wenzhou, which became the model for private-sector development in China (Wu, 2005: 295–96).

Although SEZs were conceived of by officials, individual entrepreneurs made the free-trade zones successful through prudent risk taking, hard work, and the desire to profit in the non-state sector. In particular, the Wenzhou economy depended primarily on the private sector that developed rapidly after 1978. By 1984, Wenzhou, a coastal city in southern Zhejiang Province, already had more than 130,000 family businesses. Those private firms produced the bulk of industrial output value and specialized in light industrial goods such as textiles, shoes, buttons, and electronic products. Entrepreneurship was a way of life—and Wenzhou flourished as markets deepened. With virtually no state assistance, the Wenzhou economy grew by 16 percent per year, on average, between 1978 and 1994 (Yu and Zhang, 2008: 4).

Since private enterprises (*siying qiye*) were not legally recognized until 1988, owners of private businesses with eight or more employees had a strong incentive to avoid discriminatory treatment by paying to attach themselves to SOEs (that is, becoming "hang-on household enterprises") or by registering as collective enterprises—a practice known as "wearing a red hat." Doing so would make it easier for them to obtain credit from state-owned banks. Nearly 62 percent of Wenzhou's household enterprises had attached themselves to SOEs by the mid-1980s, and 80 percent of "neighborhood and district enterprises" registered as collectives (Tsai, 2002: 130–31).

Other means of financing the growing private sector in Wenzhou emerged, including underground money houses, pawn shops, credit associations, private money houses, trade credit, and interpersonal lending. Those forms of "back-alley banking" allowed spontaneous privatization to occur in Wenzhou and other areas. Local cadres welcomed the new informal credit institutions and the newly created wealth brought about by robust private development. As one local official remarked, "If we had waited for the central government to allow certain practices, there would not be economic reform" (Tsai, 2002: 121).[12]

As Wenzhou's markets grew, there was increasing pressure to legally sanction the private alternatives to state financing. Kellee Tsai (2002: 120) cites one official at the Wenzhou City branch of the People's Bank of China as saying, "The credit services performed by [unsanctioned] financial institutions in Wenzhou are essential for the development of market socialism. . . . Private money houses should be considered within the range of 'popular' credit activities that are legal."

From the perspective of economic freedom, Wenzhou offers a prime example of how individuals, when given the opportunity to trade, can lift themselves out of poverty without state intervention. As Ma Lei (1998: 6) reported:

> The development of the private sector has fundamentally changed the way residents of Wenzhou look at the world. . . . Market forces have broadened the horizons of Wenzhou residents and educated them to the ways of the world. They have learned that in a market economy entrepreneurs frequently fail. But they have also learned that risk taking, when combined with foresight and hard work, can produce significant rewards. . . . Most important, the people of Wenzhou realize . . . that one earns his living not through coercion or brute force but by serving others. That realization has produced a climate in which private industry and private organizations—including private schools—can thrive.

Similar stories can be told about the other SEZs. They opened China to the outside world and, in so doing, widened both the market for goods and services and the market for ideas—especially regarding alternatives to central planning and control.

The Jiang-Zhu years: building the socialist market economy, 1992–2002

The decollectivization of agriculture with the HRS, the rise of TVEs, the emergence of urban private enterprises, and the creation of SEZs all contributed to making the first decade of China's economic reform a major stepping stone from plan to market—and thereby enhancing economic freedom for millions of people. Nearly everyone benefited from the reform movement: rural families, urban residents, SOEs protected by government largesse, and those who flocked to the newly created SEZs. Real incomes were rising and the future looked bright.[13] That progress, however, was brutally interrupted by the crackdown in Tiananmen Square in June 1989.

The student demonstrations began in April 1989 with the sudden death of Hu Yaobang, who was greatly revered for his stand against hardliners and his rehabilitation of those accused of being "Rightists." Hu had been ousted in January 1987 as general secretary of the CCP by so-called conservatives who wanted to protect the status quo. One of the students' demands was to restore Hu's reputation within the Party. They also wanted greater freedom of the press and assembly—demands that threatened the CCP's monopoly on power. The political crisis was also stirred up by rising inflation that threatened to reduce the growth in real incomes.

With the crackdown on June 4, 1989, conservatives gained the upper hand, and Zhao Ziyang was placed under house arrest. The reform agenda, which the public still supported, was put on hold. However, as Naughton (2007: 99) points out, "The conservative attempts to roll back reforms were completely without success." Inflation was tamed and:

> [M]arket forces corrected other imbalances in the economy with a speed that surprised conservatives and left planners far behind. As it became clear that the conservatives had no viable program, their support among the Communist Party elite began to crumble.
>
> (Naughton, 2007: 99)

In 1992, Deng exercised his leadership and support for continuing the reform movement by taking his famous Southern Tour. He visited Shenzhen and other SEZs to praise the progress that had been made since he had instituted the "open-door policy" a decade earlier. His slogan was, "It doesn't matter if policies are labeled socialist or capitalist, so long as they foster development." In October 1992, the 14th Congress of the CCP officially embraced the "socialist market economy" (Naughton, 2007: 99–100).

Deng's strong support for liberalization reignited the reform movement under the guidance of Jiang Zemin, who was appointed general secretary of the CCP in 1989 (taking the place of Zhao Ziyang), and Zhu Rongji, who became vice premier in 1993 and premier in 1998.

Many leaders still viewed the market as a mechanism for strengthening socialism. They did not want to privatize SOEs, but rather to improve their performance by introducing a "managerial responsibility contract system." After meeting a state output quota, managers were given the right to make production and resource allocation decisions based on market criteria, and were rewarded for improved performance. In this way, it was hoped that SOEs could "grow out of the plan" (Coase and Wang, 2012: 45; Naughton, 1995). The introduction of the dual-track price reform in 1984 was also meant to make SOEs more efficient.

The rise of the private sector made it essential to improve the performance of SOEs, otherwise they would put a heavy burden on the state as losses mounted. Likewise, without a unified price system reflecting supply and demand, rather than planners' preferences, markets would lack clear signals about what to produce and how best to organize production.

The problem, however, is that changing the management system, while retaining state ownership, still leaves a lot of inefficiency. The lack of bankruptcy and the absence of private owners, who have the right to capitalize enterprise income by selling assets or shares of stock, meant that no one had a strong incentive to be as efficient as private, for-profit firms.

Reform of state-owned enterprises

In 1992, as the economic reform movement gained momentum, the debate over SOE reform heated up: "It was clear that there was no way to resolve the problems with SOEs under the constraints of state ownership" (Zhang, 2015b: 19). As SOE losses mounted (overall losses for industrial SOEs exceeded profits in 1992), "fundamental thinking regarding SOEs began to change, and new thinking about privatizing them took hold" (Zhang, 2015b: 20). One of the key principles for reform adopted at the Third Plenary Session of the 14th National Congress in 1993 was "clearly established ownership." The aim was to build "a modern enterprise system" and diversify property rights (Zhang, 2015b: 20).

The ownership reform began, as usual, at the local level. However, in 1995, Jiang Zemin made it clear that only small SOEs would be allowed to "privatize," while large ones would remain in the hands of the state.[14] His idea of "grasping the large, releasing the small" (*zhua da fang xiao*) meant no radical ownership reform, but it did result in the transfer of many small- and medium-sized SOEs to the private sector, and it allowed large SOEs to diversify their ownership by transforming into joint-stock companies, especially after the 1997 Asian financial crisis (Zhang, 2015b: 20).

The poor performance of SOEs resulting from the lack of private property rights and a "soft budget constraint"—that is, an implicit promise of a government bailout for insolvent SOEs—was a major factor in bringing about SOE ownership reform. The rapid increase in non-performing loans from state-owned banks made reform of SOEs a high priority for Jiang Zemin and Zhu Rongji. By allowing debate in the market for ideas, and through strong leadership, Jiang and Zhu were able to take significant steps toward improving the ownership structure and growing the non-state sector. As Zhang (2015b: 21) notes, "In 1998 alone, about 20 million state employees were laid off when the state sector was restructured. Without Jiang and Zhu's decisiveness and courage that task would have been impossible."

The implementation of the Company Law in 1994 led to the conversion of SOEs into joint-stock companies ("corporatization") and provided the legal basis for diverse ownership forms, including private firms.[15] By 1996, the SOE share of industrial output value had fallen from 77 percent in 1978 to

33 percent (Naughton, 2007: 300–1). In terms of value added in the business sector (including agriculture), the OECD (2005: 80–83) found that when the private sector is broadly defined in terms of control rights, it accounted for 61.5 percent of value added in 2002—a gain of 8 percentage points over 1998. Meanwhile, the public sector declined by 8 percentage points (Table 9.1) because of a fall in the value added by both state- and collective-controlled enterprises. The SOE reforms shut down or divested fully state-controlled firms and injected private minority stakes in state shareholding firms. Meanwhile, collectives were transitioning to the private sector or downsizing as regional competition increased and new opportunities arose outside the planned economy.

Price reform

The dual-track approach to reforming SOEs also was applied to the price system. Under the planned economy, China's prices were set by government fiat, not market forces. Consequently, prices did not reflect reality and led to highly inefficient use of scarce resources.[16] Political/ideological constraints did not allow direct movement to market pricing; thus a mixed system of fixed state prices and flexible market prices emerged.

The first proposal for a dual-track price system was introduced in 1984 by Weiying Zhang, a young graduate economics student (Zhang, 2015a: 391, n. 6). It led to a national debate over the role of prices in a socialist economy and, eventually, to reform. Before the official dual-track price system took effect after 1984, there was an illegal price system for goods and services that was parallel to the system of planned prices. After the Third Plenary Session of the 12th Central Committee of the CCP in October 1984, there was a gradual transition to market-based product prices. In effect, "the dual-track price reform legalized the spontaneous dual-track price [system] that already existed" (Zhang, 2015a: 239).

Price reform temporarily regressed as proponents of the planned economy gained ground following Tiananmen in 1989. But after Deng's Southern Tour in 1992, there was no turning back. By 1999, 86 percent of producer goods, 95 percent of retail sales, and 83 percent of farm commodities were priced at competitively determined (market) prices (see Table 9.2).

Table 9.1 Value added in business sector by firm ownership (%)

Business sector	1998	1999	2000	2001	2002	Change
Private	53.5	54.9	56.3	59.4	61.5	+8
Public	46.5	45.1	43.7	40.6	38.5	−8
State controlled	33.1	33.0	33.1	31.2	29.9	−3.2
Collectively controlled	13.4	12.1	10.6	9.4	8.6	−4.8

Source: OECD (2005: 81)

Table 9.2 Share of transactions conducted at market prices (%)

	1978	1985	1991	1995	1999
Producer goods					
Market prices	0	13	46	78	86
State guided	0	23	18	6	4
State fixed	100	64	36	16	10
Retail sales					
Market prices	3	34	69	89	95
State guided	0	19	10	2	1
State fixed	97	47	21	9	4
Farm commodities					
Market prices	6	40	58	79	83
State guided	2	23	20	4	7
State fixed	93	37	22	17	9

Source: OECD (2005: 29)

In his book, *The Logic of the Market*, Zhang (2015a) draws various lessons from China's price reform. The most important one in helping us to understand "the evolution of economic systems" is to "know how to use the spontaneous power of the market" (Zhang, 2015a: 259). His work shows "that the dual-track system was not the result of the meticulous design . . . It arose spontaneously during the process of reform" (Zhang, 2015a: 259). Leaders realized that they did not have sufficient information to set market-clearing prices, but they learned that market participants do have the relevant information and act on it. As illegal prices became legal and state controls were relaxed, a uniform market-pricing mechanism crowded out the inferior planned system (Zhang, 2015a: 260).

Other reforms

There were other reforms during the Jiang-Zhu regime that moved China closer to a market economy—notably, the 1993 decision to establish a "socialist market economic system" (in recognition of the growing importance of marketization in China's development strategy), the 1996 decision to make the renminbi (also known as the yuan) fully convertible for current account transactions, the 1999 constitutional amendment to legitimize private ownership within the limits of the law, the 2001 decision to join the World Trade Organization (WTO), and the 2002 decision to invite private entrepreneurs to join the CCP.

Of those reforms, China's accession to the WTO in December 2001 was a particularly significant event. It helped to integrate China into the global economy and introduced China to a rules-based trade regime. However, as Nicholas Lardy (2002) has shown, China was well on its way toward global economic integration *before* entering the WTO. Tariff and non-tariff barriers had come down significantly in the decade prior to entering the WTO, and trading rights (that is, rights to export and import) were greatly extended.

The motivation behind China's ambition to join the WTO was that top leaders thought it would provide an effective means of putting pressure on vested interests, such as SOEs and state-owned banks, who sought protection from the growing non-state sector. By opening domestic producers and financial institutions to global competition, it was thought, consumers would be better served, and economic efficiency would improve. Zhu Rongji and others increased their support after the Asian financial crisis of 1997–98. They realized that "there was no viable alternative to the globalization of production" and that China "would benefit from greater participation in the trend" (Lardy, 2002: 20).[17] Opening the state sector to increased competition from foreign firms would help to downsize government, and there would be losers—but Zhu was strong in his support of structural reform and moved ahead.

The Hu-Wen era and the global financial crisis

The leadership change in 2003, with the appointment of Hu Jintao as president and Wen Jiabao as premier, ushered in a new era in which the primary goal of development became rebalancing the economy to achieve sustainable economic growth and "all-round prosperity." However, that key objective was deterred by an unforeseen event: the global financial crisis of 2008–09. A massive government "stimulus" program (RMB4 trillion, US$586 billion), designed to rapidly increase fixed asset investment and maintain China's export-led development model, kept growth positive—but it slowed progress toward rebalancing and further liberalizing the economy. Rapid credit creation, with state-owned banks funneling a large share to SOEs, misallocated credit. Moreover, in the absence of market-determined interest rates and capital freedom, financial repression remained a serious problem.[18]

Prior to the financial crisis, Premier Wen gave an important speech at Harvard. In his remarks on December 10, 2003, he expressed optimism regarding China's future. He noted that China had "found the right path of development"— namely, "building socialism with Chinese characteristics." The essential nature of that path, he said, "is to mobilize all positive factors, emancipate and develop the productive forces, and respect and protect the freedom of the Chinese people to pursue happiness." He pointed toward the success of China's economic liberalization:

> With deepening restructuring toward the socialist market economy . . ., there was gradual lifting of the former improper restrictions, visible and invisible, on people's freedom in choice of occupation, mobility, enterprise, investment, information, travel, faith, and lifestyles. This has brought extensive and profound changes never seen before in China's history.
>
> (Wen, 2003)

Most tellingly, Wen (2003) attributed China's success "to the freedom-inspired creativity of the Chinese people." To maintain that success, he argued, workers would need more capital, and to attract sufficient capital, China would need more secure property rights: "Without effective protection of the citizens' right to property, it will be difficult to attract and accumulate valuable capital."

An important step was taken toward Wen's goal when the National People's Congress amended the PRC Constitution on March 14, 2004. Article 11 now proclaims: "The State encourages, supports and guides the development of the nonpublic sectors of the economy," while article 13 holds that "Citizens' lawful private property is inviolable." However, the state reserved the right to ultimately control property rights in the "public interest," and the absence of an independent judiciary meant that private property rights were still tenuous. Moreover, land is still owned by the state, although the Property Law of 2007 extended land-use rights through long-term leases and gave stronger protection to private property rights (Zhang, 2008). Another positive development during the Jiang-Wen regime was the State Council's adoption, in February 2005, of "Guidelines on Encouraging, Supporting and Guiding the Development of the Individual, Private, and Other Non-Public Economic Sectors," which made it easier to enter certain sectors (OECD, 2005: 89, 119, n. 10).

When the global financial crisis threatened China's strong growth record, there was increasing pressure to strengthen large SOEs in pillar industries—even though the private sector had been the driving force of China's rise. However, as the global economy weakened and SOEs grew larger, China's overcapacity in steel and other state-supported industries became evident. Special interests in favor of state protection became stronger, and the pro-liberalization rhetoric of the leadership deviated from their actions. Compared to the Deng and Jiang-Zhu eras, which Weiying Zhang (2015b: 11–12) argues were characterized by "good ideas and strong leadership" (in terms of advancing marketization and reducing the scope of the planned economy), the decade under Hu-Wen is best seen as a case of "wrong ideas and weak leadership."[19]

In his recent book *Markets over Mao*, Nicholas Lardy (2014: 2) questions "the view that state firms grew in prominence during the Hu-Wen decade," finding, in particular, that "private firms continued to displace state firms throughout the period." Contrary to conventional wisdom, he also finds that "the access of private firms to bank credit has improved so much that on average new bank lending to private firms in 2010–12 was two-thirds more than to state firms" (Lardy, 2014: 4). In his view, "China's stimulus . . . was much less state-centric than is commonly charged" (Lardy, 2014: 5). Nevertheless, Lardy (2014: 107) notes that SOEs still held 48 percent of loans made by all financial institutions to enterprises in 2012, and certainly a large share of credit from *state-owned banks* still flows to SOEs.[20]

The role of private firms in China's development cannot be underestimated. Although state planning appears to have made a comeback during the Hu-Wen regime, especially after the financial crisis, Lardy (2012: 121) is correct to emphasize the continued importance of the private sector:

- "private firms have increasingly displaced state firms as the dominant source of output in most of manufacturing, mining, construction, wholesaling and retailing, and catering";
- "private industrial firms consistently make more productive use of capital, as reflected in a much higher return on assets";
- "private firms are responsible for virtually all of the growth of employment in urban China since the reform began"; and
- "private firms are now the most important contributor to China's still growing exports."

We can certainly agree with Lardy (2012: 121) that "China's economic rise in the reform era is largely the story of the expanding role of markets and private enterprise." Whether that rise continues will depend on the new leadership's commitment to fundamental reform of both the economic and legal system. As Steven N. S. Cheung (1986 [1982]) first recognized, China would "go capitalist" by allowing the spontaneous development of the market, but ultimate success requires privatization and the rule of law (Cheung, 1990).

Xi Jinping and China's future

In November 2012, Xi Jinping became general secretary of the CCP and chairman of China's Central Military Commission. He was viewed as a strong leader who would spur rebalancing and reignite economic liberalization. In March 2013, he consolidated his power by taking over as president, and Li Keqiang became the new premier. They hoped to implement policies that would achieve "all-round development," and to realize "China's Dream" of becoming a wealthy and healthy nation. However, they still had to operate within the ideological constraints of the CCP and socialism, without a free market for ideas.

The Xi-Li agenda

The first sign of progress came in November 2013, following the Third Plenary Session of the CCP's 18th Central Committee, headed by Xi Jinping, when it announced the "Decision on Major Issues Concerning Comprehensively Deepening Reforms."[21] The 60-point roadmap calls for reform on a broad front, but with a focus on economic reform:

> Economic system reform is the focus of deepening the reform comprehensively. The underlying issue is how to strike a balance between the role of the government and that of the market, and let the market play the decisive role in allocating resources and let the government play its functions better.[22]

Resource allocation is to be improved by adhering to "market rules, market prices and market competition." Officials should "encourage, support and guide the development of the non-public sector, and stimulate its dynamism and creativity."

The new roadmap for reform also emphasized the importance of property rights: "Property rights are the core of ownership. We need to improve the modern property rights system with clear ownership, clear-cut rights and obligations, [and] strict protection." In that regard, SOEs will be allowed "to develop into mixed enterprises," and "a rural property rights transfer market" will be established to help to ensure "the open, fair and procedure-based operation of rural property rights transfer." The *hukou* system will also be reformed by allowing "the eligible population to move away from agriculture and become urban residents."

Finally, there will be further efforts to "improve the mechanism for market-based Renminbi exchange rate formation, accelerate interest-rate liberalization, and . . . promote the opening of the capital market."

While the blueprint is promising, the reality is that "if people are not allowed to freely debate how to reform the political system, then it will be impossible to develop the right ideas to implement this roadmap" (Zhang, 2015b: 38).

Although President Xi has called for further economic liberalization, he has done little to advance privatization, the rule of law, or limited government; instead, he has focused on cracking down on any attempts to create a free market in ideas (Dorn, 2017). Moreover, Xi seeks to strengthen large SOEs by requiring that they operate on a commercial basis (an old socialist dream), and he plans to retain them as the heart of China's socialist market economy (Wei, 2015). The centralization of power has made local leaders more cautious in taking the initiative to advance liberalization. Without further liberalization and innovation, however, China will not be able to restructure its economy and increase efficiency.

The problem is that, without private owners and the ultimate threat of bankruptcy, socialist enterprises have little incentive to be efficient. It is well known that China's private industrial firms have a much higher return on assets than SOEs (Lardy, 2014: 121). In free private markets, firms are incentivized to be efficient and to maximize profits; firms that cannot pass the market test will fail. When government interferes with the competitive market process, the marketplace becomes politicized, and the range of choices open to people becomes more limited.

Premier Li (2015) tells us that reforms to cut bureaucracy and decentralize power will help to "get the relationship right between the government and the market." However, without widespread privatization and a free market in ideas, as expounded by Coase and Wang (2012), state power—and the rent-seeking that goes with it—will continue to be a drag on individual freedom and prosperity.

While the Party pays lip service to a free market in ideas, noting that "there can never be an end to the need for the emancipation of individual thought" (*China Daily*, 2013), Party doctrine strictly regulates that market. Consequently, under market socialism, there is bound to be ever-present tension between the individual and the state. As long as socialism trumps liberalism—in the classical sense of limited government and individual freedom—promises of further liberalization will be empty. The arbitrariness and uncertainty of state action—and the precariousness of private property and human rights—naturally breed tension. The harmony that officials promise is a false harmony designed by the state, not a true harmony spontaneously produced by limited government and freedom.

In a recent interview with the *Wall Street Journal*, President Xi expressed his view on the relationship between freedom and order: "Freedom is the purpose of order, and order the guarantee of freedom" (Xi, 2015). There is some truth to this statement, but the real meaning is that China's ruling elite will not tolerate dissent: individuals will be free to communicate ideas, but only those consistent with "socialist principles."

This socialist vision contrasts sharply with that of market liberalism, which holds that freedom is not the *purpose* of order; rather, it is the essential means to an emergent or spontaneous order. Simply put, voluntary exchange—based on the principle of freedom or non-intervention—expands the range of choices open to individuals and thus increases social wealth.[23] As James M. Buchanan (1982: 5) has argued, "The 'order' of the market emerges *only* from the *process* of voluntary exchange among the participating individuals."

At a press conference following the Third Session of the 12th National People's Congress, Premier Li Keqiang (2015) said, "We need to ensure that we run the country according to the law—everyone is equal before the law, and no one is above the law. . . . There must be no irresponsible actions or inaction on the part of government officials." He wants people to "achieve full potential in their life," and he wants the government to "eliminate roadblocks and pave the way for people to tap their entrepreneurship." Finally, he would fight corruption and rent-seeking by "institution-building." Such rhetoric is encouraging, but at the same time we hear President Xi declare: "We in the Communist Party are firm Marxists and our party's guiding thought is Marxism-Leninism, Mao Zedong Thought and Socialism with Chinese Characteristics" (Tatlow, 2014).[24]

China's future

Whether China evolves further toward the market will depend on whether Chinese leaders can "limit the power of government by adhering to a genuine constitutionalism and rule of law" (Xu, 2015: 546). What now matters is whether Xi has good ideas for liberalization and can implement them, which will depend on whether he has the wherewithal to limit his own power. When he says, "An important goal for China's current economic reform is to enable the market to play the decisive role in resource allocation and make the government better play its role," he recognizes that China needs "to make good use of both the invisible hand and the visible hand" (Xi, 2015). The problem is that the invisible hand does not work well without the freedom that stems from widespread private property—including a free market for ideas—and limited government.

Real change has come about in China because ordinary people have taken the initiative in moving from plan to market. When peasants and private entrepreneurs were successful, rulers took credit and sanctioned the spontaneous (bottom-up) privatization. Of course, "institutional development needs to fit initial conditions and to be made compatible with the interests of ruling groups" (Qian, 2003: 331). China's dual-track system of moving from plan to market was successful in that regard.[25] Moreover, as Oi and Walder (1999b: 19) note, the evolution of property rights in China has resulted from an interplay between local officials and market forces: the gradual movement from public to private or quasi-private ownership "occurred only partially as a result of explicit reforms of ownership, and . . . continued without repeated intervention by central officials seeking to implement a reform blueprint."[26]

Although ordinary people took the initiative to move outside the state sector, first in agriculture and later in industry and trade, the primary factor for China's successful reform movement, especially from 1978 to 2002, was the pairing of right ideas and strong leadership. Deng Xiaoping, Zhao Ziyang, Jiang Zemin, Zhu Rongji, and a host of other leaders—who were influenced by intellectuals sympathetic to the market mechanism and who recognized the failure of central planning—were instrumental in promoting new ways of thinking about economic organization and leading the way from plan to market.[27]

Today, the information revolution offers the Chinese people a new opportunity to expose corruption and repression, even as the CCP tries to suppress the market for ideas. However, things are not looking good. As Zhang (2015b: 38) points out, "There is every reason to be worried by the increasingly tight control of academic freedom and by the lack of publication and press freedom." China should learn from Hong Kong, which is the freest economy in the world. In a recent survey, businesses ranked "the free flow of information" near the top of the list of reasons why they moved to Hong Kong (Hong Kong Census and Statistics Department, 2015: 23).

Markets function best when there are well-defined private property rights and the free flow of information. If China hopes to establish a world-class financial market and to internationalize the renminbi, people need to be free to openly criticize existing institutions and to search for better alternatives. The history of China's economic reforms since 1978 illustrates that experimentation with market-based development—spontaneous marketization—is a proven means of advancing liberty and prosperity. Blocking the free flow of information will slow China's advance by increasing uncertainty and the tension between the individual and the state.

Conclusion

China has come a long way since the days when entrepreneurs were banned and central planning dominated economic life. Today, entrepreneurship is taught in universities, markets set most prices, and trade is seen as the path to prosperity. In Chengdu, the capital of Sichuan Province, people exchange ideas about entrepreneurship in ancient teahouses. The Rongchuang Teahouse "organizes road shows and entrepreneurship contests," as well as provides a large space for "one-stop service for selecting, breeding, incubating, and financing entrepreneurial projects" (Chengdu Government, 2016). Budding entrepreneurs in Chengdu can now obtain a business license in as little as one day.

The Chinese economy, however, is complex in terms of the interplay of plan and market. State ownership is still prevalent and investment planning, prominent. In such an environment, people seek to make themselves better off by learning how to "play the game" and evade roadblocks to market exchange. A good example is in the area of e-commerce, in which start-up firms work within the framework of monopoly platforms and the platform providers, such as Alibaba and Tencent, are active in making regulations that satisfy government bureaucrats, as well as the operators. Rent-seeking goes hand-in-hand with entrepreneurship in China. As Chen and Ku (2016: 664) explain, "Rent seeking in the real economy creates distortions and hidden opportunities that nourish innovations in the Internet sector."

To normalize markets in China, institutional change is critical. Market socialism needs to be transformed into market liberalism, with well-defined and protected private property rights. Leading reformers, such as Wu Jinglian, recognize that "all the policies encouraging the development of the private sector that are beneficial to the national economy and people's livelihood must be earnestly implemented; all the rules and regulations prejudiced against nonstate enterprises must be abolished" (Wu, 2005: 438). More importantly, Weiying Zhang (2015a: 109), the architect of dual-track pricing, understands that "the progress of humanity has been a continuous transition to the logic of the market," which is the logic of freedom.

China has opened to the outside world and moved far along the road toward a genuine market economy, but much remains to be done—especially the creation of a free market for ideas (Wang, 2017).[28] Doing so will require fundamental political change because any advancement of free speech is a threat to those in power. In this struggle between state and market, the primacy of limited government over democratic rule should be kept in mind. Also, the importance of the information age for China's future should not be underestimated. Grassroots movements have never had greater leverage than at present.

The main lesson from examining the genesis and evolution of China's reform movement since 1978 is that the spontaneous nature of many of China's key reforms, which were later sanctioned by the state, illustrate that if the government gets out of the way and allows experimentation with market-friendly institutions that reward productive activity, there will be a virtuous circle.

Notes

* The author thanks Ari Blask, Kevin Dowd, Ben Powell, Ning Wang, and Weiying Zhang for helpful comments on earlier versions of this chapter.
1 For a more detailed account of Mao's disastrous policies that took millions of lives, see Dikötter (2010, 2016).
2 Dikötter (2016: ch. 21) provides compelling evidence that, when legal markets were banned, black markets arose, especially in the poorest areas such as Yan'an, Luonan,

and Pucheng in Shaanxi Province, as early as 1974. Collective property was divided up among households, and produce was sold on the black market. Underground private factories sprung up, and peasants engaged in various trades that were banned. Local cadres looked the other way or even assisted in the illegal behavior. Similar actions were witnessed in Hunan, where peasants expanded their private plots by 50 percent in 1972. In Sichuan, farmers rented land in the early 1970s; in Guangdong, peasants returned to skilled work, such as embroidery, once trade restrictions for light industry were relaxed in 1972.

3 For a useful summary of the origins and nature of the Household Responsibility System, see Tian (2009). More detailed accounts can be found in Lin (1987) and Zhou (1996).

4 The Dazhai Commune in Shanxi, which Chen Yonggui pioneered, gained national prominence during the Cultural Revolution when Mao praised it for self-reliance and nearly miraculous productivity. In reality, Chen had created a Potemkin village to deceive officials and others into believing that state ownership and forced collectivization were working (Dikötter 2016: 219, 231).

5 In 1975, Zhao had already secretly given production teams more autonomy to decollectivize (Vogel 2011: 338).

6 Coase and Wang (2012: ch. 3) discuss these "marginal revolutions" in detail. They conclude that "the four marginal revolutions—enacted by actors marginalized in Mao's socialist economy—quickly gave birth to a dynamic private sector in China, freeing 800 million peasants from the state, allowing almost 20 million 'returned youth' in the cities to set up their own businesses, and creating a few spots for foreign and domestic entrepreneurs to flourish and inadvertently showcase the dynamism of capitalism" (Coase and Wang 2012: 65).

7 The restriction on migration to urban areas under the *hukou* system meant that the vast population in rural areas had to rely on farming within the confines of the People's Communes. As that system was dismantled, new opportunities arose for doing business in the non-state sector. Central planning and SOEs dominated the urban landscape, leaving little space for marketization and private entrepreneurs. Thus the freedom gained by peasants after the Third Plenum in 1978 gave them a head start in developing their entrepreneurial skills. See Zhang (2015a: 178) and Zhou (1996: ch. 5).

8 State-owned enterprises dominated the urban areas and left the countryside open to development by entrepreneurial farmers, who created new markets to help to relieve the shortages that were the legacy of central planning.

9 As Zhou (1996: 53) notes, "[Farmers] succeeded by making individual deals with individual cadres. They offered cadres more than the cadres expected. That broke the log jam."

10 An English translation of the PRC Constitution, with amendments, can be found at http://english.people.com.cn/constitution/constitution.html

11 Coase and Wang (2012: 68) point out that strong demand in the 1980s for consumer goods and services resulted in high incomes for small shop owners, traders, and owners of restaurants. Street vendors could earn more than scientists, and barbers could earn more than surgeons operating in the state sector.

12 See Tsai (2002: ch. 4) for a detailed discussion of the Wenzhou economic model and the emergence of private financing alternatives to state-owned banks. See also Yu and Zhang (2008) for an excellent analysis of the informal financial markets in Wenzhou and how they emerged as an example of Douglass North's notion of "adaptive efficiency."

13 Lau, Qian, and Roland (2000) refer to the 1978–88 period as "reform without losers."

14 The word "privatize" was not used by officials or in government documents because of ideological constraints (Zhang 2015b: 21).

15 Besides SOEs directly owned by the state, collective enterprises, and private firms, there are a host of other ownership forms—e.g. share cooperative enterprises, joint enterprises, limited liability corporations, and shareholding limited corporations. Meanwhile, private enterprises include sole proprietorships, partnerships, limited liability companies, shareholding limited companies, and individual businesses (Lardy 2014: 64–65).

16 See Lin, Cai, and Li (1996: chs. 2–3) for a detailed account of the distortions under China's centrally planned economy. In particular, see section 2.4 on the "Planned Resource-Allocation Mechanism," which elaborates on the pricing distortions that characterized the so-called shortage economy (Lin et al. 1996: 38–44). Planners ignored the principle of comparative advantage and gave preferential treatment to heavy industry; they suppressed interest rates and other relative prices, creating shortages; and they eliminated competition and private markets to ensure that the planners' preferences would prevail. See also Naughton (2007: chs. 3 and 19) and Zhang (2015a: 240–46).

17 Lardy (2002: 20) points to the important role that Long Yongtu, vice minister of foreign trade, played in making the case for integrating China into the global economy.

18 On the issue of financial repression, see Li (2001), Dorn (2001, 2006, 2008), and Lardy (2012: 78–88).

19 For Zhang's case against the Hu-Wen regime, see Zhang (2015b: 23–29).

20 Lardy (2012: 107), however, is careful to note that if one considers total bank credit going to households in 2012, then "loans to enterprises amounted to only 61 percent of all loans"; consequently, "loans to state-owned and state-controlled enterprises accounted for only 29 percent [48% × 61%] of all loans from the financial system in 2012."

21 Available at http://www.china.org.cn/china/third_plenary_session/2014-01/16/content_31212602.htm

22 Near the end of the first Five-Year Plan (1953–57), Gu Zhun, an economist at the Economics Institute of the Chinese Academy of Sciences, proposed that the market mechanism be given a key role in allocating resources. He was regarded as a heretic by those favoring central planning and labeled a "bourgeois Rightist." Thus his market-based development theory fell into a dark hole: see Wu (2005: 37–38).

23 Peter Bauer (1957: 113), a pioneer in development economics, held that "the principal objective and criterion of economic development" is to widen "the range of effective alternatives open to people." He understood that "the market order minimizes the power of individuals and groups forcibly to restrict the choices of other people," and that, under such a spontaneous order, "the rich . . . usually owe their prosperity to activities which have widened the choices of their fellow men, including those of the poor" (Bauer 1984: 25).

24 President Xi Jinping has also said, "We need to fully make use of the great wisdom accumulated by the Chinese nation over the last 5,000 years" (Page 2015). However, his focus has been on using classical literature to strengthen the Party's adherence to socialism, not to promote the market's invisible hand and freedom (see Dorn 2016).

25 See Qian (2003: 307–10) for a comprehensive view of the dual-track approach to market liberalization in China, as applied to agricultural, industrial, and labor markets.

26 The case studies in Oi and Walder (1999a) provide ample evidence that the emergence of the non-state sector, although often "hidden," required cooperation between local officials and private parties who sought to improve their circumstances.

27 Weiying Zhang (2015b) provides an in-depth analysis of the clash between reformers and conservatives in the transition from plan to market, and of the importance of ideas and leadership in that struggle.
28 James Madison, the "chief architect" of the U.S. Constitution, recognized the importance of a free market in ideas when he wrote, in 1825, "The diffusion of knowledge is the only guardian of true liberty" (quoted in Padover 1953: 337).

References

Bauer, P. T. 1957. *Economic Analysis and Policy in Underdeveloped Countries.* Durham, NC: Duke University Press.

Bauer, P. T. 1984. *Reality and Rhetoric: Studies in the Economics of Development.* Cambridge, MA: Harvard University Press.

Becker, J. 1998 [1996]. *Hungry Ghosts: Mao's Secret Famine.* New York: Henry Holt.

Becker, J. 2000. *The Chinese.* New York: Free Press.

Buchanan, J. M. 1982. Order Defined in the Process of Its Emergence. *Literature of Liberty,* 5(4): 5–18.

Chen, T. J., and Ku, Y. H. 2016. Rent Seeking and Entrepreneurship: Internet Startups in China. *Cato Journal,* 36(3): 659–688.

Chengdu Government. 2016. "Makers" Grow by 680 People per Day: Chengdu Becomes City of "Entrepreneurship." *Wall Street Journal,* July 15.

Cheung, S. N. S. 1986 [1982]. *Will China Go "Capitalist"?* 2nd edn, London: Institute of Economic Affairs.

Cheung, S. N. S. 1990. Privatization vs. Special Interests: The Experience of China's Economic Reforms. In J. A. Dorn and X. Wang (eds.), *Economic Reform in China: Problems and Prospects,* pp. 21–32. Chicago, IL: University of Chicago Press.

China Daily. 2013. The Decision on Major Issues Concerning Comprehensively Deepening Reform in Brief. *China Daily,* November 16.

Coase, R., and Wang, N. 2012. *How China Became Capitalist.* New York: Palgrave Macmillan.

Deng, X. P. 1987. *Fundamental Issues in Present-Day China.* Trans. Bureau for the Compilation and Translation of Works of Marx, Engels, Lenin, and Stalin under the Central Committee of the Communist Party of China. Beijing: Foreign Languages Press.

Dikötter, F. 2010. *Mao's Great Famine: The History of China's Most Devastating Catastrophe, 1958–62.* New York: Walker.

Dikötter, F. 2016. *The Cultural Revolution: A People's History, 1962–1976.* New York: Bloomsbury Press.

Dorn, J. A. 2001. Creating Real Capital Markets in China. *Cato Journal,* 21(1): 65–75.

Dorn, J. A. 2006. Ending Financial Repression in China. *Cato Institute Economic Development Bulletin,* 5: 1–4.

Dorn, J. A. 2008. Creating Financial Harmony: Lessons for China. *Cato Journal,* 28(3): 535–553.

Dorn, J. A. 2016. China's Challenge: Expanding the Market, Limiting the State. *Man and the Economy,* 3(1): 23–41.

Dorn, J. A. 2017. China Needs a Free Market for Ideas. *Orange County Register,* February 4.

Friedman, M. 1989. Using the Market for Social Development. *Cato Journal,* 8(3): 567–579.

Friedman, M. 1990. *Friedman in China*. Hong Kong: Chinese University of Hong Kong Press.

Hong Kong Census and Statistics Department. 2015. *Report on 2015 Annual Survey of Companies in Hong Kong Representing Parent Companies Located Outside Hong Kong*. Available at https://www.censtatd.gov.hk/hkstat/sub/sp360.jsp?productCode=B1110004

Huang, Y. 2008. *Capitalism with Chinese Characteristics: Entrepreneurship and the State*. New York: Cambridge University Press.

Lardy, N. R. 2002. *Integrating China into the Global Economy*. Washington, DC: Brookings Institution.

Lardy, N. R. 2012. *Sustaining China's Economic Growth after the Global Financial Crisis*. Washington, DC: Peterson Institute for International Economics.

Lardy, N. R. 2014. *Markets over Mao: The Rise of Private Business in China*. Washington, DC: Peterson Institute for International Economics.

Lau, L., Qian, Y., and Roland, G. 2000. Reform without Losers: An Interpretation of China's Dual-Track Approach to Transition. *Journal of Political Economy*, *108*(1): 120–143.

Li, D. 2001. Beating the Trap of Financial Repression in China. *Cato Journal*, *21*(1): 77–90.

Li, K. 2015. *Full Transcript of Premier's Press Conference*. Third Session of the 12th National People's Congress, March 15. Available at http://english.gov.cn/premier/news/2015/03/15/content_281475071837425.htm

Lin, J. Y. 1987. The Household Responsibility System Reform in China: A Peasant's Institutional Choice. *American Journal of Agricultural Economics*, *69*(2): 410–415.

Lin, J. Y., Cai, F., and Li, Z. 1996. *The China Miracle: Development Strategy and Economic Reform*. Hong Kong: Chinese University Press.

Ma, L. 1998. Private Education Emerges in China. *Cato Policy Report* (March/April): 6.

Naughton, B. 1995. *Growing out of the Plan: Chinese Economic Reform 1978–1993*. New York: Cambridge University Press.

Naughton, B. 2007. *The Chinese Economy: Transitions and Growth*. Cambridge, MA: MIT Press.

Oi, J. C., and Walder, A. G. (eds.). 1999a. *Property Rights and Economic Reform in China*. Stanford, CA: Stanford University Press.

Oi, J. C., and Walder, A. G. 1999b. Property Rights in the Chinese Economy: Contours of the Process of Change. In J. C. Oi and A. G. Walder (eds.), *Property Rights and Economic Reform in China*, pp. 1–24. Stanford, CA: Stanford University Press.

Organisation for Economic Co-operation and Development (OECD). 2005. *OECD Economic Surveys: China*. Paris: OECD.

Padover, S. K. (ed.). 1953. *The Complete Madison: His Basic Writings*. New York: Harper & Bros.

Page, J. 2015. In China Confucius Makes a Comeback. *Wall Street Journal*, 21 September.

Qian, Y. 2003. How Reform Worked in China. In D. Rodrik (ed.), *In Search of Prosperity: Analytic Narratives on Economic Growth*, pp. 297–333. Princeton, NJ: Princeton University Press.

Schumpeter, J. 1942. *Capitalism, Socialism, and Democracy*. New York: Harper & Bros.

Tatlow, D. K. 2014. Xi Jinping on Exceptionalism with Chinese Characteristics. *New York Times*, October 14.

Tian, Q. 2009. Household Responsibility System. In L. Cheng (ed.), *Berkshire Encyclopedia of China*, pp. 1066–72. Great Barrington, MA: Berkshire.

Tsai, K. S. 2002. *Back-Alley Banking: Private Entrepreneurs in China*. Ithaca, NY: Cornell University Press.

Vogel, E. F. 2011. *Deng Xiaoping and the Transformation of China*. Cambridge, MA: Belknap Press/Harvard University Press.

Wang, N. 2017. China's Future and the Determining Role of the Market for Ideas. *Cato Journal*, 37(1): 149–165.

Wei, L. 2015. China to Overhaul State Sector. *Wall Street Journal*, September 14.

Wei, Z. 2003. The Changing Face of Rural Enterprises. *China Perspectives*, 50(Nov–Dec): 1–17.

Wen, J. 2003. Full Text of Premier Wen's Speech at Harvard. *People's Daily*, December 12.

Wong, C. H. 2016. Xi Warns Party Not to Waver on Ideology. *Wall Street Journal*, July 2–3.

Wu, J. L. 2005. *Understanding and Interpreting Chinese Economic Reform*. Boston, MA: Thompson/South-Western.

Xi, J. 2015. In Rare Interview, Xi Discusses Ties with the U.S. *Wall Street Journal*, September 22.

Xu, C. 2015. China's Political-Economic Institutions and Development. *Cato Journal*, 35(3): 525–548.

Yu, G., and Zhang, H. 2008. Adaptive Efficiency and Financial Development in China: The Role of Contracts and Contractual Enforcement. *Journal of International Economic Law*, 11(2): 459–494.

Zhang, M. 2008. From Public to Private: The Newly Enacted Chinese Property Law and the Protection of Property Rights in China. *Berkeley Business Law Journal*, 5(2): 317–363.

Zhang, W. 2015a. *The Logic of the Market: An Insider's View of Chinese Economic Reform*. Trans. M. Dale. Washington, DC: Cato Institute.

Zhang, W. 2015b. The Power of Ideas and Leadership in China's Transition to a Liberal Society. *Cato Journal*, 35(1): 1–40.

Zhao, Z. Y. 1987. *Advance along the Road of Socialism with Chinese Characteristics*. Report Delivered at the 13th National Congress of the Communist Party of China, October 25. In *Documents of the Thirteenth National Congress of the Communist Party of China*. Beijing: Foreign Languages Press.

Zhou, K. X. 1996. *How the Farmers Changed China: Power of the People*. Boulder, CO: Westview Press.

Part III

Keynote addresses

10 Freedom versus coercion in economic development

William Easterly

One of the most important, yet underappreciated, ideas in the history of economic thought is that of the "spontaneous order" of economic development. Development outcomes for good or ill are often the result of a general equilibrium process of markets and politics, in which the outcomes were not intended by any one individual or leader. The key insight of economics is that individual freedom will generally induce good outcomes in a spontaneous order, while coercion generally induces bad outcomes. Yet the issue of freedom versus coercion in economic development gets much less attention than it should.

The idea of spontaneous order goes back to the 18th-century Scottish Enlightenment. Adam Ferguson (1995 [1767]: 119) said, in 1782, that economic development is "the result of human action, but not the execution of any human design." Adam Smith (1776: locs. 7132–36) noted how a business person "intends only his own gain [but] he is led by an invisible hand to promote an end which was not part of his intention"—namely, benefits to consumers. Smith argued that the unintentional benefits of self-interested participants in markets were greater than benefits conveyed by altruists: "By pursuing his own interest he frequently promotes that of the society more effectually than when he really intends to promote it." Smith went even further: "I have never known much good done by those who affected to trade for the public good."

In the 20th century, F. A. Hayek (2011 [1960]: 1980) was the economist who offered the most insight on spontaneous order, saying about competitive markets, "we trust the independent and competitive efforts of many to induce the emergence of what we shall want when we see it." He argued, like Ferguson, that human design plays little role in such outcomes: "The curious task of economics is to demonstrate to men how little they really know about what they imagine they can design" (Hayek, 1988: 76).

Although the idea of spontaneous order is associated with economists oriented towards support for market solutions, other less pro-market economists celebrate the same idea. Kenneth Arrow (1983: 107–8) noted that "effects may be very different from intentions through the workings of an entire system," and declared that this is "surely the most important intellectual contribution that economic thought has made" to the study of social processes. Larry Summers quoted in Yergin and Stanislaw, 1998: 150–51) affirmed Hayek's insight: "Things will happen in well-organized efforts without direction, controls, plans. That's the consensus among economists." What Arrow and Summers understood is that even a system with extensive government intervention is still a spontaneous order and that outcomes in such a system will still not necessarily match intentions.

Despite the widespread support among economists for the idea of spontaneous order, it is a profoundly unpopular idea in the field of economic development. Development policymakers and experts seek to address tragic outcomes among the world's poorest people with intentional efforts to achieve a better outcome: if there is hunger, send food; if there are inefficient subsistence farms, replace them with efficient cash crops or forestry. Development agencies favor plans combining many such interventions, the best known of which was the United Nations' Millennium Development Goals effort of 2000–15, which has since been superseded by the Sustainable Development Goals for 2015–30.

Development advocates seem to fear that emphasizing ideas like unintentional and undesired outcomes in a spontaneous order will induce passivity and hopelessness about development efforts. Compared to the promise and simplicity of direct action towards a goal, spontaneous order is usually raised to explain why something will *not* work. As Hayek (2011 [1935]: locs. 152–57) noted, "the person who actually does things" is always likely to be more popular than "the economist [who is] the odious individual who explains why the well-meaning efforts of the former are frustrated."

Another uncomfortable angle reinforces the unpopularity of the idea of spontaneous order in development. It seems to leave us development intellectuals nothing to do. Combined with our idealism and altruism, it is also in our self-interest, as development experts, to remain employed. So we might have a bias towards ideas that feature a larger role for experts compared to those that have a lesser role.

These sensitive topics are beginning to get some attention in economics, such as the *Journal of Economic Perspectives* symposium in 2016 on self-motivated beliefs (e.g. Epley and Gilovich, 2016). Levy and Peart (2016) offer a brave recent consideration of the self-interest of experts and technocrats in economic policymaking.

Historian of the Russian intelligentsia Richard Pipes (1990: locs. 3817–23) had one of the best insights on this: "Although the intelligentsia likes to see itself as selflessly dedicated to the public good . . . its members . . . also share common interests—interests which may well clash with their professed ideals. The intelligentsia has difficulty admitting this."

Pipes (1990: locs. 3881–88) also gave a dire warning that could help us to see why the topic of self-interest of experts has remained off limits for so long: "Historical experience indicates that any movement that questions the ideology and interests of intellectuals dooms itself to defeat, and that any intellectual who challenges his class condemns himself to obscurity."

Despite all of these good reasons for the unpopularity of spontaneous order, it cannot simply be wished away. Attempting to plan outcomes in the presence of a spontaneous order simply generates a different spontaneous order, in which it is still unlikely that planners have enough knowledge and control to reach the intended outcomes. And the politics that decides what are "desirable outcomes"—whether under democracy, autocracy, competing warlords, or a Soviet system—is itself a spontaneous order that keeps throwing up new leaders with far from complete control of their own societies. The only choices are a good or bad spontaneous order.

Economists have long understood the basic principle that distinguishes good from bad spontaneous orders. The key principle for a good spontaneous order is that each agent receives private returns to their activity that are equal to their social returns to that activity. This alignment of returns is possible when there is individual liberty that allows the individual to do anything they want, as long as they do not coerce anybody else.

Adam Smith understood that a competitive marketplace with voluntary exchange makes possible the alignment of public and private returns for private goods. The sales price of a good reflects what consumers are willing to pay and hence the private benefits to the consumer, while the same price is what the suppliers are willing to accept and so reflects social benefits to suppliers.

Coercion destroys the alignment of private and public returns. If the consumer forces the supplier to turn over goods for free at gunpoint, he generates positive private returns for himself, but negative returns for the supplier.

The alignment of private and public returns is also vital in political systems, as the field called "public choice" or "political economy" has long studied. Government officials have opportunities for coercion of private individuals, generating private returns to those officials and negative social returns for citizens. Free political systems that feature individual rights protections, democratic accountability, and freedoms of speech, assembly, and protest are attempts to align private and social returns for public officials. In free systems, public officials that do harm to private individuals can suffer negative political consequences, while public officials who supply honest contract enforcement, protections for property rights, and public goods demanded by the citizens will get rewarded.

Economic freedom of choice in international trade is central to economic development because it finds both the top income-earning opportunities for the poor and the cheapest prices for essential goods for the poor.

If U.S. corporations such as Cargill and Monsanto succeed in exporting US$20 billion in soybeans, it is only because global consumers choose their cheaper prices over those available from domestic suppliers. Cargill and Monsanto generate private returns for their shareholders while they generate the social return of alleviating world hunger.

Freedom to choose what to export similarly opens up a wide range of often surprising income-earning opportunities for poor countries. Using international trade data on very specific product exports by source and destination, we find that Egypt gets substantial revenue from exporting toilets to Italians. Kenya profits from sending cut flowers to the Netherlands, while Ecuador sends cut flowers to Russia. Each country's top specializations by product and destination account for a surprisingly high share of its total exports, but these specializations also change from one period to the next. Global trade is indeed a spontaneous order, with no designer. It would be hard to imagine a planner deciding that Egyptians should do the toilets for the Italians, while Ecuadoreans do the flowers for the Russians.

In aid and development, when things go wrong, it is sometimes because there is coercion rather than freedom to choose. The U.S. Agency for International Development gives aid with shipments of U.S. wheat to alleviate famine, which start off as more altruistic than Cargill and Monsanto on fighting world hunger. Yet a study by Nunn and Qian (2014) found that food aid, on average, has an unintentional consequence of increasing violence in countries receiving that aid. The problem is that food aid is injected into a spontaneous order based on coercion rather than choice, such as the wars in Somalia and Afghanistan. Somali warlords or the Taliban in Afghanistan succeed in capturing some of the food aid shipments and then use these shipments to pay for more weapons or feed more soldiers, to inflict even more violence. Warlords thus generate a positive private return, but a negative social return.

Economic policies based on a high degree of coercion also can cause a big divergence between private and social returns, to the detriment of overall development. A common example has been the policy that forces exporters to sell all of their foreign exchange to only the government central bank, at a highly unfavorable exchange rate, and forbids them selling it on any private foreign exchange market. This policy inevitably leads to a black market in foreign exchange, in which the amount of domestic currency offered for a dollar of foreign exchange is much higher than the official (unfavorable) exchange rate. The difference between the black-market exchange rate and the official rate is called the black-market premium. It has been relatively common in the history of development policies for the black-market premium to exceed 40 percent (and sometimes to be much higher, at even hundreds of percent). The exporter often does not get access to the official exchange rate for buying foreign exchange for its own imported inputs. So the exporter is buying at the black-market exchange rate and selling at the much more unfavorable official exchange rate, and thus getting a negative or very low private return, even though the exporter is producing a social return by exporting. Meanwhile, corrupt government insiders can get the foreign exchange at the official rate from the exporters, and resell it at the much higher black-market rate. The corrupt insiders thus generate a private return, but not a social return.

One example of a high black-market premium as described here lies in Ghana in the late 1970s and early 1980s. There is, of course, some temptation for exporters to try to evade the coercion to sell their foreign exchange on the black market instead of at a punitive exchange rate, but this can simply cause the government to ratchet up the coercion. Indeed, at one point Ghana even imposed the death penalty for black-market transactions. This coercive policy had the effect of killing off many of Ghana's exports, including that of cocoa, in which it used to dominate the world market.

Another type of coercion in aid and development is exemplified by forced resettlement projects. For example, in the district of Mubende, Uganda, in 2010, the World Bank's International Finance Corporation (IFC) developed a forestry project that was supposed to increase the productivity of the land compared to its existing use for subsistence crops. According to the usual development metrics, the project was a success in doing what it intended—but there were unintended negative consequences because the World Bank project was based on coercion instead of consent. Armed men showed up in Mubende to confront the farmers who had been living on the land for several generations. The soldiers burned the farmer's homes and crops, shot their livestock, and marched the farmers away at gunpoint from their own lands. The owners of the land thus realized negative returns from a World Bank development project with positive returns. The positive returns were captured by somebody else: a private British company financed by IFC/World Bank.

This violation of the Mubende farmers' economic, political, and human rights was so outrageous that it generated an unusual amount of attention. British charity Oxfam wrote a report about what happened, and the story appeared on the front page of the *New York Times* in September 2011. Laura Freschi and I wrote about the story in our blog, Aid Watch, after the *Times* story appeared. The World Bank told me on Twitter that it was "taking allegation seriously" and that it was "lkg into it." On the Aid Watch blog, we started a public clock ticking until the World Bank investigation into its own conduct in Mubende was completed.

That clock is still ticking today seven years later. While the IFC/World Bank mediated a (very inadequate) settlement from the private British company for the victims in Mubende, the Bank never investigated how or whether its own conduct led to the tragedy or announced any remedies to prevent future occurrences. What was discouraging to other observers and to me was how little the general development community seemed to care about consent versus coercion. Human Rights Watch (Evans, 2013) later documented how pervasive rights violations are in World Bank projects, while a group of investigative journalists documented many other cases of forced resettlement in World Bank development projects.[1]

This chapter began with the observation that the idea of a beneficial spontaneous order under individual liberty seems to leave the development intelligentsia nothing to do. Yet the examples given here suggest ways in which development experts, as advocates and educators, can suggest principles that will improve outcomes.

(1) The case of food aid and violence is suggestive that injecting aid into a spontaneous order based on coercion and violence will not have good outcomes. Understanding this would have prevented some of the aid debacles in places such as Afghanistan and Somalia, and challenged one of the popular development mantras of the past decade of *increasing* aid to the so-called fragile states (that is, states in the middle of conflict and terrorism).

(2) The case of coercive policies that lead to high black-market premiums is suggestive of how economists can advocate economic reforms that improve outcomes. Indeed, such advocacy (including by economists from the "bad

policy" countries themselves) has been successful in generating economic reforms that have largely done away with high black-market premiums around the world. Other reforms have succeed at mostly eliminating very high rates of inflation and punitive controls on nominal interest rates under high inflation that led to negative real interest rates, as well as the most extreme policies that repress international trade, including tariffs, quotas, and overvalued currencies. Despite the backlash against markets and globalization, the median worldwide ratio of trade revenues to gross domestic product (GDP) has maintained an upward trend, as shown in Figure 10.1. Indicators of these reforms are correlated with economic growth recoveries, including the decent economic growth in Africa and Latin America since the "Lost Decades" of the 1980s and 1990s.

How is this progress on market reforms possible despite the anti-market and anti-globalization backlash? Economists in rich and poor countries have a powerful ally in those who are themselves the victims of coercive policies that violate their freedom to make a living in their own way. For example, protest against coercion and corruption and democratic activism have been growing in Africa. A recent book documents "over ninety popular protests in forty countries during the 2005–14 period" (Branch and Mampilly, 2015: loc. 357)

In Ghana, resistance to punitive economic policies and democratic activism, combined with advice by Ghanaian and foreign economists, led first to

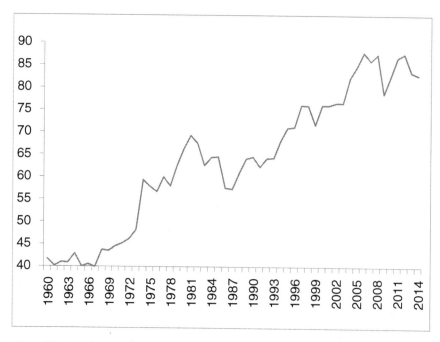

Figure 10.1 Median trade share of worldwide GDP

a major increase in economic freedom after 1984 that revived the Ghanaian economy, and then to activism that resulted in competitive democratic elections by 2000. Ghanaians now enjoy relatively high values of both economic and political freedom.

(3) There is still some way to go in getting the development community to take seriously the principle of consent instead of coercion. For me, personally, the Mubende debacle in 2011 made me realize how futile it was to lobby the existing aid structures that ignore the rights of the poor. Soon afterward, I ended the blog Aid Watch and devoted my efforts instead to writing a book, *The Tyranny of Experts: Economists, Dictators, and the Forgotten Rights of the Poor* (Easterly, 2014). These and many other education and advocacy efforts by non-tyrannical experts and economists have uncertain payoffs. However, getting ideas and ideals right should never be based on a calculus of payoffs; rather, it is an end in itself.

I did not sufficiently appreciate, while writing *The Tyranny of Experts*, how much the battle for freedom still needed to be fought at home in the United States and in Western Europe, and not only for developing countries. Perhaps we development experts from the West are now paying for our indifference to the rights of the Rest with new threats to our rights at home. As Abraham Lincoln warned a long time ago, "Those who deny freedom to others deserve it not for themselves, and under a just God, cannot long retain it."

Economists' understanding of the gains from consensual trade, investment, and migration enriches a positive-sum view of beneficial interactions between nations and ethnic groups. We have seen instead, in the United States and Europe, a resurgence of primitive zero-sum thinking in which groups can gain only at the expense of other groups. This thinking has contributed to rising xenophobia, along with a resurgence of support for highly coercive controls on trade and migration.

In 2014, I quoted Hayek:

> The contrast between the "we" and the "they," the common fight against those outside the group, seems to be an essential ingredient in any creed which will solidly knit together a group for common action . . . [for] the unreserved allegiance of huge masses. From [autocrats'] point of view it has the great advantage of leaving them greater freedom of action than almost any positive program.
>
> (Easterly, 2014: 30, quoting Hayek, 2010
> [1940–43]: loc. 3893)

I thought then that I was talking about the threat of rising authoritarianism in poor countries, not realizing that the same threat was emerging in my home country. The battle for a spontaneous order based on equal liberty for all still needs to be fought everywhere, in both poor and rich countries.

Note

1 See the International Consortium of Investigative Journalists on World Bank evictions, online at https://www.icij.org/investigations/world-bank/

References

Arrow, K. 1983. *Collected Papers of Kenneth J. Arrow, Vol. 2: General Equilibrium.* Cambridge, MA: Harvard University Press.

Branch, A., and Z. Mampilly. 2015. *Africa Uprising (African Arguments).* London: Zed Books (Kindle Edition).

Easterly, W. 2014. *The Tyranny of Experts: Economists, Dictators, and the Forgotten Rights of the Poor.* New York: Basic Books (Kindle Edition).

Epley, N., and T. Gilovich. 2016. The mechanics of motivated reasoning. *Journal of Economic Perspectives, 30*(3): 133–140.

Evans, J. 2013. Abuse-free development: How the World Bank should safeguard against human rights violations. *Proceedings of the Annual Meeting (American Society of International Law), 107*: 298–302.

Ferguson, A. 1995 [1767]. *An Essay on the History of Civil Society.* Cambridge: Cambridge University Press (Kindle Edition).

Hayek, F. A. 1988. *The Fatal Conceit: The Errors of Socialism.* Chicago, IL: University of Chicago Press (Kindle Edition).

Hayek, F. A. 2010 [1940–43]. *The Collected Works of F. A. Hayek, Vol. 2: The Road to Serfdom—Text and Documents.* Ed. B. Caldwell. Chicago, IL: University of Chicago Press (Kindle Edition).

Hayek, F. A. (ed.). 2011 [1935]. *Collectivist Economic Planning: Critical Studies on the Possibilities of Socialism by N.G. Pierson, Ludwig von Mises, Georg Halm, and Enrico Barone.* London: Routledge & Kegan Paul (Kindle Edition).

Hayek, F. A. 2011 [1960]. *The Collected Works of F. A. Hayek, Vol. 17: The Constitution of Liberty.* Ed. R. Hamowy. Chicago, IL: University of Chicago Press (Kindle Edition).

Levy, D. M., and S. J. Peart. 2016. *Escape from Democracy: The Role of Experts and the Public in Economic Policy.* Cambridge: Cambridge University Press (Kindle Edition).

Nunn, N., and N. Qian. 2014. U.S. food aid and civil conflict. *American Economic Review, 104*(6): 1630–1666.

Pipes, R. 1990. *The Russian Revolution.* New York: Knopf Doubleday (Kindle Edition).

Smith, A. 1776. *The Wealth of Nations* (Illustrated). London: Strahan & Cadell (Kindle Edition).

Yergin, D., and J. Stanislaw. 1998. *The Commanding Heights: The Battle between Government and the Marketplace that is Remaking the Modern World.* New York: Simon & Schuster.

11 The case for free trade since David Ricardo

Douglas A. Irwin

Introduction

Ever since Adam Smith published the *Wealth of Nations* in 1776, economists have generally supported the policy of free trade and opposed the imposition of trade barriers.[1] This position was solidified by the classical economists – notably, David Ricardo, who is credited with developing the theory of comparative advantage. This theory was set out in the famous chapter on "Foreign Trade" in his *On the Principles of Political Economy and Taxation*, published just over 200 years ago, on April 19, 1817.

Smith and Ricardo, as well as many later economists, were not satisfied with only making a theoretical case for more open trade policies; they also tried to influence politicians and shift government policy toward freer trade. Smith once spent a week in a stagecoach with the Earl of Shelbourne, while both were traveling from Edinburgh to London in 1761. Over the course of that trip, Smith helped to persuade Shelbourne about the merits of open trade and, as Morrison (2012) has detailed, Shelbourne attributed his intellectual conversion to this journey. In 1815, Ricardo wrote an *Essay on the Influence of a Low Price of Corn upon the Profits of Stock* in which he argued that the Corn Laws (restrictions on the importation of wheat) raised the rent on land and reduced the profit on capital. He later became a Member of Parliament from 1819 to 1823, where he continued to speak out in favor of freer trade.

What arguments did Smith and Ricardo, and then later generations of economists, use to persuade others about the merits of free trade? How have these arguments changed in the 200 years since Ricardo outlined the idea of comparative advantage? In essence, there have been four broad intellectual arguments for free trade: a theoretical case, a moral case, a political case, and an empirical case. In this chapter, I will briefly address each of these arguments, assess their strengths and weaknesses, and look to the future of trade policy.

The theoretical case

The theoretical case for free trade, at least as made by economists, is often based more on the Ricardian theory of comparative advantage than on Smith's case for the division of labor across countries. The theory of comparative advantage, which has the advantage of being modeled mathematically, suggests that trade will be mutually advantageous between two countries even if one of them is less efficient at producing goods than the other. Paul Samuelson (1972, 683) famously told the story that, when challenged by the mathematician Stanislaw Ulam to name one proposition in the social sciences that was both true and non-trivial, Samuelson proposed the theory of comparative advantage.

Of course, the problem with making an exclusively theoretical case for free trade is that theory is difficult for economists to explain and for non-economists to understand. Consider Ricardo's famous chapter on "Foreign Trade." In it, Ricardo explains how England and Portugal, producing cloth and wine, could both gain from exchange because it takes 100 workers to produce cloth in England and 120 workers to produce wine, and . . . well, you get the picture.[2]

In trying to keep track of all of the labor requirements and exchange ratios, any layperson reading Ricardo would likely come away more confused than convinced about the merits of trade. As George Stigler (1982, 58) once quipped: "The import this layman is likely to embrace is not the English theory of free trade but a bottle of Portuguese wine."

In a superb essay, "Ricardo's Difficult Idea," Paul Krugman (1998) examines why non-economists have such a hard time grasping the implications of trade based on comparative advantage, aside from the inherent difficulty of the concept. The reason, he concludes, is not only that many people fail to grasp the positive-sum nature of trade, wanting instead to view it as a zero-sum competition or rivalry; equally important is that many ancillary assumptions that economists take for granted (such as labor mobility, full employment, flexible wages and prices, balanced trade, and so forth) are needed for it to fully make sense.

This discussion points to some of the problem with using theory to persuade others about the merits of free trade. The issue is not simply that theory is abstract and difficult to understand, but also that it depends upon certain assumptions. The skeptic can always question those assumptions and thereby bring into doubt the conclusion that free trade will work out for the best. Indeed, as Max Corden (1974, 7–8) reminds us, "theory does not say, as is often asserted by the ill-informed or wrongly taught, that 'free trade is best.' It says that given *certain assumptions* it is best." And one can always question those assumptions in any particular case and thereby bring into doubt the wisdom of the policy conclusion.

For example, in my book, *Against the Tide: An Intellectual History of Free Trade*, published in 1996, I systematically went through the various instances in which leading economists have argued that the case for free trade can break down: if tariffs can influence the terms of trade, if markets are distorted by market failures, if trade affects income distribution in undesirable ways, if infant industries fail to develop, and so forth. For example, economists have long noted that if a country could use tariffs to improve its terms of trade (the prices of its exports relative to its imports), it might gain by imposing an "optimal" tariff. Economists did not necessarily think that this theoretical possibility had many practical implications, as least for Britain in the nineteenth century when the theory was developed, but they could not deny the theoretical validity of this case against free trade. As F. Y. Edgeworth (1908, 555–56) said, "the direct use of the theory is likely to be small. But it is to be feared that its abuse will be considerable. . . . Let us admire the skill of the analyst, but label the subject of his investigation POISON."

The main complaint about the classical theory of trade was that it was static in nature, focusing exclusively on exchange and consumption, and that it ignored the dynamic aspects of trade, including the importance of expanding production and increasing economic growth. The principle interlocutor here was Friedrich List, whose book *The National System of Political Economy* (1841) argued that developing countries would be ill-served by a policy of openness to trade, which would lock them into a static specialization of primary products from which they would never escape. Over the decades, this doctrine has been much more influential among policymakers in developing countries than has Ricardo's doctrine of comparative advantage.[3]

Furthermore, no matter how robust or powerful the case for free trade is as a matter of theory, there is not much evidence that this matters for policymakers. The decisions of policymakers are influenced by a wide variety of political forces and interest groups, not intellectual argumentation. Furthermore, they may even dismiss the prevailing economic theory – sometimes wisely – as it is presented to them. For example, Robert Peel, the British prime minister who was responsible for the repeal of the Corn Laws in 1846, rejected the contemporary theory of economists that the real wages of workers would not improve with the importation of cheap wheat. (Real wages were considered fixed, for Malthusian reasons.) As Irwin (1989) shows, Peel was convinced by empirical evidence that real wages would rise with tariff reductions, contrary to the views of economists, and this allowed him to move forward with more extensive reforms.

The moral case

The moral case for free trade comes in two variants. The first is that individuals have a natural right to trade with other people in other countries without government interference. The invocation of natural rights may be satisfying for some – particularly those with a philosophical bent – but it is not a method of argumentation that economists are sympathetic to. Jeremy Bentham famously referred to natural rights as "simple nonsense: natural and imprescriptible rights, rhetorical nonsense, – nonsense upon stilts." All rights, he insisted, were specific and legal, not something to be dreamed up. Most economists have accepted this view. In his essay *On Liberty*, John Stuart Mill (1859, 62) said:

> The so-called doctrine of "free trade" . . . rests on grounds different from, though equally solid with, the principle of individual liberty . . . Restraints on trade . . . are indeed restraints; and all restraint, *qua* restraint, is an evil; but the restraints in question . . . are wrong solely because they do not really produce the results which it is desires to produce by them . . . The principle of individual liberty is not involved in the doctrine of free trade.

The second variant of the moral case for free trade is more of a religious one. In his book *The Age of Atonement*, historian Boyd Hilton (1988) argues that the religious and evangelical thought in early nineteenth-century Britain had a greater impact on the thinking behind economic policy than did the arguments of the classical economists. This was the period in which ideas about free trade were flourishing, and yet Hilton argues that many of the discussion at the time – even political discussions – had religious overtones rather than narrowly economic ones. For example, Richard Cobden's Anti-Corn Law League spread its views with envelopes decorated with biblical texts. And Cobden himself argued, as Hilton (1988, 246) notes, that "providence had designed commerce to unify and 'moralize' mankind, and that Free Trade was the international law of God, to 'spread Christianity through commerce, over the world'."

While Hilton's views have been challenged, there is something to his case – at least at that particular time and place.[4] Regardless of their validity or efficacy, however, most economists do not invoke religious or moral arguments in the case for freer trade.

The political case

The main political case for free trade is that it contributes to good relations among nations. Therefore, it is reasoned, trade tends to preserve peace and may even help to prevent war. The person most associated with this line of reasoning is Charles-Louis de Secondat, Baron de Montesquieu. Many authors have cited Book XX of his 1748 *Spirit of the Laws*, in which Montesquieu claims: "The natural effect of commerce is to bring peace. Two nations that negotiate between themselves become reciprocally dependent, if one has an interest in buying and the other in selling. And all unions are based on mutual needs." However, as Robert Howse (2006, 2–3) warns us:

> For those who are inclined to reduce philosophy to a set of slogans, Montesquieu is a dangerous thinker to cite and an impossible one to understand. There is hardly a generalization in his *Spirit of the Laws* that is not qualified or contradicted by another generalization, or put in question by Montesquieu's own examples.

For example, Montesquieu is acutely aware that conquest and colonialism went hand in hand with the expansion of commerce.

David Hume and Adam Smith were sympathetic to the argument that increased commerce would make the world more peaceable, but thought that the argument could be taken too far. As a result, they did not put a great deal of stress on it (Manzer, 1996). Paganelli and Schumacher (2017) even argue that Hume and Smith believed that more commerce might lead to more war because economic development allowed the use of public debt, which lowers the perceived cost of starting a military conflict. Their theories did not suggest that the world would automatically become more peaceful as a result of economic progress and commerce.

However, the argument that trade – and freer trade policies – was associated with peace was an idea that gained ground in the nineteenth century, as Bosanquet (1924) notes. The argument was taken up with great enthusiasm by British political activist Richard Cobden, the leader of the Anti-Corn Law League. Cobden and others after him argued that trade and peace were strongly interrelated, as Cain (1979) and Stringham (2004) note.

This political argument complements the economic argument about the benefits of trade, but economists have rarely invoked it because international relations are outside their field of expertise. At some intuitive level, the argument makes sense. In fact, going further than most economists have, John Stuart Mill (1909 [1848], 582) endorsed the idea wholeheartedly in writing that commerce:

> . . . is rapidly rending war obsolete, by strengthening and multiplying the personal interests which are in natural opposition to it. And it may be said without exaggeration that the great extent and rapid increase in international trade, in being the principal guarantee of the peace of the world, is the great permanent security for the uninterrupted progress of the ideas, the institutions and the character of the human race.

This argument took a hit with the outbreak of World War I. This war came only a few years after Norman Angell wrote his book *The Great Illusion* in 1910. Angell argued that growing economic interdependence as a result of trade would render warfare and territorial conquest futile. He was widely misinterpreted as saying that economic interdependence would make war less likely; rather, his main point was that the world had changed, so that there were fewer advantages to starting a military conflict. Ever since then, historians and political scientists have debated whether globalization and increased trade would make war more likely or less likely (Gartzke and Lupu, 2012).

The idea that trade and peace are related has motivated many a policymaker. One person who took up the Cobdenite mantle after World War I was American Cordell Hull. Trained as a lawyer, Hull represented Tennessee in Congress when, in 1933, U.S. President Franklin Roosevelt asked him to become secretary of state. Personifying the long-standing opposition to high tariffs in southern states, Hull had long believed that excessive import duties discouraged exports, harmed consumers and workers by increasing the cost of living, promoted the growth of monopolies and trusts, and redistributed income from poor farmers in the south and midwest to rich industrialists in the north.

But it was World War I that opened Hull's eyes to the international ramifications of trade policies. The war marked "a milestone in my political thinking," Hull (1948, 81) recalled in his memoirs. "When the war came in 1914, I was very soon impressed with two points. . . . I saw that you could not separate the idea of commerce from the idea of war and peace [and that] wars were often largely caused by economic rivalry conducted unfairly." In Hull's view, the quest of the European powers to gain access to foreign markets – particularly the competitive rivalry to establish colonial empires and to secure preferential access to the world's raw materials – was a factor behind the international tensions that eventually led to military conflict, and he:

> . . . came to believe that if we could eliminate this bitter economic rivalry, if we could increase commercial exchanges among nations over lowered trade and tariff barriers and remove unnatural obstructions to trade, we would go a long way toward eliminating war itself.
>
> (Hull, 1948, 81)

Having fought for lower tariffs solely for domestic reasons in the past, Hull (1948, 84) found that "for the first time openly I enlarged my views on trade and tariffs from the national to the international theater."

Therefore Hull (1948, 81) recalled:

> Toward 1916 I embraced the philosophy that I carried throughout my twelve years as Secretary of State. . . . From then on, to me, unhampered trade dovetailed with peace; high tariffs, trade barriers, and unfair economic competition, with war. Though realizing that many other factors were involved, I reasoned that, if we could get a freer flow of trade – freer in the sense of fewer discriminations and obstructions – so that one country would not be deadly jealous of another and the living standards of all countries might rise, thereby eliminating the economic dissatisfaction that breeds war, we might have a reasonable chance for lasting peace.

As secretary of state, Hull led the fight for the passage of the Reciprocal Trade Agreements Act of 1934, which allowed the president to conclude trade agreements with other countries to reduce tariff barriers.[5] While this policy met with limited success in the 1930s, it became the basis for postwar U.S. foreign economic policy. Speaking at Baylor University in March 1947, as the final meeting to conclude the General Agreement on Tariffs and Trade (GATT) was about to start, President Harry Truman stated:

> At this particular time, the whole world is concentrating much of its thought and energy on attaining the objectives of peace and freedom. These objectives are bound up completely with a third objective – reestablishment of world trade. In fact the three – peace, freedom, and world trade – are inseparable. The grave lessons of the past have proved it.[6]

Is there empirical evidence to support the contention that the economic interdependence that comes with trade either promotes peace or prevents war? In recent years, political scientists have investigated this question at length. The hurdles in establishing such a relationship are formidable and the empirical methods most often used (simple regression analysis) are so fraught with difficulties that most economists could easily poke holes in them. Despite these problems, the consensus among political scientists is that trade does promote peace. As examples of this, see the work of, as well as the many case studies examined by, McDonald (2009) and Copeland (2015).

The empirical case

While generally satisfied with the theoretical case for freer trade, over the past few decades economists have sought to have their policy positions be "evidence-based." Setting aside the issue of what constitutes sound and robust evidence, and how evidence can be used selectively to buttress one's position rather than to reveal actual impacts, there is often a professional consensus about whether the weight of evidence tends to be on one side or another on any particular policy issue.

The evidence that most economists find persuasive is empirical evidence, and there are two types of empirical evidence: quantitative and historical. In the realm of trade and trade policy, quantitative evidence usually involves the collection of cross-country data and then the analysis of how different trade regimes affect outcomes such as the level or growth rate of gross domestic product (GDP) or investment. Historical evidence usually involves case studies of the actual experience of particular countries under different policy regimes (such as, in the case of trade and development, import substitution versus export promotion). There are methodological pros and cons to each type of evidence, but each is worth pursuing.

Let us consider quantitative evidence first. Here, we should differentiate between empirical analysis of the relationship between trade and income and that of the relationship between trade policy and income. The relationship between trade and income – that countries that engage in more trade enjoy a higher real income – is well established. The obstacle here is that trade and income have a two-way relationship: it is not only that countries with more trade will have a higher income, but also that countries with higher income may be able to engage in more trade. Therefore one could not make any causal inferences from this observed correlation. However, Jeffrey Frankel and David Romer (1999) were able to overcome this simultaneity problem by using geographic distance as an instrument for trade – that is, they exploited the fact that distance from trading partners is an important determinant of trade, but is unrelated to income. They found that countries with more trade did, in fact, enjoy a higher level of income for reasons unrelated to a country's income level.

Subsequent work by James Feyrer (2009) employed a geography-based instrument for trade that varies over time, and this time series variation allows for controls for country fixed effects (eliminating the bias from time invariant variables such as distance from the equator or historically determined institutions). Like Frankel and Romer, Feyrer found that trade has a significant effect on income with an elasticity of roughly one half. Furthermore, differences in predicted trade growth can explain roughly 17 percent of the variation in cross-country income growth between 1960 and 1995. These studies showed that the positive relationship between trade and income is statistically robust, and that the direction of impact runs from trade to income.

The relationship between trade policy and income has been more difficult to determine in the context of cross-country regression analysis. First, it is difficult to develop a single summary statistic for trade policy. Trade policy consists of not only tariffs, but also import quotas and foreign exchange restrictions. Each one of these policies is difficult to measure at the sectoral level, let alone to gather into an aggregate country-based index. Second, it is difficult to find "exogenous" changes in trade policy that one can use to identify impacts on income. Third, policy is often an "endogenous" variable that should not be taken as exogenous in such regressions (Rodrik, 2012).

Nevertheless, a number of studies on the relationship between trade policy and income were published in the 1990s. In general, this literature found that more open trade policies were associated with more rapid growth.[7] Perhaps the most famous paper in this literature is that by Jeffrey Sachs and Andrew Warner (1995), who developed a 0–1 indicator variable of whether a country is "open" to trade, based on such factors as tariffs and the black-market premium on foreign exchange. They could then assess the impact of countries becoming more open to trade as policies changed in the 1980s, concluding that open economies experienced more rapid growth than closed economies.

However, this literature soon suffered a devastating blow in 2001. In "Trade Policy and Economic Growth: A Skeptic's Guide to the Cross-National Evidence," Francesco Rodriguez and Dani Rodrik (2000) argued that the most cited papers in this area suffered from mis-specification, poor measures of trade openness (protectionist policies were highly correlated with other bad economic policies, making identification difficult), and fragile results. Simply put, the existing studies were not robust and their strong conclusions were unwarranted. While the authors did not conclude that higher trade barriers were good for growth, they did not find much evidence that lower trade barriers would improve economic performance (or, at least, that we could have confidence that was the case).

Fortunately, economists rose to the occasion and improved the empirical methods that they were using to examine these questions. The first paper to do so was by Romain Wacziarg and Karen Welch (2008). They extended the Sach–Warner dataset into the 1990s, when many more developing countries had begun to open up to trade, and used more precise measures of trade policy. Unlike Sachs and Warner, who focused on the cross-sectional relationship between trade policy and economic growth, Wacziarg and Welch had enough data to examine the within-country impact of policy liberalization. They found that, over the period 1950–98, countries that liberalized their trade regimes experienced annual growth rates that were 1.5 percentage points higher than before liberalization. They also found that liberalization raised investment rates by 1.5–2.0 percentage points and lifted the trade-to-GDP ratio by roughly 5 percentage points.

Similarly, Antoni Estevadeordal and Alan Taylor (2013) focus on countries that reduced their import duties on intermediate goods. Looking at a panel of countries with data into the 1990s, they found that countries that reduced their tariffs on capital goods and imported intermediate goods grew about 0.7–1.0 percentage points faster than non-liberalizers. In addition, the growth effects came mainly from reducing tariffs on capital goods rather than reducing tariffs on consumer goods, as theory would lead one to expect.

Additional evidence came from Andreas Billmeier and Tommaso Nannicini (2013), who create synthetic control countries to investigate the impact of economic liberalization on per capita GDP. The synthetic control method compares the post-liberalization trajectory of real GDP of "treated" economies (those that undertake reforms) with the trajectory of a combination of similar, but untreated, economies (those that did not reform). They found that economic liberalization (moving to a more market-oriented economy, including trade reforms) had a positive impact of real income in most regions, although later reformers (in the 1990s, principally in Africa) did not realize such gains. A host of other recent papers have used the synthetic control method to evaluate policy changes and mostly reach comparable conclusions.

Together, these papers have overcome many of the methodological problems identified by Rodriguez and Rodrik, and have enhanced our understanding of the empirical – that is, quantitative – relationship between trade policy and economic growth.

The other type of evidence is based on historical experience, meaning case studies. This sort of evidence can be traced back to the National Bureau of Economic Research (NBER) study of trade and development policy overseen by Jagdish Bhagwati and Anne Krueger in the 1970s, summarized in Bhagwati (1978) and Krueger (1978). Another important work during this era was the book *Industry and Trade in Some Developing Countries* by Ian Little, Tibor Scitovsky, and Maurice Scott, published in 1970. The somewhat impressionistic findings of these volumes was that a more open trade policy was related to better economic performance.

Bhagwati and Krueger (1973) noted a common pattern in the trade policies of developing countries. Countries tended to allow their currencies to become overvalued relative to others, either unintentionally (by fixing the exchange rate, but pursuing looser monetary policies than partner countries) or deliberately (to make imported capital goods cheaper, or to make debt repayment easier). The overvalued exchange rate, however, reduced export earnings and led to a loss of foreign exchange reserves. To prevent the loss of reserves, import licenses would be imposed as a way of rationing foreign exchange. (This would often lead to a black-market premium on foreign exchange away from the official exchange rate.) Those import licenses would generate enormous rents, leading to rent-seeking behavior, as discussed by Krueger (1974). Governments would also impose higher tariffs to extract those rents from domestic firms – but those tariffs were not a binding constraint on imports; rather, the import licenses were the binding constraint.

At some point, these extreme measures to ration foreign exchange would fail to achieve their objective, with countries experiencing the continued loss of reserves, the continued economic distortions caused by the trade measures (particularly in terms of lost exports), and the continued appreciation of the real exchange rate. This would lead to a crisis, which could only be resolved by devaluation of the currency to reduce the real exchange rate, along with the removal of import licenses and the reduction in tariffs to permit export expansion. Perhaps the central role in all of this is played by the real exchange rate. It is often said that the most important price in an open economy is the exchange rate. And, as Peter Timmer (1973, 76) once quipped: "While 'getting prices right' is not the end of development, 'getting prices wrong' often is." And if one undertakes policies that result in a severely overvalued exchange rate, doing so often kills exports and leads to foreign-exchange rationing and import compression.[8]

Since the Bhagwati–Krueger studies of the 1970s, many developing countries have followed the script of embracing a reform package that entails a devaluation, a lifting of import licensing, and a reduction of import tariffs. A classic case is India. In 1991, the government faced a loss of foreign-exchange reserves. The country's foreign trade had long been hampered by the "license raj," in which firms had to obtain scarce licenses from the government to import goods from abroad. Thanks to a handful of reform-minded economists and ministers, the government devalued the rupee and abolished the license raj in one swoop, and the existing high tariffs on imported capital goods were slashed. The result was a large increase in imports of intermediate goods that, subsequent studies have shown, vastly increased the productivity of Indian producers (Goldberg et al., 2010). More broadly, the economic reforms shifted India from the slow "Hindu" rate of growth of about 2–3 percent to a higher growth path of 6–8 percent (Panagariya, 2004).

This type of evidence – specific historical case studies, conclusions drawn from several reform episodes, or what one might call reform storytelling – is often more persuasive to non-economists than a battery of regression results or a bunch of theoretical models. What gave the Bhagwati and Krueger studies, as well as Little and colleagues' (1970) book, such force and influence was that they were based on the on-the-ground reality in many, many countries. The evidence presented was not theoretical and could not be dismissed on the basis of its assumptions. It presented a stark reality of economic policy that had to be confronted and alternatives that could be embraced.[9]

Milton Friedman once argued that "people are persuaded by the evidence of experience."[10] More than regression results, these country findings presented the evidence of experience – experience with import substitution and with trade reforms. As noted earlier, Robert Peel, the conservative British prime minister who went against his party in proposing the repeal of the Corn Laws in 1846, did so in part because he was persuaded by empirical evidence, not by the abstract doctrine of political economy. The same is true of Cordell Hull in the United States many decades later. If this is the case, relating the experience of different economic policies through stories and illustrations would seem to be a worthwhile endeavor.

Conclusion

Economists have been making the case for freer international trade ever since the publication of Adam Smith's *Wealth of Nations* more than 240 years ago. There is still a healthy debate about whether ideas can play a role in convincing policymakers and others about the merits of freer trade and the costs of protectionist policies. Perhaps that debate should shift from "whether" ideas matter for policy formation to "what type of ideas" matter for policy formation. Theoretical ideas or data-heavy quantitative evidence are perhaps least likely to make major inroads with non-specialists, whereas simple storytelling – with concrete examples – may make the main message more likely to stick with others.

One might have thought that there is less of a need to make the case for freer trade policies because many policies in developing countries have been reformed over the past several decades. Yet there still are many developing countries with trade policies in desperate need of improvement, and there are many in the developed world too. The Trump Administration's nostrums on U.S. trade show that economists will continue to play a role in educating policymakers and the general public about the broad benefits of free international trade.[11]

Notes

1 As Harry Johnson (1960, p. 327) once put it: "The proposition that freedom of trade is on the whole economically more beneficial than protection is one of the most fundamental propositions economic theory has to offer for the guidance of economic policy."

2 John Chipman (1965, p. 480) remarked: "It does not seem to have been recognized that Ricardo's own statement of the law is quite wanting, so much so as to cast some doubt as to whether he truly understood it; at best, his version is carelessly worded." For further background on Ricardo's discovery, see Ruffin (2002) and the critique by Gerhrke (2015).

3 Krugman (1996, pp. 31–32) said that "more people should read the works of Friedrich List. If they do, they may wonder why this turgid, confused writer – whose theory led him to predict that Holland and Denmark would be condemned to permanent economic backwardness unless they sought a political union with Germany – has suddenly become a favorite [of free trade critics]." In another piece, Krugman (1996, p. 32) attacks the journalist James Fallows, since "his praise for List shows clearly that he does not understand Ricardo. For List's old book ... is the work of a man who, right from the beginning, just didn't get it; who could not get straight in his mind how trade between two countries could raise incomes in both. (A sample List argument: he points out that agricultural land near cities is more valuable than that far away, and concludes that tariffs on manufactured goods will help farmers as well as industrialists)."

4 See the insightful review of Gash (1989), who argues that Hilton exaggerates his evidence.

5 This fight is recounted in Irwin (2017a).

6 Address on Foreign Economic Policy, delivered at Baylor University, March 6, 1947, available at http://www.presidency.ucsb.edu/ws/?pid=12842

7 Early papers in this genre were summarized by Sebastian Edwards (1998).
8 Friedman (1962, p. 57): "Interferences with international trade appear innocuous . . . yet there are few interferences which are capable of spreading so far and ultimately being so destructive of free enterprise. There is much experience to suggest that the most effective way to convert a market economy into an authoritarian economic society is to start by imposing direct controls on foreign exchange. This one step leads inevitably to the rationing of imports, to control over domestic production that uses imported products or that produces substitute for imports, and so on in a never-ending spiral."
9 Panagariya (2018) is the most recent manifestation of this type of analysis.
10 "The Rising Risk of Recession," *Time*, December 19, 1969,
11 I have tried to do so elsewhere (see Irwin 2016, 2017b).

References

Bhagwati, Jagdish. 1978. *Anatomy and Consequences of Exchange Control Regimes.* Cambridge, MA: Ballinger.

Bhagwati, Jagdish, and Anne Krueger. 1973. Exchange Control, Liberalization, and Economic Development. *American Economic Review, 63*: 419–427.

Billmeier, Andreas, and Tommaso Nannicini. 2013. Assessing Economic Liberalization Episodes: A Synthetic Control Approach. *Review of Economics and Statistics, 95*(3), 983–1001.

Bosanquet, Helen D. 1924. *Free Trade and Peace in the Nineteenth Century.* Kristiania, Oslo: H. Aschehoug & Co.

Cain, Peter. 1979. Capitalism, War and Internationalism in the Thought of Richard Cobden. *British Journal of International Studies, 5*: 229–247.

Chipman, John S. 1965. A Survey of the Theory of International Trade, Part 1: The Classical Theory. *Econometrica, 33*(3): 477–519.

Copeland, Dale C. 2015. *Economic Interdependence and War.* Princeton, NJ: Princeton University Press.

Corden, W. Max. 1974. *Trade Policy and Economic Welfare.* Oxford: Clarendon Press.

Edgeworth, F. Y. 1908. Appreciation of Mathematical Theories. *Economic Journal, 18*: 541–556.

Edwards, Sebastian. 1998. Openness, Productivity and Growth: What Do We Really Know? *Economic Journal, 108*(447): 383–398.

Estevadeordal, Antoni, and Alan M. Taylor. 2013. Is the Washington Consensus Dead? Growth, Openness, and the Great Liberalization, 1970s–2000s. *Review of Economics and Statistics, 95*(5): 1669–1690.

Feyrer, James. 2009. *Trade and Income: Exploiting Time Series in Geography.* NBER Working Paper No. 14910.

Frankel, Jeffrey A., and David H. Romer. 1999. Does Trade Cause Growth? *American Economic Review, 89*(3): 379–399.

Friedman, Milton. 1962. *Capitalism and Freedom.* Chicago, IL: University of Chicago Press.

Gartzke, Eric, and Yonatan Lupu. 2012. Trading on Preconceptions: Why World War I Was Not a Failure of Economic Interdependence. *International Security, 36*(4): 115–150.

Gash, Norman. 1989. Review of *Age of Atonement* by Boyd Hilton. *The English Historical Review, 104*(410): 136–140.

Gerhrke, Christian. 2015. Ricardo's Discovery of Comparative Advantage Revisited: A Critique of Ruffin's Account. *European Journal of the History of Economic Thought, 22*(5): 791–817.

Goldberg, Pinelopi, Amit Khandelwal, Nina Pavcnik, and Petia Topalova. 2010. Imported Intermediate Inputs and Domestic Product Growth: Evidence from India. *Quarterly Journal of Economics, 125*(4): 1727–1767.

Hilton, Boyd. 1988. *The Age of Atonement: The Influence of Evangelicalism on Social and Economic Thought, 1795–1865.* Oxford: Clarendon Press.

Howse, Robert. 2006. Montesquieu on Commerce, Conquest, War and Peace. *Brooklyn Journal of International Law, 31*(3): 693–708.

Hull, Cordell. 1948. *The Memoirs of Cordell Hull.* New York: Macmillan.

Irwin, Douglas A. 1989. Political Economy and Peel's Repeal of the Corn Laws. *Economics and Politics, 1*(1): 41–59.

Irwin, Douglas A. 1996. *Against the Tide: An Intellectual History of Free Trade.* Princeton, NJ: Princeton University Press.

Irwin, Douglas A. 2016. The Truth about Trade: What Critics Get Wrong about the Global Economy. *Foreign Affairs, 95*(4): 84–95.

Irwin, Douglas A. 2017a. *Clashing over Commerce: A History of U.S. Trade Policy.* Chicago, IL: University of Chicago Press.

Irwin, Douglas A. 2017b. The False Promise of Protectionism: Why Trump's Trade Policy Could Backfire. *Foreign Affairs, 96*(3): 45–56.

Johnson, Harry G. 1960. The Cost of Protection and the Scientific Tariff. *Journal of Political Economy, 68*(4): 327–345.

Krueger, Anne. 1974. The Political Economy of a Rent Seeking Society. *American Economic Review, 64*(3): 291–303.

Krueger, Anne. 1978. *Liberalization Attempts and Consequences.* Cambridge, MA: Ballinger.

Krugman, Paul. 1996. *Pop Internationalism.* Cambridge, MA: MIT Press.

Krugman, Paul. 1998. *Ricardo's Difficult Idea.* Available at http://web.mit.edu/krugman/www/ricardo.htm

Little, Ian, Tibor Scitovsky, and Maurice Scott. 1970. *Industry and Trade in Some Developing Countries.* Oxford: Oxford University Press.

Manzer, Robert A. 1996. The Promise of Peace? Hume and Smith on the Effects of Commerce on Peace and War. *Hume Studies, 22*(2): 369–282.

McDonald, Patrick. 2009. *The Invisible Hand of Peace: Capitalism, the War Machine, and International Relations Theory.* New York: Cambridge University Press.

Mill, John Stuart. 1859. *On Liberty.* London: Longmans.

Mill, John Stuart. 1909 [1848]. *Principles of Political Economy.* Ed. William J. Ashley. London: Longmans.

Morrison, James A. 2012. Before Hegemony: Adam Smith, American Independence, and the Origins of the First Era of Globalization. *International Organization, 66*(3): 395–428.

Paganelli, Maria P., and Edward J. Schumacher. 2017. *More Commerce, More Wars: Adam Smith and David Hume on the Effects of Economic Development on Warfare.* Working Paper.

Panagariya, Arvind. 2004. *India in the 1980s and 1990s: A Triumph of Reforms.* IMF Working Paper No. 04/43.

Panagariya, Arvind. 2018. *Free Trade and Prosperity: How Openness Helped the Developing Countries Grow Richer and Combat Poverty.* New York: Oxford University Press.

Rodriguez, Francisco, and Dani Rodrik, 2000. Trade Policy and Economic Growth: A Skeptic's Guide to the Cross-National Evidence. *NBER Macroeconomics Annual, 15*: 261–325.

Rodrik, Dani. 2012. Why We Learn Nothing from Regressing Economic Growth on Policies. *Seoul Journal of Economics, 25*(2): 137–151.

Ruffin, Roy. 2002. David Ricardo's Discovery of Comparative Advantage. *History of Political Economy, 34*(4): 727–748.

Sachs, Jeffrey D., and Andrew Warner. 1995. Economic Reform and the Process of Global Integration. *Brookings Papers on Economic Activity, 26*(1): 1–118.

Samuelson, Paul. 1972. *The Collected Scientific Papers of Paul A. Samuelson, Vol. 3.* Cambridge, MA: MIT Press.

Stigler, George J. 1982. *The Economist as Preacher and other Essays.* Chicago, IL: University of Chicago Press.

Stringham, Edward. 2004. Commerce, Markets, and Peace: Richard Cobden's Enduring Lessons. *Independent Review, 9*(1): 543–549.

Timmer, C. Peter. 1973. Choice of Technique in Rice Milling on Java. *Bulletin of Indonesian Economic Studies, 9*(2): 57–76.

Wacziarg, Romain, and Karen H. Welch. 2008. Trade Liberalization and Growth: New Evidence. *World Bank Economic Review, 22*(2): 187–231.

12 Manifesto for a new American liberalism

Or, how to be a humane libertarian

Deirdre Nansen McCloskey[1]

I make the case for a new and humane American "libertarianism."

Outside the United States, libertarianism is still called plain "liberalism," as in the usage of French President Emmanuel Macron, with no "neo-" about it. That's the L-word I'll use here. The economist Daniel Klein calls it "Liberalism 1.0," or, channeling the old C. S. Lewis book *Mere Christianity* on the minimum commitments of faith (1942–44, 1952), "mere Liberalism."[2] In 1997, David Boaz of the Cato Institute wrote a lucid guide, *Libertarianism: A Primer*, reshaped in 2015 as *The Libertarian Mind*. I wish David had called it *The Liberal Mind*.

In desperate summary for you Americans, Liberalism 1.0 is Democratic in social policy and Republican in economic policy and non-interventionist in foreign policy. It is, in fact, mainly against "policy," which of course has to be performed, if there is to be a policy at all, through the government's monopoly of violence. (To confirm this experimentally, try not paying your taxes; then try to escape from prison.) Liberals 1.0 believe that having little or no policy is a good policy.

That does not put the Liberals 1.0 anywhere along the conventional one-dimensional right–left line, stretching from a compelled right-conservative policy to a compelled left-"liberal" policy. The real liberals instead sit happily up on a second dimension, the non-policy apex of a triangle, so to speak, the base of which is the conventional axis of policy by violence, right or left. We Liberals 1.0 are neither conservatives nor socialists. Both of them believe, with the legal mind, as the liberal economist and political philosopher Friedrich Hayek (2011 [1960]: 532) put it, in that "order [is] . . . the result of the continuous attention of authority." Both conservatives and socialists, in other words, "lack the faith in the spontaneous forces of adjustment which makes the liberal accept changes without apprehension, even though he does not know how the necessary adaptations will be brought about" (Hayek, 2011 [1960]: 522).

Liberals 1.0, to put it another way, don't like violence. They are friends of the voluntary market order, as against the policy-heavy feudal order or bureaucratic order or military-industrial order. They are, as Hayek (2011 [1960]: 529) declared, "the party of life, the party that favors free growth and spontaneous evolution," against the various parties of right and left, which wish "to impose [by violence] upon the world a preconceived rational pattern."

At root, then, Liberals 1.0 believe that people should not push other people around. As Boaz (2015: 39) says at the outset of *The Libertarian Mind*, "In a sense there have always been but two political philosophies: liberty and power." Real, *humane* Liberals 1.0—political philosophers Jason Brennan and John Tomasi call themselves "neoclassical liberals," and contribute to a lively website called "bleeding heart libertarians"—believe that people should of course help and protect other people when we can. That is, the humane liberals are very far from being against poor people. Nor are they ungenerous, or lacking in pity. Nor are they strictly pacifist, willing to surrender in the face of an invasion. But they believe that, in achieving such goods as charity and security, the polity should not turn carelessly to violence, at home or abroad, whether for rightish or leftish purposes, whether to police the world or to help the poor. We should depend chiefly on voluntary agreements, such as exchange-tested betterment, or treaties, or civil conversation, or the gift of grace, or a majority voting constrained by civil rights for the minority.

To use a surprising word, we liberals, whether plain 1.0 or humane, rely chiefly on a much-misunderstood "rhetoric," despised by the hard men of the seventeenth century such as Bacon and Hobbes and Spinoza, but a practice anciently fitted to a democratic society. Liberalism is deeply rhetorical, the exploration (as Aristotle said) of the available means of non-violent persuasion. For example, it's what I'm doing for you now. *For* you, understand, not *to* you. It's a gift, not an imposition. (You're welcome.)

Yes, I know: *some* imposition by violence is necessary. Got it. But a big, modern state depends too much on violence, by bombing foreigners, jailing people for smoking pot, protecting favored occupations, seizing their property by eminent domain, breaking into homes in the middle of the night. A little, non-modern state depends on it, too. States, with their tempting monopolies of violence, tend to.

By contrast, the market for goods, like the markets for art and ideas, relies on persuasion, "sweet talk."

"Here's $3."
"Thank you, ma'am. Here in turn is your de-caf caramel macchiato grande."

Or:

"Let me make a painting by dripping colors on a big canvas and see if you like it."
"Wow! A late Jackson Pollock!"

Or:

"Libertarianism is actually the original theory of liberalism."
"Oh, I get it."

No pushing around.

The Blessed Adam Smith (1723–90) recommended, in 1776, "the liberal plan of equality, liberty, and justice" (Smith, 1981 [1776]: 664). Professor Smith's triad begins with a hoped-for equality in social standing, which he favored. Smith, contrary to the country club, was an egalitarian. A man's a man for a' that.[3] The second item hoped for—equal *liberty*—is the economic right you should have, equal to anyone else's, to open a grocery store or enter an occupation when you want. Especially occupations: Smith was outraged by the restrictions on the right of a working man to use his powers, restrictions such as the fine-enforced rule in Oregon that you cannot publish remarks about engineering matters, such as the timing of traffic lights, without being a duly state-licensed engineer, even if you are in fact trained as an engineer. The third hoped-for item, justice, is another equality: your equal standing with any other individual before the executive powers of the state, and before the courts of the state when used by other people against you. What philosophers call "commutative" justice—a justice in the procedures for getting income as against justice in how income after it is gotten will be "distributed," as it were—is summarized in the modern idiom by Klein and Boaz as the just procedure of "not messing [without consent] with other people's stuff." We should all be so constrained, equally in justice.

The theme in liberalism, you see, is equality, derived from the equal natural rights of each.[4] Although a commonplace now, the liberal idea that each person should have equal rights was, in the eighteenth century, highly original and was, to many people, shocking. In earlier centuries of agriculture and its accompanying hierarchy, a liberal equality was held in fact to be quite absurd. And dangerous. In 1381, Lollard priest John Ball was drawn and quartered for asking, "When Adam delved and Eve span / Who then was the gentleman?" In 1685, Richard Rumbold, an English Leveler condemned to the scaffold under James II, declared—to the amusement of the crowd standing by to mock him—"I am sure there was no man born marked of God above another, for none comes into the world with a saddle on his back, neither any booted and spurred to ride him." In 1685 such an egalitarian ideal was deemed to be madness.

In northwestern Europe a century or so after Rumbold, the idea that no man was born marked of God above another was becoming a commonplace, at any rate among Old Whigs and radicals. Smith and his avant-garde allies of the eighteenth century, from John Locke and Voltaire to Thomas Paine and Mary Wollstonecraft, were recommending a voluntaristic egalitarianism. Liberals. They were persuaders, not enforcers. They recommended sweet talk, not guns. (Well, perhaps a *few* guns, at the Boyne and Saratoga and Valmy, in aid of equal liberty for free male citizens espousing the appropriate religious rhetoric.) Mainly, when they heard the word "guns," they reached for their rhetoric. Smith's first paid job was teaching rhetoric to Scottish boys, and he retained his conviction that "everyone is practicing oratory on others through the whole of his life" (Smith, 1982 [1762–66]: 352). A liberal society practices oratory, not physical, compulsion. Women and apprentices and servants and sailors in the eighteenth century were routinely beaten. Then, after a while, they were not.

In its fitful development after 1776, such a "liberalism," from a *liberalitas* long understood by the slave-holding ancients as "the leading characteristic of a non-slavish person," came to mean the theory of a society consisting *entirely* of free people. No slaves at all. No pushing around. Humane. Sweet-talking. Persuasive. Rhetorical. Voluntary. Minimally violent. Tolerant. No racism. No imperialism. No unnecessary taxes. No dominance of women by men. No messing with other people's stuff. It recommended a maximum liberty to pursue your own project, if your project does not employ physical violence to interfere with other people's projects.

The management theorist of the 1920s Mary Parker Follett defined democracy not merely as majority voting (and perhaps after the election, then, a bit of violent messing with the stuff belonging to the minority), but as the program of discovering, in her coinage, "win–win." It is the best version of being an American, or being a liberal and pluralistic human. In 1935, African-American poet Langston Hughes got it right: "O, let America be America again— / The land that never has been yet / —And yet must be—the land where *every* man is free."

Such a humane liberalism has, for two centuries, worked, on the whole, astonishingly well. For one thing, it produced increasingly free people, which (we moderns think) is a great good in itself. Slaves, women, colonial people, gay people, disabled people, and above all the poor, from which almost all of us come, have been increasingly allowed since 1776 to pursue their own projects consistent with not using physical violence to interfere with other people's projects. As someone put it: in the eighteenth century, kings had rights and women had none. Now it's the other way around.

And—quite surprisingly—the new liberalism, by inspiriting for the first time in history a great mass of ordinary people, produced a massive explosion of betterments. Steam, rail, universities, steel, sewers, plate glass, forward markets, universal literacy, running water, reinforced concrete, automobiles, airplanes, washing machines, antibiotics, the pill, containerization, free trade, computers, the cloud. It yielded, in the end, an increase in real income per head by a factor of *30*, and a startling rise in the associated ability to seek the transcendent in Art or Science or God or Baseball.[5]

I said 30. It was a stunning Great Enrichment, material and cultural, coming well after the classic Industrial Revolution.

The Enrichment was—I say again, in case you missed it—*3000* percent per person, near enough, utterly unprecedented. The goods and services available to even the poorest rose by that astounding figure, in a world in which mere doublings, rises of merely 100 percent, had been rare and temporary, as in the glory of fifth-century Greece or the vigor of the Song Dynasty. In every earlier case, the little industrial revolutions had reverted eventually to a real income per head in today's prices of about $3 a day, which was the human condition since the caves. Consider trying to live on $3 a day, as many people worldwide still do (although during the past forty years their number has fallen like a stone). After 1800 there was no reversion. On the contrary, in every one of the forty or so recessions since 1800 the real income per head after the recession exceeded what it had been at the previous peak. Up, up, up. Even including the $3-a-day people in Chad and Zimbabwe, real-world income per head has increased during the past two centuries by a factor of 10—and by a factor of 30, as I said, in the countries that were lucky, and liberally wise. Hong Kong. South Korea. Botswana. The material and cultural enrichment bids fair to spread now to the world. Halleluiah.

And the enrichment has been equalizing. Nowadays, in places like Japan and the United States, the poorest make more, corrected for inflation, than did the top quarter or so of two centuries ago. Jane Austen lived more modestly in material terms than the average resident of east Los Angeles. Equality of real comfort for the poor in adequate food, housing, clothing, education, health, entertainment, and most other goods and services has steadily increased since 1800 peak to peak. In countries fully experiencing the enrichment, the average (and, with it, the median and the comfort of the poorest) has increased from that $3 a day in 1800 to over $100 a day now. The poorest have been the greatest beneficiaries. As Austrian-American economist Joseph Schumpeter (1883–1950) put it in 1942:

> Queen Elizabeth owned silk stockings. The capitalist achievement does not typically consist in providing more silk stockings for queens but in bringing them within the reach of factory girls in return for steadily decreasing amounts of effort. [. . .] [T]he capitalist process, not by coincidence but by virtue of its mechanism, progressively raises the standard of life of the masses.
>
> (Schumpeter, 1950 [1942]: 67–68)

By 2018, the standard of life for the American masses was four times higher than that in the early 1940s, when average American real income was about what it is now in Brazil. Washing machines. Antibiotics. Autos. A bedroom for every child. An education for most.

Recently in China and India an economic liberalism has succeeded in enriching the places in spectacular fashion. They are still poor, but wait: in the next century—and sooner, if conservatives and socialists will abandon their schemes for pushing people around—everyone on the planet will be U.S.-rich. The museums and concert halls will be filled; the universities will boom; a full life will be open to the poorest.

§

Yet, alas, late in the nineteenth century, even in the Anglosphere, a clerisy of artists and journalists and professors commenced rebelling against this splendidly productive liberalism. The Great Enrichment didn't come fast enough, they declared. It was a project of our vulgar fathers. It was not governed by our pre-conceived rational patterns. By the time, in the 1940s, that Schumpeter wrote *Capitalism Socialism, and Democracy*, most of the clerisy expected comprehensive socialism in the future. Even Schumpeter did. And most of the clerisy had long welcomed the prospect. As early as 1919, the American journalist Lincoln Steffens, returning from the young and turbulent Soviet Union, declared, "I have seen the future, and it works."

By 1910 at the latest, the New Liberals in Britain and the new Progressives in America had, for what they assured us were the best of motives, redefined the L-word to mean its opposite, a slow socialism. Slow socialism was supposed to raise up the working man, right now, by compulsion—without, to be sure, the sort of violence urged by the harder-left socialists in more of a hurry.

The liberal philosopher Jason Brennan (2004), among other observers, adopts the terminology for the resulting version of slow socialism in the United States as "High Liberalism." In High Liberalism the equal right I have to make a voluntary arrangement with you was extended to a novel right of mine to seize with violence your goods to give me a set of "positive" liberties. I am to have a liberty from want, for example, regardless of my supply of goods to you. "Every man a king," said Huey Long in 1934, and his way of achieving it was that of both Bad King John and his enemy Robin Hood, characteristic of the feudal and the socialist order: "[I]t is necessary to scale down the big fortunes," said Huey, "that we may scatter the wealth to be shared by all of the people."[6] Scale down by violence one person to give to another, and all will be well. Zero sum.

And I am to have a liberty to regulate through the government's monopoly of violence your trade in ways beneficial to me, and a liberty to prevent your entry into my trade, forcibly backed by police, and a liberty to wage a war to end all wars financed by your goods appropriated for the purpose. In short, the New or High or Progressive "Liberal," however one names her, advocated a regime of pushing people around. As implemented in the twentieth century, her regime had little of voluntary agreement about it, and a good deal of violent illiberal rhetoric, and a zero-sum economics, and not much of a search for win–win.

Our friends on the left would do well to reflect on the authoritarian cast of American Progressivism c. 1910 and High Liberalism c. 1960 and so-called Liberalism c. 2018.[7] Then our friends on the *right* should reflect on the authoritarian cast of their conservatism. The very word "liberty" in the rhetoric of both left and right has reverted to its medieval and violent meaning, in the plural, "liberties"—"a liberty," such as "the liberty of the City of London," being a special and distinct privilege to this or that person or group, violently enforced against any who would presume to claim it without the gracious permission of the government. It is government-enforced protection for tire companies in Ohio, or relaxed policing of drugs in white suburbs. It contradicts the liberal principle articulated by Thomas Paine, "Give to every other human being every right that you claim for yourself—that is my doctrine."

Slow socialism recommended, and eventually achieved, an astonishingly high share of national income spent by the government out of coerced taxes, a higher and higher share taxed out of personal income—higher than in any historical instance but the most appalling tyrannies. It achieved medieval standards of regulations of one's stuff by experts imposed on more and more people, more governmental intervention in the wage bargain, more eugenic sterilization of undesirables, more economic protection offered to this or that group, more police-enforced licensing of occupations, more electronic inspection of the residents, more armies and empires and aggressive alliances, more nationalizations of the means of production. It resulted in the stagnant growth of the 1970s in the United Kingdom and the arrogant policing of the world since 1945 by the United States. The slow socialist motto is, "I'm from the government, and I'm here to help you, by messing with someone's stuff . . . maybe yours." Or, "Don't tax him, / Don't tax me: / Tax that man / Behind the tree."

Such, then, is "liberalism," as defined in these latter days in parts of the Anglosphere. Boaz (2015: 34) quotes Schumpeter's witticism about the theft of the word "liberal": "As a supreme, if unintended, compliment, the enemies of private enterprise have thought it wise to appropriate its label." The appropriation was not "mere" rhetoric. It vividly illustrates the non-mereness of how we talk to each other. The historian Kevin Schultz (2015) has written a dual biography of that odd couple, conservative William Buckley (1925–2008) and radical Norman Mailer (1923–2007), *Buckley and Mailer: The Difficulty Friendship That Shaped the Sixties*. Schultz documents how both men were in revolt against the High Liberalism of the 1950s and 1960s. Yet in policy High Liberalism won, with a good deal of conservative approval, and crowded out the adult projects of a free people, such as families as ethical schools, or the self-provision for old age, or a trade-union insurance against unemployment, or a prudent wariness about foreign entanglements.

Mailer and Buckley, each in his flamboyant way, sought civil discourse. But they lost. The left–right quarrel has finally yielded the fact-free dogmatisms of left and right we hear nowadays, even among otherwise adult and benevolent folk. One hears: "If there is *any* spillover, then the government of the United States should step in with police powers to stop it." Or: "If there are *any* bad people in the world, then the government of the United States should bomb them." When someone asked Michael Bloomberg, the brilliant businessman and three-time mayor of New York City, what he thought about legalizing marijuana, he brought out the fact-free line that marijuana is a "gateway drug." When someone challenged Lindsey Graham, the brilliant senior senator from South Carolina, about America's overreach abroad, he brought out the fact-free line, "If we don't fight them in Syria, we'll have to fight them in Charleston."

The slow-socialist, New-High-Progressive "liberals" of the late nineteenth and early twentieth centuries, such as Lloyd George and Woodrow Wilson, and then also their supposed enemies the Burkean Conservatives, such as Buckley and Graham, seized what they imagined to be the ethical high ground. It turned out to entail coercion by governmental violence. The New Liberals and the Progressives have been declaring since around 1900—joining in this the Conservatives since Thomas Carlyle (who had long made a similar declaration)—that:

Our motives for extending the scope of governmental violence are pure and paternalistic. Our policy of physical coercion is designed to help the pathetic, childlike poor and women and minorities, so incapable of taking care of themselves. To leave their business to themselves and to their peaceful markets would be highly dangerous, unlike our proposals for coercion at home and wars abroad. You Humane Liberals criticize our splendid policies. You must hate the poor and women and minorities, and love only the rich. And you do not sufficiently love our king and country, the Land of Hope and Glory, the Land of the Free. For shame, for shame! Why should we listen to bad people like you?

Thus Senator Elizabeth Warren, bless her, or Senator John McCain, bless him.

Yet as great (American-definition) liberal Lionel Trilling wrote in 1950, the danger is that "we who are liberal and progressive [or indeed Burkean and conservative] know that the poor are our equals in every sense except that of being equal to us."[8] The "us" are the natural governors, graduates of Columbia University, New York, or of Trinity College, Dublin, or of Sciences Po, Paris. In 2016, such arrogance among the elite was detected and punished by those who voted for Trump, and worldwide by populists from Britain to the Philippines. High Liberals and conservatives suppose that the poor and the rest are incompetent to manage their own affairs. Therefore we of the clerisy—a regiment of what Boaz (2015) calls "court intellectuals," gathered in the District of Columbia, with a lively regiment of Eurocrats, too, stationed in Brussels—are supposed to guide the poor and the mere citizens remotely from the royal courts of Washington, DC, or Brussels, or from Springfield or City Hall, and will do so better than the poor or the mere citizens can guide themselves.

Beyond the surface implausibility of the supposition, its paternalism has dangers. Elsewhere Trilling wrote that "we must be aware of the dangers that lie in our most generous wishes," because "when once we have made our fellow men the object of our enlightened interest [we] go on to make them the objects of our pity, then of our wisdom, ultimately of our coercion."[9] Every nurse or mother knows the dangers. And when she loves the beloved for the beloved's own sake, she resists them.

The progressives and the conservatives kindly left the word "libertarianism," a coinage becoming common in the 1950s, for the mere Liberals 1.0, who, in a collectivist age, remained loyal to Smith and John Stuart Mill, Tocqueville and Bastiat, Lord Acton and Macaulay. The mere liberals were people like Hayek (1899–92) and Milton Friedman (1912–2006) all their adult lives, the philosopher Robert Nozick (1938–2002) in his early middle age, and Deirdre McCloskey (1942–) in her maturity. Deirdre's father was an eminent political scientist (1915–69), a New-Deal Democrat drifting rightward, and she vividly remembers him around 1960 using "libertarian" as a term of contempt. For a long time, it kept her from taking humane liberalism seriously.

§

I was in fact, at age 16 or 17, a Joan-Baez socialist, singing the labor songs. I dreamt I saw Joe Hill. Then, in college in the early 1960s, the better to help the poor and disadvantaged—which remains my sole political object, as it is for all of us humane liberals (although we want to *actually* help, rather than resting at signaling how superior in pity we conceive ourselves to be)—I majored in economics and became a standard-issue Keynesian. I was making my fellows the object of my pity, then of my newly acquired wisdom—ultimately of my coercion.

One of we three college roommates, a brilliant electrical engineer, used to read liberal Ludwig von Mises' *Human Action* (1949) in breaks from solving second-order differential equations. I remember David leaning perilously back in his swivel chair, his feet up on the desk, smoking Galoises cigarettes, Castro's speeches from Cuba via shortwave set at low volume serving as a droning background, with the old tan-bound Yale Press edition of Mises perched on his knees. The other roommate and I, both leftish Democrats, both studying economics à la Harvard College out of Paul Samuelson's elementary textbook in those happy days, scorned the engineer's non-orthodox, voluntaristic, and "conservative" economics. We favored instead a pity-driven coercion in the style of Keynes and Samuelson and Stiglitz. Yet in reading Mises during work breaks our David undoubtedly learned more of the economics of a free society than the two of us did attending hundreds of hours of classes in Keynes and slow socialism.

A couple of years later, beginning in graduate school still at Harvard, I intended to join the other proudly elite economists down in Washington as a *social* engineer, "fine-tuning" the economy. At the time only a handful of graduate programs, such as those at UCLA, the University of Virginia, and above all the University of Chicago, doubted the Ivy League and slow-socialist theory of expertise. Yet a year or two into my graduate studies, it began to dawn on me what the core of economics actually said—see *Human Action* and its Liberalism 1.0. The core denied the premise of social engineering, left and right, that the social engineer (as again the Blessed Smith put it) "can arrange the different members of a great society with as much ease as the hand arranges the different pieces upon a chessboard" (Smith, 1982 [1759]: 234). And, about then, the most prominent piece of social engineering on display, the American invasion of Vietnam, didn't seem to be working out quite as planned. By the time I got my first academic job in 1968, at that same University of Chicago, a version of humane liberalism, as against coercive social engineering, was beginning to make sense.

Chicago was then notorious in the Ivy League for being "conservative." (We of the left did not distinguish conservatives—who admire old evolutions, but fear new ones—from liberals, who welcome future evolutions as well: Hayek, 2011 [1960].) Back as a senior at college, in the fall of 1963, still a vaguely Keynesian leftie, I had not so much as considered applying to Chicago's large and distinguished graduate program. Why listen to such bad people? My undergraduate essays in economics were denunciations of the Chicago School for its lack of pity and for its idiotic misunderstanding of the theory of monopolistic competition devised by my teacher Edward Chamberlain. Yet a dozen years after spurning the Chicago School, I became its director of graduate studies. A textbook on Chicago-style microeconomics that I subsequently wrote contains a showing that monopolistic competition is self-contradictory. As the Dutch say, *Van het concert des levens krijgt niemand een program* ("In the concert of life no one gets a program"). You're telling me.

By the late 1960s, then, I had become a Chicago School economist, and in the uses of supply and demand I remain one. As a rough guide to the flourishing of ordinary people in market economies such as those of Sweden or Japan or the United States, the supply-and-demand argument has never been overturned scientifically, despite what you may have heard from Paul Krugman or Robert Reich. My earliest big paper in economic history, entitled "Did Victorian Britain Fail?" (McCloskey, 1970), was an early "supply-side" rejection of using the Keynesian demand-side economics for the long run. Krugman might want to have a look at it. Another paper a few years later, "New Perspectives on the Old Poor Law" (McCloskey, 1973), distinguished the effects of intervening in the wage bargain from the effects of giving a tax-supported cash subsidy to the poor to bring them up to a respectable standard. Reich might want to have a look at it. The cash subsidy as against intervention in the wage bargain is what the left and right in economics have, since the 1950s, been calling the "negative income tax," or nowadays the "earned income tax credit," such as the $9 a month the Indian government proposed in 2016 to replace its hundreds of corrupt and cumbersome subsidies. It is Liberalism 1.0, made "Christian" (or Hindu, or "bleeding heart") by a preferential option for the poor.

§

The essence of real, humane liberalism, in short, is a small government, honest and effective in its modest realm. Otherwise, leave people alone to pursue their non-violent projects voluntarily, *laissez faire, laissez passer*. But do not ignore other people, or disdain them, or refuse to help them, issuing a country-club sneer, "I've got mine." Humane liberalism is not atomistic and selfish, contrary to what the High Liberals believe about it—and as some misled libertarians in fact talk in their boyish ways as if they believed about it, too. It is, on the contrary, an economy and polity and society of equal dignity.

The routine arguments against such a humane liberalism are, as I gradually came to realize after the 1960s, mostly feeble. For example, it's not true, as slow socialists argue, that the taxation and spending and regulation by big governments are innocent because, after all, they are voted on by "us" and anyway "give back services." The humane liberal will inquire mildly of the High Liberal: did you vote for the 81,640 pages of new regulations promulgated by the federal government during 2016? Did your representatives in Congress or the White House know what was in them? Did you or they properly understand the economic consequences, as against what the lawyers claimed the regulations were "designed" to do? (Design is good for furniture and trucks, but then the design has to sell in voluntary purchases. Not if the design is governmental.) And do you actually want the fixed-price menu of national parks and state licensing requirements and local schools that government now provides, or would you rather order à la carte, at a lower price and better quality?

Another feeble objection to *laissez faire*, even in some true-liberal theory after Locke, is the notion that the government is composed of highly ethical philosopher-monarchs, who can therefore be trusted to run a government kindly, giving us stuff out of taxes (taxes taking out of our stuff)—a government that now spends and redistributes 30 percent and more of what we mere citizens make, and regulates much of the rest. In France, the governmental share is higher, at 55 percent. (Henry Kissinger joked that France was the only successful communist country.)

When Commissioner of the U.S. Food and Drug Administration Margaret A. Hamburg retired in 2015, she was introduced on National Public Radio as having regulated fully a fifth of the American economy. The statistic startles, but it is correct (Walker and Nardinelli, 2016). Food. Drugs. Was Hamburg a wonder woman—a wholly ethical and wholly wise philosopher queen? It's unlikely, although I am sure she is very nice. Therefore the cancer treatment that works in Berlin, Germany, is inaccessible to you in Boston, Massachusetts, awaiting a certified finding from the FDA, after many years of delay, during which you will die in agony, about the drug's "efficacy," tested in unethical, but "gold standard," double-blind experiments guided by meaningless tests of statistical significance, and going far beyond the original brief of the FDA to test merely for safety, not for an elusive efficacy.[10]

A premise that government is in fact in the hands of philosopher kings and queens seems, on its face, naive, which is what late economist James Buchanan's notion of "public choice" avers. The naivety is well illustrated by the perils of the U.S. Constitution, from the Alien and Sedition Acts of 1798 down to Donald Trump. The kings and queens and tsars and commissioners are regularly corrupted by governmental power, the tempting ability to compel by violence. Try using in Massachusetts that cancer therapy from Germany without the FDA's approval and see what happens to you. And, anyway, the royal governor, whoever she is, does not have to be careful with other people's money, or with other people's lives. She waxes proud in her "program" to spend money and regulate lives, and proud, too, in her power to enforce her decisions concerning one fifth of the U.S. economy. Power, you might say, tends to corrupt.

As Paine wrote in the liberal birth year of 1776, "government even in its best state is but a necessary evil, in its worst state an intolerable one." Better keep the power to compel modest. By 1849, at the first maturation of liberalism 1.0, Thoreau could declare, "I heartily accept the motto, 'That government is best which governs least'; and I should like to see it acted upon more rapidly and systematically." In that same year, in far Torino, Italian liberal economist Francesco Ferrara (quoted in Mingardi, 2017: 29) wrote that "taxation is the great source of everything a corrupt government can devise to the detriment of the peoples. Taxation supports the spy, encourages the faction, dictates the content of newspapers." As humane liberal Donald Boudreaux wrote recently in his regular blog *Café Hayek*, "The only sure means of keeping money out of politics is to keep politics out of money."[11] The bumper sticker on my little Smart car reads, "Separation of Economy and State."

Even at this late hour, reducing the size and power of government, and letting free people have a go, is practical—achievable by parts whether or not a Painean or Thoreauesque or Ferrarite ideal is finally achieved. It's not true, to note another feeble argument against *laissez faire*, that the more complicated an economy is, the more regulatory attention it needs from the governors. No, quite the contrary. A complicated economy far exceeds the ability of any collection of human intellects to govern it in detail. A person's own life, or her little household, or maybe even her big company might be so governed— although any adult knows that even small societies are hard to plan in detail, offering endless surprises. You get no program. But governing sensibly the trillions of shifting plans made daily by the 324 million individuals in the American economy, much less nation-building abroad, is impossible—because, as Smith (1982 [1759]: 234) again put it, "in the great chess-board of human society, every single piece has a principle of motion of its own." The principles of motion are idiosyncratic, because people are motivated in varying proportions by prudence and temperance and courage and justice and faith and hope and love. By way of such virtues, and less happily their corresponding vices, you and I pursue our endlessly varied projects. Such a liberal plan is appropriate to a society in which people are taken as free and equal—equal even to the Columbia/Trinity College/Sciences-Po graduates of the clerisy.

What to do, then, in leashing the power to coerce? The practical proposals are legion, because illiberal policies are by now legion, as they also were during the feudalism that the early liberals overturned. Cut the multiple levels of corrupt government in Illinois. Kill off, as much-maligned Liberal 1.0 and billionaire Charles Koch wishes, the vast programs of corporate welfare, federal and state and local. Close the agricultural programs, which allow rich farmers to farm the government instead of the land. Sell off "public" assets, such as roads and bridges and street parking, which, in an age of electronic transponders, can be better priced by private enterprise. Close the American empire. Welcome immigrants. Abandon the War on Drugs. Give up eminent domain and civil forfeiture and military tanks for police departments. Implement the notion of Catholic social teaching of "subsidiarity," placing modest responsibilities such as trash collection or fire protection down at the lowest level of government that can handle them properly. Then outsource the trash collection and the fire protection. To finance K-12 education—socially desirable, but sometimes out of reach of the poor—give families vouchers to cash in at private schools, as Sweden has done since the 1990s and as Orleans parish has done for poor families since 2008. To achieve universal K-12 education, and a select few of other noble and otherwise privately unfundable purposes, such as universal vaccination or accessible buildings or rational policies against global warming or a war of survival, by all means tax you and me, not only the man behind the tree. But eliminate the inquisitorial income tax, replacing it with a tax on personal consumption declared on a one-page form, as long proposed by economists such as Robert Hall and Arthur Laffer. Still better, use only an equally simple purchase tax on businesses, to reduce the present depth of personal inquisition. Eliminate the so-called corporate income tax, because it is double taxation and because economists have in fact little idea which people actually end up paying it. (The old bumper sticker saying "Tax corporations, not people," when you think about it, doesn't make a lot of sense.) Give a poor person cash in emergencies, from those modest taxes on you and me. Quit inquiring into whether she spends it on booze or her children's clothing. Leave her and her family alone. No pushing around.

A government does of course "have a role"—as in indignant reply to such proposals my progressive and conservative friends put it to me daily, predictably, relentlessly. George Romney, the automaker and conventional 1950s Republican, opposing the Liberal 1.0 and conservative Barry Goldwater in 1964 (in Schultz, 2015: 77), declared, "Markets don't just *happen*. There must be some role for government." Well, yes, of course, government has "some role," although, contrary to Romney, most markets do in fact "just happen," because people find them mutually beneficial, with or without governmental action. There are markets inside jails and prisoner-of-war camps, for example, as there were among Australian aborigines buying their boomerangs from better-skilled bands hundreds of miles distant (Radford, 1945; Berndt and Berndt, 1964).

Anyway, only briefly, at age 15 or so, did I think of myself as a literal "anarchist," *an-archos*, Greek meaning "no ruler, at all." Government has an essential role in those wars of survival, for example, in which a singular purpose is exactly what we need and can achieve with justified, if often overapplied, coercion for the duration. Then, after the victory, we can hope that we can get rid of the coercion—without a great deal of hope, actually, as the economist Robert Higgs (1987) has shown. Do arm the little government, therefore, to protect us from invasion by, say, those toque-wearing Canadians and, rather more urgently, from nuclear threats by Russian neo-tsars.

And, yes, by all means let us have a government, a small one, to protect us from force and fraud by fellow Americans— although, of course, such private arrangements as door locks and high-reputation suppliers and competition in markets do accomplish the protections in most cases much better, to speak quantitatively, than does their alleged "ultimate" backing by governmental courts and police. Protect us especially from government itself, from its habit of abridging the right to vote, or spying on civil rights leaders, or enforcing bedroom and bathroom norms, or suspending the right to *habeas corpus*, or beating up on sassy citizens.

But the government should leave off giving *economic* "protection," such as President Trump promised against the nefarious plot by Chinese and Mexicans to sell us, at low prices, very long ties for men and very good parts for cars.

Let us have separation of economy and state. As in Mafia usage, governmental "protection" is regularly corrupted for the benefit of the rich. It is a tax on enterprise and violates the equal liberty of other people--Americans or foreigners or non-Mafiosi—to compete without violence in offering good deals to us American consumers. Such taxation is, of course, the very purpose of the Mafia, extracting protection money by making an offer you can't refuse. And it is the purpose, too, of the Chicago City Council, encouraged by well-placed bribes . . . uh . . . campaign contributions to prevent by ordinance the poor-person-supplying Ikea or Wal-Mart from opening in town. Extortion and protection and rent-seeking by elites exercising the monopoly of violence puts a fatal drag on betterment, stopping people with new ideas from competing for our voluntary purchases. In the extreme, it stops economic growth cold, as it did during the grinding millennia of poverty before 1800, and before liberalism.

Would you want governmental "protection" from new ideas in science or music or cooking? Probably not. Would you always "buy American" in music or spices or medical innovations? No. Consider this: if you really do think protection and buying American is a good idea, to be enforced by governmental tariffs and jail terms, why not still better buy Illinoisan or Chicagoan or Printers' Rowian? Or, for that matter, why not make everything you want yourself in your own home, thereby achieving plenty of "jobs"? Grow your own wheat. Make your own accordion. Invent your own Internet. Bravo.

Or ask this: do you so fear the multinational corporation, which is trying in its evil way to sweet-talk you into buying its running shoes, that you are willing to erect a comprehensive socialist monopoly backed by guns to prevent you from getting any shoes other than government-issue? Witness the quarter of the world ruled once by communism, or the recent history of Venezuela. As another Italian liberal, and anti-fascist, Benedetto Croce, put it in 1928 (quoted in Mingardi, 2017: 35), "Ethical liberalism abhors authoritarian regulation of the economic process because it considers it a humbling of the inventive faculties of man." To protect the Postal Service's monopoly, inspectors in trench coats used to go around in December putting the arm on little children distributing Christmas cards for free in neighborhood mailboxes. In Tennessee by law nowadays, to open a new company for moving furniture you must get permission from . . . wait for it . . . the existing companies.[12]

Economic protection as actually implemented—contrary to the sweet if naive theory that the implementers are wise and ethical philosopher kings and queens, such as those imagined on the blackboards of Cambridge or New Haven or Princeton, or (without the lovely mathematics) on the political stump nationwide—regularly hurts the helpless more than it helps them. But it always favors the few protected, who are easy to see up on the stage, to be favored over the unseen multitudes damaged off stage. Usually, the protected have made that nice contribution to a congressperson's welfare. Thus we get useless tanks and planes to stop the Canadian invasion, built with parts made in every congressional district, and garnering votes for every congressperson.

Tariff protection, for example, pushing up profits and wages in American-made steel, will at the same time, of course, hurt American consumers of steel off-stage. Obviously. That is what it designed to do, and, unusually for "designed" policies, what it actually achieves. (Let us set aside the hurt to foreigners. Yet since when is a cosmopolitan concern for foreigners not to be recommended ethically? And what sort of childish nationalism thinks that hurting Mexicans is good for Americans?) Regularly, in dollar terms, such off-stage damage imposed on unprotected Americans is many times larger than the on-stage favor granted to the protected Americans. When, in 2017, the American government agreed with Mexican sugar producers to restrict imports of Mexican sugar and keep sugar anyway at the high, protected American price (nice, too, for the sellers of sugar producers from Mexico), the jobs saved in U.S. sugar production were a tiny fraction of those destroyed in sugar-using production. When it comes to protecting sugar, the four senators from Florida and Louisiana are very, very interested, with the six from Texas, Hawaii, and North Dakota, too, expressing a strong opinion on the matter. Odd. One wonders why.

When, in the 1970s, the American government imposed quotas on Japanese automobiles, the additional cost every year to American consumers of autos outweighed the annual wages in Detroit thus protected by a ratio of ten to one. The net beneficiaries were United Auto Workers accustomed to receiving a share of the monopoly profit extracted from Americans buying their cars from the lonely and protected Big Three. The other beneficiaries were, of course, the stockholders of the Big Three and, less obviously, a Toyota Company in far Japan enabled to capture still more of its very own monopoly profit—by restricting its supply to the United States and thereby pushing the U.S. price above the world price of Toyotas, like the Mexican sugar producers. Swell.

A worse case, still deemed sacred on the left, is the worldwide assault through job protections on young or unskilled seekers of any job at all. Job protections in slow-socialist regimes have created in Greece and South Africa and the slums of the United States a dangerously large class of unemployed youths. A quarter of French people who are under 25 years of age and out of school are unemployed, and the rest are employed mainly on monthly temp contracts, because regular jobs in France are fiercely protected. The bosses therefore are terrified to hire in the first place, because they cannot dismiss workers who steal from the till or insult the customers or are in other ways unproductive. And even the honest and productive workers cling in terror to the wrong jobs, because they are unlikely to get the right ones. The protection-caused unemployment is higher still in Greece, and appalling in South Africa.

In the United States, the protections have caused the ghettos to require armed occupation. The south and west sides of Chicago should be hives of industrial activity, employing at low starter wages the unemployed youths now instead standing on street corners and joining gangs to enforce local monopolies of drug distribution. Interventions in the wage bargain in Chicago, such as the governmentally enforced minimum wage, and interventions in the location of economic activity, such as zoning, and interventions in consumption, such as the war on drugs itself, make such places economic deserts. No factories; no grocery stores; no incomes.

§

Yet we are speaking of a *humane* liberalism. Helping people in a crisis, surely, or raising them up from some grave disadvantage, such as social or economic or physical or mental handicap, by giving help in the form of money to be spent in unprotected markets, is a just role for the government, and is still more justly admirable for individuals giving effective help voluntarily. Give the poor in Orleans parish the vouchers for private schools. Give money to the very poor of Chicago to rent a home privately. Turn over your book royalties from *Capitalism in the Twenty-First Century* to an effective charity.

Yet do not, please, ever, supply schooling or housing directly from the government, because governmental ownership of the means of production, a literal socialism, is regularly a bad way to produce anything but, say, national defense (and even that's pretty badly done), and anyway makes the poor into serfs of the government, or of its good friends the teachers' union in the public schools and the bureaucrats in the public housing authority. The Swedes, whom American think are socialists, gave up their state monopoly of local pharmacies, which any elderly Swede can tell you were maddeningly arrogant and inefficient.

Libertarians have a reputation for not being charitable, as mere apologists for rich people. Not so. Look at the numbers. And anyway the indictment from the left depends on an implausible psychological theory. It supposes that a whole class of political thinkers claim disingenuously that they *do* have the poor in mind, but secretly want to make the rich even richer. Why would anyone want such an outcome? What would be his motive? Corrupting pay from the corporations? Fellowships from humane-liberal billionaire Charles Koch? If that's how psychology works, consider the pay from the government to teachers in state schools and universities, or fellowships from slow-socialist George Soros, which might be supposed on such a psychological theory to be equally corrupting. Surely not.

Admittedly, a certain strain of conservatives and the more brotherly libertarians exhibit just such a lack of sympathy for the disadvantaged. It is too often the attitude of the country club. William Buckley's startling defense back in the 1960s of the tyranny directed at the poor among African Americans exhibited one version of it. But a lack of concern for the less fortunate of our brethren is by no means intrinsic to humane liberalism. On the contrary. Dr. Adam Smith was much given to acts of secret charity. For half a century, Charles Koch, bizarrely demonized by Jane Mayer in *The New Yorker* and in her book *Dark Money* (which lets George Soros off the hook), has given many billions to causes such as the United Negro College Fund. Check it out. On a somewhat smaller scale, I myself supported two homeless people for many years in my own apartment. A lack of concern for others is not at all implied by humane liberalism, or by Christian libertarianism, or neoclassical libertarianism, or a liberalism of the bleeding heart.

Ayn Rand had here a bad effect, with her masculinist doctrine of selfishness, and her uniformly male, self-absorbed, and reckless heroes in her novels, ever-popular with college freshmen. Especially fresh-men. Senator *Rand* Paul, in his run for the Republican presidential nomination in 2016, got disproportionately fewer votes from women than from men. Yet his policies of stopping the drug war against Black families and reducing the flow of body bags from foreign wars, like most of his proposals, were the most family-friendly on offer from any candidate, including (in their actual, as against their "designed," effects) those from frankly socialist Bernie Sanders. As for charity, Dr. Paul regularly contributes his skill as an eye surgeon to sight-saving operations in poor countries. I urge Dr./Senator Paul, for the good of our shared humane liberalism, to ditch that misleading "Rand," and change his first name to, say, Adam.

Mainly let people create by themselves a growing economy, as they did spectacularly well from 1800 to the present, when liberalism inspirited the masses to devise betterments and open new enterprises and move to new jobs. The stunning Great Enrichment of a fully 3,000 percent increase since 1800 in real wages, which was especially important for the poorest, happened not because of the nudging and protecting and regulating and subsidizing and prohibiting and unionizing and drafting and enslaving by politicians and organizers and bureaucrats and thugs armed with a monopoly of violence. Mostly it happened despite them, by way of an increasingly free people. The government's rare good deeds in the story were the passing of laws to make people free, as in the Civil Rights Acts of 1866 and of 1964—passed in the interludes between the government's enslaving or re-enslaving or manhandling people in the Dred Scott decision or *Plessy v. Ferguson* or the Palmer Raids or Bull Conner's dogs or the deportation of Dreamers.

The Enrichment and its associated Liberation, that is, did not arise chiefly from government, beyond its modest role of the prevention of some portions of force and fraud and the few cases of genuine defense from foreign aggression, such as the unsuccessful War of 1812–14 and the successful Pacific War of 1941–45. Yet, strangely, the economists since around 1848 have mainly made their scientific reputations by proposing this or that pro-governmental "imperfection in the market," to the number of more than 100 imagined, almost all of them proposed without evidence that they matter much to the economy (McCloskey 2018). Monopoly. Spillovers. Ignorant consumers. The economists have claimed again and again that a brilliant government of philosopher-monarchs, advised by the very economists, can offer simple solutions. Antitrust. The FDA. Industrial policy. And yet the most important fact about modern economic history, occurring at the very time the economists were bemoaning our "disgrace with fortune and men's eyes / Alone beweeping our outcast state" from the horrible imperfections in the market, was that the wretchedly distorted and imperfect exchange-tested betterment was delivering a Great Enrichment to the poorest among us of thousands of percent. Some imperfections.

For instance, the governmental choosing of winners in the economy, an industrial policy, is designed to repair the shocking imperfection of foresight in private investment, so obvious to the economists, without the bother of measuring whether the imperfection is actually large or the industrial policy actually works. Industrial policy in fact seldom works. Why, actually, would such choosing of winners work? Why would an official high up in the government, stipulating even that she is equipped with economic models and is thoroughly ethical, being an extremely bright, if recent, graduate of Harvard College, know better what would be a good idea to make and sell and buy than some ignorant hillbilly out in the market facing the prices registering the value ordinary people place on goods and services and facing the opportunity cost in production, and going bankrupt if he chooses badly? Why would it be a good idea to subsidize wind power in advance of a showing that spending on it in fact makes us better off, net of opportunity costs? As the economist Don Lavoie (1985: 4) concluded from a detailed study of such governmental planning, "any attempt by a single agency to steer an economy constitutes a case of the blind leading the sighted."

The hubris of industrial planning is a very old story. An instance was the Europe-wide mercantilism that Adam Smith deprecated. In Sweden, the Göta Canal was built 1810–32 by military conscripts, before Sweden adopted liberalism. It was a singularly ill-advised project, immensely expensive in real costs, eventually used chiefly for a bit of pleasure boating. In the United States, in the nineteenth century, the "internal improvements" financed by the government were mostly bad ideas (such as canals in Pennsylvania and Indiana during the 1830s, built, like Sweden's, on the eve of railways making most of the canals unprofitable) and were, of course, corrupted into favors for the few. Under the Obama Administration, the Solyndra fiasco gave away a $535 million "loan" from the government to subsidize U.S.-made solar panels, promptly undersold by the Chinese. Both big political parties do it. A humane liberal party would not.

§

Worry not at all about inequality if it is achieved by smart betterment. Such inequality pretty much dissipates within a couple of generations, and often within a couple of years, through the entry of imitating betterments. Meanwhile we poor slobs get the betterments. The imitation of Henry Ford's assembly line or Steve Jobs' smartphone spreads the benefit to us all, soon, in lower prices and higher quality and frenetic, ongoing improvements. Such a result of entry is not hypothetical. It has been the economic history of the world since the beginning, when not blocked—as until 1800 it commonly was blocked—by monopolies supported by the ur-monopolies of governmental violence, and now again increasingly under High Liberalism by the administrative state. The economist William Nordhaus (2004) reckons that inventors in the United States since World War II have kept only 2 percent of the social value of the betterment they produce. Look at your computer. Two percent of the social gain arising from Wal-Mart's early mastery of bar codes and mass purchasing—great better-ments compared with the older and worse models of retailing—left a great deal of money for the children of Sam and Bud Walton. But the rest of us were left with the 98 percent.

Local fortunes a century ago were built on local banking and local depart-ment stores. Their business models were soon imitated, and at length bettered, and anyway eroded from the beginning by rapidly falling transport costs. Sears Roebuck and Montgomery Ward competed with the brick-and-mortar gen-eral store charging high prices, shipping the new mail orders at lower prices, as Amazon is doing again a century on. The market share of United States Steel attained its highest level, fully two-thirds of the steel produced in America, on the day it was founded in 1901. Its share of American steel production fell steadily thereafter, with Bethlehem and other companies entering. Look at the 30 companies in the Dow-Jones industrial average. Only five date from before the 1970s. The 25 others have been replaced by such "industrials" as Visa and Verizon and Coca Cola.

The sheer passage of human generations works, too. How many rich Carnegies have you heard of? Andrew might have made his daughter and her four children and their children—or for that matter his cousins back in Scotland—fabulously wealthy, down to the fourth generation and beyond. But he didn't. Instead he built the library in Wakefield, Massachusetts in which I found and devoured at age 15 Prince Peter Kropotkin's sweet anti-capitalist anarchist classic *Mutual Aid* (1902). If you want to see how the dissipation of wealth through families works, look at the Wikipedia entry for "Vanderbilt Family," noting that old Cornelius (1794–1877), the richest American at the time, had 13 children (pity Mrs. Sophia Johnson Vanderbilt). His great-great-granddaughter, Gloria Vanderbilt (born 1924), made her own money, by providing goods and services that people were willing to pay for. Her son, Anderson Cooper of CNN, does so, too.

But you should indeed worry about inequality if it is achieved by using the government to get protection for favored groups. That is what a large govern-ment, worth capturing to get the protection, is mainly used for, to the detri-ment of most of the people off-stage. We humane liberals, such as Charles Koch, who puts his money where his mouth is, agree with the slow socialists about the evil of an inequality caused by what economists call "rent-seeking"—that is, using the powers of the government to extract profitable favors for, say, big oil companies. But we liberals are then startled that our friends the slow socialists advocate . . . well . . . giving still more power of extraction to the same government. Put the fox in charge of the hen house, they cry. Surely Mr. Fox is a good and honest civil servant.

Guilds with governmental protection such as the American Medical Association, and government regulations in building codes to favor plumbers, protect the well-off, who in turn fund the politicians enforcing the guilds and regulations. Neat. How many Huey and Earl and other Longs have dominated Louisiana politics since the 1920s? Look at Wikipedia for that one, too. Such inherited political power allied to corruption is ancient. Political candidates in the late Roman Republic routinely bought votes, and anyway the rich of Rome had more power in the system of voting itself. There is nothing new about politicians and businesspeople and billionaires buying Congress for special protection, and gerrymandering the voting system to boot. Mark Twain said, "It could probably be shown by facts and figures that there is no distinctly American criminal class except Congress." Better keep it under parole.

§

Understand that the greatest challenges facing humankind are *not* terrorism or inequality or crime or population growth or climate change or slowing productivity or recreational drugs or the breakdown of family values or whatever new pessimism our friends on the left or right will come up with next, about which they will write urgent editorials until the next "challenge" justifying more governmental coercion swims into their ken.

The greatest challenges have always been poverty and tyranny, which have the effect through governmental violence of not allowing ordinary people to have a go. The use of "liberal" is a language game, but not therefore "mere" (Skinner, 1969). It has consequences, in allowing or not allowing people to have a go. If you eliminate poverty through liberal economic growth, as China and India are doing nowadays, and as did the pioneering instances of liberalism back to Holland during the seventeenth century, you will get equality of real comfort, the educating of engineers to control flooding (and latterly to lessen global warming), and the educating of us all for lives of flourishing. If you eliminate tyranny, replacing it with liberalism 1.0, you will get the rise of liberty for slaves and women and the handicapped, and then still more fruits of the Great Enrichment, as more and more people are liberated to seek out exchange-tested betterments. You will get stunning cultural enrichments, the end of terrorism, the fall of the remaining tyrants, and riches for all.

How do I know? Because it happened in northwestern Europe gradually from the seventeenth century onward, accelerating after 1800, and now at a headlong pace in large parts of the rest of the world. It can happen soon everywhere.

By contrast, keep on with various versions of old fashioned kingship, or with slow or fast socialism, with their betterment-killing policies protecting the favored classes, especially the rich or the Party or the cousins, Bad King John or Robin Hood—in its worst forms, a military socialism or a tribal tyranny; in its best, a stifling regulation of new cancer drugs by the FDA—and you get the grinding routine of human tyranny and poverty. The agenda of humane liberalism, ranged against tyranny and poverty, is achieving human flourishing, in the way it has always been achieved. Let my people go. Let ordinary people have a go. Stop pushing people around.

I realize that you will find some of the items we humane liberals propose hard to swallow. You've been told by our progressive friends that we need to have policies and programs and regulations or the sky will fall. Or you've been told by the conservative side that we need anyway to occupy and govern by the gun all sorts of communities of poor people, among them the lesser breeds without the law east and west of Suez, from the 800 American military bases worldwide. You may view as shocking the contrary proposals to let people be wholly free to flourish in a liberal economy—right-wing madness, you will say, enriching the rich; or left-wing madness, leading to chaos. You will say from the left that liberalism has allowed monopoly to increase. (It has not. Illiberalism has, when it could get away with it—although monopoly in fact has been dramatically reduced since 1800 by liberty of movement and by free trade, by the railway and the telephone and the Internet: McCloskey, 2018.).You will say from the right that liberalism has allowed terrorism to increase. (It has not. Illiberalism has—although in fact terrorism in the West has *declined* rapidly in the past few decades: Mueller, 2006.) If you cannot actually think of any fact-based arguments against a humane liberalism, you will assert anyway with a sneer that it is impractical, out of date, old-fashioned, nineteenth-century, a dead parrot. (It is not. The illiberal national socialism practiced by most governments is.)

But you owe it to the seriousness of your political ideas, my dear misled friends, to listen a little, and to consider. Lavoie (1985: 8) noted "the impossibility of refuting a theory without first trying to see the world through its lenses." Try out the lenses, too.

§

I am optimistic, and I want to dispel the sky-is-falling gloom that seems always to command a ready market and which is routinely reused by populists and other tyrants to justify their tyrannies, and anyway is used even by good-hearted slow socialists and moderate authoritarians to push people around . . . by first absolutely terrifying them. Terrorism works with more than guns and bombs.

On the contrary, we are *not* doomed by the New Challenges. We need to avoid shooting ourselves in the feet. It is a lively possibility, because we have done it before, by way of traditionalism and nationalism and socialism and national socialism, and now again populism. Think of August 1914. But if we can avoid such disasters of clumsy politics, we will rejoice over the next 50 or 100 years in the enrichment through humane liberalism of the now-poor, a permanent liberation of the wretched of the earth, and a cultural explosion in arts and sciences and crafts and entertainments beyond compare.

I urge you to reconsider. I want you to become less self-satisfied in your progressivism or your conservatism or even your amiable middle-of-the-road-ism. I want you to realize that they all depend to a greater or lesser degree on an exercise of the monopoly of violence. I want you to come to rely on sweet talk, liberal rhetoric, peaceful exchange. I want you, above all, to become much less certain than you are now that The Problem is "capitalism," or the Enlightenment, or that liberty can be Taken Too Far, or that government programs, protections, regulations, and prohibitions are usually innocent exercises by wise bureaucrats to better the lives of Americans.

With an open mind and a generous heart, my dears, you will tilt towards a humane real liberalism, 1.0. Welcome, then, to a society held together by sweet talk rather than by violence.

§

What, then, are the prospects for such a new American liberalism? What steps can we take to encourage a society of sweet talk?

Well, for one thing, we can keep on doing the talk, making the intellectual case, such as sketched here, and explored in some depth in the trilogy *The Bourgeois Era* (McCloskey, 2006, 2010, 2016). From that experience, I draw a couple of Rules for Humane Liberal Rhetoric, if we are to succeed in changing people's minds.

Rule 1: We *must* declare in a prominent position in everything we write or say that we are for the poor and disadvantaged, because it is true and because it is routinely misunderstood. The "preferential option for the poor" is Catholic social teaching, which unhappily is largely slow socialist. But I take it that every humane liberal in fact also wants to help the poor and disadvantaged—although, as I noted, *our* help is efficacious, unlike the corrupting handouts or the violent police actions on offer from the left or the right. We need to say, and say again, that we are for opportunity, to lean against the strange assumption of the High Liberals that we low liberals 1.0 are against it. We aren't.

The journalists classify us as "pro-business," and classify our leftward opponents as "pro-labor." The classification comes from the rule of journalistic balance and from an unexamined belief in the one-dimension, left–right spectrum that most people have taken to be political reality since the French Assembly initiated it. If humane liberals keep being characterized as pro-business, understood as favoring the rich, it will be little wonder that we will have little influence. It's hard to get across to a journalist innocent of economics that, for example, abandoning rent controls on apartments will in fact increase the supply of housing for the poor. But let's keep teaching it, for the benefit of the poor.

Rule 2: We *must* criticize conservatives, not merely progressives. At the end of *The Constitution of Liberty*, Hayek added a Postscript I have often quoted here, "Why I am Not a Conservative." If we are going to change anyone's mind, we must extract ourselves from our automatic characterization as "conservative." The left–right spectrum, which most people believe is a wonderfully true and simple way of classifying all politics, puts us on the right side of the spectrum, well into the blue. We need to emphasize instead the triangle, or, in the other visualization, the *two* dimensions, of economic liberty (high for conservatives, sometimes, and always high for liberals) and of personal liberty (high for progressives, sometimes, and always high for liberals). Liberalism lives in the northeast corner of such a pair of axes, high in economic liberty and high in personal liberty.

Rule 3, which is something of a theorem derivable from rules 1 and 2: We should make common cause with radicals. Liberalism 1.0 was the original radicalism, from the Levelers in England to the Hippies in America. Do your own thing. For example, we should make common cause with gender minorities, such as was done brilliantly by Sarah Rose interviewing me for *FreedomWorks*.[13] We should make common cause with the young, because they are the victims of High Liberalism and Old Conservatism, blocked out of jobs. We should make common cause with the oppressed. If you don't think that women and Blacks and poor people worldwide are oppressed by the slow socialists and the conservatives, you must not be acquainted with many women or Blacks or poor people. We *are* the radicals.

The intellectual case needs to be made, and is being made at think tanks such as Cato or the Charles Koch Institute or the American Enterprise Institute, and elsewhere at the Fraser Institute in Canada or the Institute for Economic Affairs in Britain. The Atlas Network is spreading the word, salting the globe with liberal think tanks, the head salters being people such as the inimitable Tom Palmer, smuggling through the old Iron Curtain in his luggage disguised copies of *Capitalism and Freedom*.

And, thinking about the form of words, it would be good to focus on journalists, providing plenty of fellowships to give them the leisure to read Hayek or Smith (Vernon, as much as Adam). Very few journalists are humane liberals in the mold of Steve Chapman at the *Chicago Tribune*. Neither the *Times* or the *Washington Post* has a humane liberal columnist, although David Brooks sometimes talks like one, and on those occasions we applaud. And George Will, once a Buckleyite conservative, reads more and more like a humane liberal. *Reason* magazine is now a serious force, although tending a bit to the harsh, brotherly sort of libertarianism, unlike the sisterly version of humane liberalism I preach here. Yet the magazine is not yet an outlet like *Harpers* or *The New Yorker* that gets quoted for its authority. It should be.

The truth, of course, will set you free. Yet writing or talking the truth has limits in changing hearts. One might suppose that a careful reading of *The Wealth of Nations* or *On Liberty* or *Free to Choose* or *Anarchy, State, and Utopia* would convert anyone instantly to humane liberalism 1.0. It doesn't. The reason is that people acquire their politics early, too early, late in adolescence. Then they never think about it again and resist kind offers from humane liberals to set them straight. It becomes part of their personal identity to be "a good social democrat" or, for that matter, a "Randian." (The same is true, by the way, about religious ideas, which is why one hears adolescent attacks on theology coming out of the mouths of 50-year old men, who have not reconsidered since they first had such clever ideas at age 14.)

Most adolescents in a rich economy come from loving, non-farm, non-small-business families, and therefore have no idea where meat comes from, or how its price will change how much Dad makes. Mom in the little economy that most of us nowadays come from is a benevolent and all-wise central planner of meals, the materials for which appear to fall from the sky like manna. A loving family is a nice little socialist society. No wonder that young people imagine that it is easy and virtuous to extend it to what Hayek called, in advance of President Lyndon Johnson, the Great Society, of 324 million Americans. No wonder that each new generation since we stopped living mainly on farms has flirted with socialism, as I did age 16, and as did the younger of the British electorate in the May 2017 general election, or the Bernie Sanders' voters in the U.S. primaries in 2016. The natural socialism of bourgeois youth is a big problem in persuading people of humane liberal ideas.

Therefore I thank my Anglican God for the energy of Students for Liberty in spreading the new old/liberal ideology. Ideology does, after all, change, so it must not be hopeless to try to push it along. It changed from 1700 to 1848 in a liberal direction, and from 1848 to 1970 in a socialist direction. Ideology depends on enthusiasm. The point I'm making is that energy, enthusiasm, emotion are as important for lasting ideological change as are rational findings that rent-seeking is hard to stop, or that Great Societies have a problem of free-riding. A certain kind of libertarian (I use the term precisely) believes that Logic Alone suffices. It has never been true.

We need, of course, at least somewhat free institutions to advance a free society. I have met with Russian liberals a little and know who the real heroes of Putin's Russia are. By comparison, Americans have little to fear in espousing humane liberal ideas, aside from the stunned incomprehension of friends and relatives at Thanksgiving under the spell of High Liberalism or standard-issue conservatism.

But to get beyond the wholly intellectual appeal of humane liberalism—the intellectual routine is all I myself can do as an academic with no artistic gifts— we need to enlist the artists, especially the storytellers in the movies and novels and country music lyrics. It's what Fred L. Smith, founding director of the Competitive Enterprise Institute, advocates these days. I know well, as a former Joan-Baez socialist, that the left has the best ballads. And the right has the best marching tunes. I think we can do humane liberalism with stories, as Fred says. I've recently seen two Hollywood movies praising enterprise, *Joy* (2015) about Joy Mangano's business success with a self-wringing mop, and *The Founder* (2016) about Ray Kroc making McDonald's into a national and international chain. Neither is uncritical about business, but both are less hostile than the productions by corporate executives in Hollywood assaulting corporate executives elsewhere, such as in the two *Wall Street* movies (1987 and 2010), and in *The Man in the Grey Flannel Suit* (1956).

Maybe the tide is turning. Ideologies do change, and ideas in statistics and in stories do it. Or so we liberals believe. As Hayek (2011 [1960], p. 526) said, "liberalism [has a] fundamental belief in the long-range power of ideas." Surely.

Young and poor and women of all countries unite. You have nothing to lose but your governmental chains.

Notes

1   The essay is a much-revised version of the introduction to a book manuscript, *How to Be a Humane Libertarians: Essays in a New American Liberalism*. I thank the Charles Koch Institute for providing me with the time in its Washington, DC, office to do the revisions.

2 See his lecture, available at http://econfaculty.gmu.edu/klein/Assets/Liberalism%20 1.0%20version4.pptx David Boaz (2015, p. 145) uses a similar locution. On the US/UK definition, as against the Continental definition, see Schlesinger (1962 [1956]).

3 The phrase is, of course, from Burns in the 1790s, but Smith showed, in all of his writings, that he was just such an egalitarian. Levy and Peart (2008) call his premise, carried forward in Liberalism 1.0, "analytic egalitarianism" and offer many examples.

4 It seems to me a fault in the book by Hayek from which I have quoted that he depends on instrumental reasons for liberty, such as economic productivity (see, e.g., Hayek 2011 [1960], pp. 84–85), rather than the natural and equal right we should all have to liberty, regardless of payoff.

5 For the factual evidence for these remarks, and for much else, consult McCloskey (2006, 2010, 2016).

6 *Every Man a King*, Radio speech to the nation delivered February 23, 1934, available at http://www.americanrhetoric.com/speeches/hueyplongking.htm

7 When I use, as I will, the locution "our friends on the left" (or the right), I am speaking sincerely. I have many good friends on the left (and the right), whom I love ... but who I believe are mistaken.

8 The late James Seaton (1996, p. 35) alerted me to Trilling's worry. His references are to Trilling's essay on Henry James, "Princess Casamassima," and "Manners, Morals, and the Novel," both reprinted 1950.

9 As quoted in Seaton (1996, p. 35).

10 On the FDA, see Briggeman (2015) and Bhidé (2017, p. 28). On the meaninglessness of tests of statistical significance, see Ziliak and McCloskey (2008), and Wasserstein and Lazar (2016).

11 *Café Hayek*, March 5, 2017, available at https://cafehayek.com/2017/03/quotation-of-the-day-2005.html

12 I believe I learned this fact from the sainted John Stossel in one of his TV shows.

13 FreedomWorks, *Transgender Rights*, Episodes 1, 2, and 3.

References

Berndt, Ronald M., and Catherine H. Berndt. 1964. *The World of the First Australians*. Sydney: Ure Smith.

Bhidé, Amar. 2017. Constraining Knowledge: Traditions and Rules that Limit Medical Innovation. *Critical Review*, 29(1): 1–33.

Boaz, David. 1997. *Libertarianism: A Primer*. New York: Free Press.

Boaz, David. 2015. *The Libertarian Mind: A Manifesto for Freedom*. New York: Simon & Schuster.

Brennan, Jason. 2004. Illiberal Liberals: Why High Liberalism Is Not a Liberal View. *Review Journal of Political Philosophy*, 2: 59–103.

Briggeman, Jason. 2015. *Search for Justification of the Policy of Pre-Market Approval of Pharmaceuticals*. Ph.D. dissertation, George Mason University. Available at http://mars.gmu.edu/bitstream/handle/1920/9656/Briggeman_gmu_0883E_10872.pdf

Hayek, Friedrich A. 2011 [1960]. *The Constitution of Liberty*. Ed. Ronald Hamowy. Chicago, IL: University of Chicago Press.

Higgs, Robert H. 1987. *Crisis and Leviathan: Critical Episodes in the Growth of American Government*. New York: Oxford University Press.

Lavoie, Don. 1985. *National Economic Planning: What Is Left?* Cambridge, MA: Ballinger.

Levy, David M., and Sandra J. Peart. 2008. Social Inequality, Analytical Egalitarianism, and the March towards Eugenic Explanations in the Social Sciences. *American Journal of Economics and Sociology*, 67(3): 473–480.

McCloskey, Deirdre N. 1970. Did Victorian Britain Fail? *Economic History Review*, *23*(3): 446–459.

McCloskey, Deirdre N. 1973. New Perspectives on the Old Poor Law. *Explorations in Economic History*, *10*(4): 419–436.

McCloskey, Deirdre N. 2006. *The Bourgeois Virtues: Ethics for an Age of Commerce*. Chicago, IL: University of Chicago Press.

McCloskey, Deirdre N. 2010. *Bourgeois Dignity: Why Economics Can't Explain the Modern World*. Chicago, IL: University of Chicago Press.

McCloskey, Deirdre N. 2016. *Bourgeois Equality: How Ideas, Not Capital or Institutions, Enriched the World*. Chicago, IL: University of Chicago Press.

McCloskey, Deirdre N. 2018. The Two Movements in Economic Thought, 1700–2000: Empty Economic Boxes Revisited. *History of Economic Ideas*, *26*(1): 63–95.

Mingardi, Alberto. 2017. Classical Liberalism in Italian Economic Thought, from the Time of Unification. *EconJournalWatch*, *14*(1): 22–54.

Mueller, John E. 2006. *Overblown: How Politicians and the Terrorism Industry Inflate National Security Threats, and Why We Believe Them*. New York: Free Press.

Nordhaus, William D. 2004. *Schumpeterian in the American Economy: Theory and Measurement*. NBER Working Paper No. W10433.

Radford, R. A. 1945. The Economic Organisation of a P.O.W. Camp. *Economica* (New Series), *12*(48): 189–201.

Schlesinger, Arthur, Jr. 1962 [1956]. Liberalism in America: A Note for Europeans. In *The Politics of Hope*. Boston, MA: Riverside Press.

Schultz, Kevin M. 2015. *Buckley and Mailer: The Difficult Friendship That Shaped the Sixties*. New York: Norton.

Schumpeter, Joseph A. 1950 [1942]. *Capitalism, Socialism and Democracy*. 3rd edn. New York: Harper & Row.

Seaton, James. 1996. *Cultural Conservatism: Political Liberalism—From Criticism to Cultural Studies*. Ann Arbor, MI: University of Michigan Press.

Skinner, Quentin. 1969. Meaning and Understanding in the History of Ideas. *History and Theory*, *8*(1): 3–53.

Smith, Adam. 1981 [1776]. *An Inquiry into the Nature and Causes of the Wealth of Nations*. Eds. R. H. Campbell, A. S. Skinner, and W. B. Todd, two vols. Indianapolis, IN: Liberty Classics.

Smith, Adam. 1982 [1759]. *The Theory of Moral Sentiments [TMS]*. Eds. D. D. Raphael and A. L. Macfie. Indianapolis, IN: Liberty Classics.

Smith, Adam. 1982 [1762–63]. *Lectures on Jurisprudence*. Eds. R. L. Meek, D. D. Raphael, and P. G. Stein. Oxford: Oxford University Press.

Walker, Sheri, and Clark Nardinelli. 2016. Consumer Expenditure on FDA Regulated Products: 20 Cents of Every Dollar. *FDA Voice*, November 1. Available at https://blogs.fda.gov/fdavoice/index.php/2016/11/consumer-expenditure-on-fda-regulated-products-20-cents-of-every-dollar/

Wasserstein, Ronald L., and Nicole A. Lazar. 2016. The ASA's Statement on *p*-Values: Context, Process, and Purpose. *American Statistician*, *70*(2): 129–133.

Ziliak, Stephen, and Deirdre N. McCloskey. 2008. *The Cult of Statistical Significance: How the Standard Error Costs Us Jobs, Justice, and Lives*. Ann Arbor, MI: University of Michigan Press.

Index

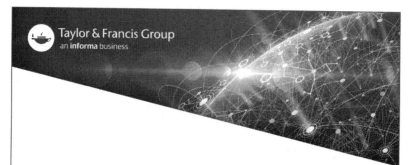